A
PHILOSOPHICAL STUDY
of
RELIGION

David Hugh Freeman
in
collaboration with David Freeman

THE CRAIG PRESS
Nutley, New Jersey

To

Deanna and Renée,

daughters and granddaughters

A

PHILOSOPHICAL STUDY

of

RELIGION

PUBLISHER'S NOTE

A *Philosophical Study of Religion* was written by Dr. David Hugh Freeman, Chairman of the Philosophy Department at the University of Rhode Island, in collaboration with his father, Dr. David Freeman. The latter is largely responsible for the sections dealing with Christianity, Judaism, and Islam. An educator, he is the author of *The Bible and Things to Come*. David Hugh Freeman is the editor of the *Modern Thinkers Series* in the International Library of Philosophy and Theology, has translated many scholarly Dutch works into English, and is the author of *Tillich* and *Recent Studies in Philosophy and Theology*.

The authors wish to thank Estelle Boisclair and Mary Johnson for their careful assistance in typing and proofreading, Mr. John Murphy and Dr. Robert Reymond for their suggestions and criticisms, and Dr. William Oliver Martin and Dr. William Young for many hours of stimulating conversation.

CONTENTS

CHAPTER I

CAN RELIGION BE DEFINED?

Religion is found in every society. However, to admit its universality does not answer the question: What is religion?

There are different perspectives from which religion may be studied. The various systems of beliefs and practices within diverse cultures can be compared, and the internal development of religious beliefs can be treated in the order of their historical appearance. However, the study of a comparison and/or of the history of religions is not the same as a philosophical investigation of religion. The nature of such an investigation should not be decided arbitrarily. A philosophical inquiry depends upon the perspective of the investigator and the nature of the subject matter. Further, the choice of perspective depends upon what a person wants to know, while the nature of the object to be studied is independent of subjective interests. It is not an arbitrary whim of the astronomer that he uses a telescope instead of a microscope to study the stars. His choice of instrument depends upon what he is studying and not conversely.

The first problem in a philosophical examination of religion is to understand the nature of religion. Anyone who denies that religion or philosophy has a nature cannot, of course, embark upon such a study. For, if in principle we cannot determine what religion is, then we also cannot determine what it is not, and if this were the case there would be no point in studying it. Likewise, if there is no such thing as philosophy, then everyone can be a philosopher, which of course means that no one can. If everyone were to be regarded as an historian, a chemist, a biologist, or a physicist, then there would be no need in

1

calling attention to the special kinds of knowledge that an historian, a chemist, a biologist, or a physicist has. Surely, if one were to hold that every person in the United States is a physicist, and that all physicists are equal, then sanity would demand the mental reservation that while all are equal, "some are more equal than others."

The reader may subsequently disagree with our analysis of what "religion" and "philosophy" properly are, but in order to express his denial he will have to commit himself to another analysis.

Our concern is not simply to propose a series of definitions that are so general and vague that they mean nothing. The textbooks are filled with such definitions. We shall rather undertake the more difficult task of deciding whether it is possible to state what religion and philosophy are. Is a definition possible? We make no claim to have considered every definition that has every been given. We shall, however, try to be as comprehensive in our analysis as the subject matter and space permit.

1. *The Problem of Objectivity*

The problem of objectivity is especially acute in the study of religion. An investigation may be objective in that it simply describes structural states of affairs as they occur to everyone. Such objectivity may in fact never be completely attainable.

A study is also objective when the investigator is not neutral on the issues involved, provided that he conducts his inquiry honestly and does not knowingly withhold relevant evidence that would prejudice his own position. We shall strive to be objective in our description of religion, and when we make critical judgments, we shall not knowingly withhold information prejudicial to our point of view. We do not attempt the impossible; we do not pretend to be neutral where neutrality cannot exist. We make no effort to disguise the fact that we possess what we believe to be a universal characteristic of man: we cannot escape being religious. We are not free of religious beliefs. Such neutrality and objectivity is not possible for any man. Religious beliefs may be disguised and masked under other names. The worst form of dogmatism is to hide the fact that such beliefs are there. Man may be a rational being, but he is more than rational; he is a religious being. It is not possible, therefore, to be "objective" in the study of religion in the sense that the person making the study is absolutely neutral in the matter of religious beliefs. A critical examination of the nature of religion discloses that the notion of absolute neutrality depends upon question-begging assumptions.

2. Is a Single Definition of Religion Possible?

There are several means by which an effort might be made to state what religion is. We might simply make a survey and find out what people think religion is. Modern views might then be compared with those held in the past, both in our own and in other cultures. Such a procedure, like consulting a dictionary, is useful, but it does not solve the problem.

Actually, the problem of definition can be illustrated by turning to a dictionary. *Webster's Collegiate Dictionary* defines "religion" as:

> 1. The service and adoration of God or a god as expressed in forms of worship. 2. One of the systems of faith and worship. 3. The profession or practice of religious beliefs; religious observances collectively; rites. 4. Devotion or fidelity; conscientiousness. 5. An awareness or conviction of the existence of a supreme being, arousing reverence, love, gratitude, the will to obey and serve, and the like.

Such a definition is adequate for certain purposes. If we already know what it means to worship and to adore God, we may then know how some people use the word "religion." The dictionary is of no help to us if we do not already recognize acts of worship, religious rites, and religious attitudes; and we can only know what the latter are by knowing what it means to be religious.

3

When Webster states that "religion is the service and adoration of God or a god as expressed in forms of worship," he is giving a partial description of the way the word is used. Whether religion really is capable of serving God or a god depends upon whether or not God or a god really exists. That people engage in what they understand to be acts of adoration in no way establishes the reality of what they would serve or adore.

To give a verbal or nominal definition, we need only mention a word or phrase equivalent to the word "religion," and we can stop with Webster. Our problem, however, is not simply to define the word "religion" by tracing its customary usage. We wish to discover how people conceive of religion and whether their idea of religion is what religion really is.

Every concept has a comprehension, often called a connotation or intension, and an extension, often called a denotation. The *comprehension* of the concept of a horse, for example, is the set of traits that makes an animal a horse. It is that which describes what makes a horse the kind of animal it is. However, the various types of individual horses, e.g., race horses, work horses, cow-ponies, five-gaited horses, etc., are a part of the *extension* of the concept.

When the question as to what is the meaning of the concept of religion is asked, much confusion can arise unless the distinction between the comprehension and the extension of the concept of religion is carefully noted. For example, the impression is sometimes given that the concept of religion is adequately defined by simply pointing to its extension, i.e., to the various individual types of things that are called religion: e.g., Buddhism, Shintoism, Taoism, Judaism, Christianity, Islam, etc. Such a procedure refers to the extension of the concept of religion and neglects the comprehension of the term. It simply overlooks the question as to whether there is in fact a single concept of religion. We shall subsequently see that the word "religion" is ambiguous; it refers to more than one concept. We shall see that there is no single concept of religion, and

4

that the various world religions do not have a common essence which enables them to be placed upon the same coordinate level. We shall see that the assumption that all religions are essentially the same is uncritical in that it assumes what ought to be demonstrated. It simply begs the question to assume that because certain accidental features may be shared by the world religions they are essentially the same. Yet this uncritical assumption lies at the foundation of many works on comparative religion and the philosophy of religion. It is in fact frequently proclaimed to be the very mark of scientific objectivity!

The problem ought to be considered as to whether there is in actuality a single concept of religion. If there are in fact several concepts of religion, then each will have its own comprehension; and consequently the extension of each concept will also be different. The comprehension of a concept may be stated in a definition; the extension of a concept may be adequately classified or divided in terms of a single principle of division. Any adequate analysis of the concept of religion must be clear as to whether the concern is with the comprehension or the extension of the concept.

If our concern were simply with the meaning of concepts, it would then only be necessary to state what people understand when they form a concept of religion. The problem of truth would then never arise. But since we are not simply concerned with the meanings of words and concepts, it is necessary to go beyond conceptual analysis.

To state what something is, we must give a definition in which the comprehension of a concept becomes a part of the predicate of a proposition and is asserted to exist in a certain way. Our purpose is not simply to analyze the meaning of words and concepts; it is to find out what religion is. Concepts must be integrated into propositions before we can raise the question as to whether something is factual and truthful.

Analysis of the customary meaning of the word "religion" and of the concepts of religion is necessary, but it can never tell us whether religion is what people conceive it to be. It is possible, for example, to understand what people might mean by the term unicorn; it is also possible to form a concept of a unicorn and to give a conceptual definition of it, but whether or not unicorns are imaginary or actual animals does not depend on what people may think about them but upon non-verbal and non-conceptual states of affairs.

A proposition is concerned with existence. It may be true or false. To know what a thing is, is not the same as knowing whether it is. Mere concepts are not sufficient for knowledge. To have knowledge about religion, we must know the facts about religion. We must know whether that which religious propositions assert to be the case is actually the case. The truth of a proposition depends upon whether or not what the proposition asserts conforms to what is, to states of affairs as they are.

A proposition is not true because it satisfies some human purpose, because it works. We understand "truth" to mean the conformity to things as they are. A false proposition may be satisfying. The truth or falsity of a proposition has nothing to do with whether a human purpose is served by the belief that a proposition is true. Either there is truth or there is not, and if a proposition is true, it is true no matter what a person may think about it.

Our effort to state what religion is, is concerned with the truth about religion. We want to know more than how the word religion is used, and we want to know more than the meanings of the various concepts of religion. We want to know whether propositions which state what religion is are true.

The term "religion" is notoriously ambiguous. Its possible meanings must, therefore, be noted carefully before any attempt can be made to define the concept of religion or to give a real definition of religion. The reason why the term "religion" is ambiguous is that it is used by different people to stand for totally different things and concepts; even the same person may on different oc-

6

casions use the word to signify entirely different aspects of the same thing.

Few, if any, would use the word "religion" to refer to the behavior of animals. The term "religion" usually is used to refer to some form of human experience. However, it may refer exclusively to man's behavior and have nothing to do with any non-human point of reference, or it may refer to the activity of man and to some non-human point of reference, or it may refer to the non-human point of reference and have nothing to do with man. Moreover, the non-human element that the term "religion" is frequently used to designate may be the occasion of further ambiguity. The term may refer to various aspects of the world, to nature, to one God, to many gods, or to spirits. When the term is used to refer to man's behavior, it may then refer to the feelings, beliefs, social customs, and the ethical practices to which the term "religion" is somehow thought to be appropriate.

The word "religion" may refer to things and events in the present or the past. Such things and events may be real or imaginary. It is possible for "religion" to refer to certain concepts that people have; on other occasions, it may refer to what the concepts intend. "Religion" may refer to the object of beliefs, to the beliefs themselves, to the act of believing, to acts associated with beliefs, or to the statements in which beliefs are expressed. "Religion" may refer to the comprehension of a concept of religion, to what is thought to be essential to religion; or the term may refer to the extension of a concept of religion.

Whenever different concepts of religion are held, the word "religion" may refer to entirely different conceptions. For example, if a Marxist conceives of religion to be a weapon in the hands of a ruling class, when he uses the term "religion" he uses it in an entirely different way from a person who conceives of religion to be man's relation to a sovereign Deity. Even when two people have the same concept of religion in mind they may still use "religion" to refer to different aspects intended by the concept or to the concept itself. Moreover, the term "religion"

7

may not refer to any particular concept of religion but to all concepts of religion, no matter how diverse they may be.

How people use the term "religion" will depend in part upon what they conceive religion to be and in part upon what they wish to discuss. Suppose, for example, that two devout adherents of a particular religion use the term "religion." They may mean to refer solely to their own religion, for they may regard everything else as forms of superstition. When they use the term "religion," they may refer to their concept of it, to what they consider to be its essence; or they may refer to its concrete historical manifestations. They may think of their own personal relation to whatever they consider to be of supreme importance within their religion—their relation to a God or gods, or they may refer to a set of beliefs that express the tenets of their religion. They may refer to the practices that are occasioned by such beliefs, or they may refer to what the beliefs are about—to the events, and things that constitute the basis for such beliefs and practices. Or "religion" may simply be used to refer to all these aspects in their totality. Unless it is clear as to what the term "religion" is meant to refer to, intelligent discussion is not possible. The failure to distinguish what is meant by the term "religion" results in hopeless confusion.

The point has been made that while the term "religion" is ambiguous, concepts of religion are not. Concepts are simply what they are. Different religions give rise to different concepts of religion, and wherever there are different concepts of religion, the difference in conception may be the occasion of different conceptual and real definitions.

Concepts of religion are in part formed because certain practices, observances, and beliefs are observed and held by various peoples throughout the world. Such states of affairs have their own peculiar features. A person who kneels for hours in a beautifully constructed building is not working to achieve an economic goal, nor is he simply concerned with the aesthetic qualities of the building. He is doing something, but what is he doing? Are there any

8

reasons for such behavior? And if so, what are they? Does the ground for such behavior lie within himself, or is there some non-subjective basis for his action? If it lies solely within himself, what fact or factors are the occasion of it? If the reason for such behavior is outside himself, what fact or factors are the occasion of it?

The concepts that people hold as to what religion is depend in part upon how they answer such questions. When these questions are answered differently, people form different concepts of religion. Let us suppose that a person holds that all such practices that are usually understood to be acts of worship, e.g., prayer, sacrifice, singing, etc., have no basis other than in the mind of the worshiper. Now either such is the case, or it is not. If it is true that there is never an objective basis for worship, then the person who understands acts of worship to be merely subjective is correct, and his concept of worship comprehends the essence of worship. He not only conceives of worship as being subjective, but it *really* is subjective. On the other hand, suppose that there is an objective basis for worship. Suppose a supreme Being had commanded it. The person who concluded that there was no objective basis for worship would then be wrong. His concept of worship would be a concept of something other than worship. Any definition of his concept of worship could still be adequate to express what he understood by worship, but worship would really be quite different from what he thought it to be. Conceptual definitions state what some people understand by the concept of religion, and real definitions seek to state what religion really is. It is only the latter that can properly be said to be true or false.

Many definitions of religion have been given. If such definitions are simply verbal and conceptual, they simply tell us how people use the word "religion" or what they understand by their concept of religion. A concept of religion has either comprehended what religion really is, or it has comprehended something else. If it has grasped what religion really is, it is then possible to give a definition of what religion really is.

9

Basically, there are only two types of definitions of religion that purport to be real definitions. The first assumes that there is some basis for religious beliefs and practices outside of man. The second simply denies that there is any non-human fact or factors to which man is related. Either there is a God or there is not. Either there are non-human powers that are conscious of man or there are not. If a God exists, then either he is concerned with man or he is not. And if gods or spirits exist, then either they are concerned with men or they are not. A person's concept of religion will vary, depending upon which sides of the above disjunction he chooses. And his concept of religion will in turn become a part of his real definition of religion. Consider the first disjunction: Either there is a God or there is not. If God exists then he exists. It obviously is not possible for God to exist and for God not to exist. But how does one decide? If a person decides that God exists, has he not already made a religious commitment or assumption? And if a person decides that God does not exist, has he not also made a religious commitment or assumption? And since either God exists or he does not, can anyone avoid making religious assumptions?

We seem, however, to be involved in a difficulty. On the one hand, any real definition of religion appears to depend upon a religious assumption about the existence of God; and yet on the other hand, any religious assumption would itself seem to presuppose some prior concept and real definition of religion. Otherwise how would we know it was religion? One way of avoiding this difficulty is to recognize that decisions that are made about the existence or non-existence of God are not always the result of theoretical reflection and analysis. There is a level of experience that is prior to any theoretical reflection—the level of everyday, common-sense experience, the level of naive experience. It is on this level, before any theoretical questions ever arise, that a person makes certain decisions that precede his conceptual and real definitions of religion. The difficulty as to which is first, the religious assumption or the real definition of religion, arises because of a failure

10

to consider a difference of priority. On the theoretical level of experience, on the level of logical abstraction, on the scientific or philosophical level, concepts and definitions of religion are needed to explain the nature of religious assumptions. In the actual course of a person's life, religious assumptions are chronologically prior to theoretical concepts and definitions. The failure to distinguish logical priority from chronological sequence may result in the mistaken notion that a person can look at religion in a purely neutral and objective way, that he can form concepts and definitions without being involved in any religious assumption. What is forgotten, however, is that prior to engaging in such theoretical analysis, i.e., during the course of his own life history, each person either believes that God exists or that he does not. There is no middle ground. Philosophical examinations of religion often try to conceal that the investigator has religious beliefs, or if they are stated openly, the impression is given that they are the result of the present study and were made only after careful theoretical consideration. To admit that he has made religious commitments chronologically prior to his theoretical study of religion frequently is thought to be enough to disqualify the investigator from the academic game. A truly critical attitude, however, demands the recognition that even professors of philosophy have usually lived a long time before they became professors. As human beings either they believe that God exists, or they do not. Their beliefs are chronologically prior to any theoretical analysis.

An analogous situation would exist if language teachers insisted that since languages presuppose grammar, grammar comes first. But in what sense does grammar come first? Logically or historically? In the actual process of learning his own language, a child learns to speak prior to learning any grammar. In fact, one can speak a language without ever studying its grammar. To demand that a person must be free of any religious beliefs prior to the theoretical study of religion is similar to the demand that a person ought not to speak a language prior to the study of its grammar.

11

No person is free of religious beliefs. The agnostic may think he can avoid taking sides. However, the truth is that like anyone else the agnostic believes that God either exists or does not exist. If he believed that God existed, he would not be an agnostic. This is not to imply that there is no difference between the agnostic and the atheist. In part the difference is psychological. The agnostic may not share the avowed atheist's strong feeling of certainty that there is no God. The agnostic may not feel that the evidence for the existence of God is adequate, so in the absence of adequate evidence, he is unwilling to believe in God. The atheist's stronger conviction, however, may in turn be fortified by the notion that the evidence against the existence of God is overwhelming, so that he *knows* that God does not exist. The point is, however, that neither the atheist nor the agnostic *believes* that God exists.

Everyone who approaches the study of religion is either a believer or a non-believer, i.e., he believes or does not believe in a god. It is possible that in the course of his study a believer may become a non-believer, or vice versa, but there is no middle ground. It is for this reason that complete neutrality about religious matters is impossible, and if objectivity depends upon such neutrality, then no one is ever objective. Yet, no matter what a person's beliefs may be it is still possible for him to be objective in the sense that he is willing to examine critically the evidence that would destroy his own beliefs as well as the evidence that would support them.

At this point, it ought to be evident that what a person understands by the concept of religion depends upon several factors. We have seen that every form of human behavior that gives rise to a concept of religion has two aspects— a subjective aspect and an allegedly objective aspect. The subjective factor is concerned with a person or persons that are engaged in some act or acts to which the adjective "religious" is customarily applied. Such acts may be internal—they may occur within the mental life of a person, in his beliefs, and attitudes; or they may be external,

12

expressed in propositions, acts of worship, prayer or sacrifice.

This second factor purports to be objective; it includes the object or objects, real or imaginary, about which beliefs are entertained and to which acts of worship, prayer, and sacrifice are directed. This objective aspect claims to provide a religion with an objective basis.

A person's concept of religion depends upon his conception of the relation between the subjective and the objective aspect of such phenomena as beliefs about a God, gods, spirits, powers, forces, and such acts as worshiping, praying, etc. A person may hold that no religion ever has an objective aspect, or he may hold that some religions do not have any objective aspect. Obviously, if no religion ever has an objective basis, then it is false to say that all religions have an objective basis, and it is equally false to say that some religions have an objective basis. If no religion ever has an objective basis, then all religions are subjective, so that the study of religion is really the study of human behavior and nothing more. Religion is then a part of anthropology. If the assumption is made, however, that some religions do not have an objective basis, then it would follow that it is false to hold that all religions have an objective basis, but the possibility would still exist that some religions, at least one, have an objective basis.

The proposition "no religion has an objective basis" is precisely the point at issue. If it is true, then all religion is really subjective, and all religions ought to be defined and studied as such. If the proposition is false, then some religions, at least one, have an objective aspect, and at least one religion ought to be defined in such a way that its objectivity is included as a part of its definition.

Many philosophers of religion assume the point in question: "no religion has an objective basis." To assume what is at issue without evidence is uncritical. We prefer to ask: What evidence is there that "no religion has an objective basis"? How would anyone know that all religions are subjective? What would the evidence for such an assumption be like? Has anyone ever examined all religions?

13

If so, how did he find out that the God or gods that were alleged to exist do not exist? What type of evidence is relevant to the truth or falsity of the proposition "no religion has an objective basis"?

Suppose a person wanted to know whether it is true or false that all religions are wholly subjective, i.e., that they lack any objective basis outside of human nature. Is there any specialist to whom he could go to find out? Are there any experts who *know* the answers to his questions? Could the mathematician help? Does the mathematician have some special knowledge, as a mathematician, that would be relevant to the truth or falsity of the question as to whether or not all religions lack an objective aspect? Does what a person knows about numbers, whether natural, irrational, negative or imaginary, have anything to do with the point at issue? Can any algebraic operation be of help? Will any geometry, calculus, or trigonometric function provide an answer? The mathematician, as a man, may entertain *opinions* about the truth or falsity of religions; but if he *knows* anything about religion, that is, if he has evidence, the nature of the evidence that he has is not mathematical.

Religious people are sometimes disheartened when they read that a great mathematician has launched an attack upon religion. But what a mathematician has to say about religion, whether pro or con, has nothing to do with mathematics, and it will be wise or foolish depending upon whether the mathematician knows something other than mathematics, specifically something about religion.

While it may be admitted that mathematics is irrelevant to questions about religion, perhaps the physicist *knows* something about religion. A moment's reflection, however, should make it clear that the position of the physicist is analogous to that of the mathematician. If the physicist *knows* anything about the objectivity of religion then he knows it because he knows something else besides physics. The study of the physical aspect of our world in terms of such a concept as an electron might be relevant to some religions, e.g., to those that deny the

14

reality of the physical world— but it could not prove that "no religion is objective." Christianity, for example, does not deny that the world the *physicist* studies is real. On the contrary, we shall see that Christianity insists that the world is real. In part, this is what the Christian doctrine of creation means. Some religions, at least Judaism, Christianity, and Islam, do not identify the world that the physicist studies with what they hold to be God. Other religions are pantheistic.

If the mathematician and the physicist are not able to offer evidence that is relevant to the truth or falsity of the statement that "no religions are objective," what about the biologist? We shall examine in some detail the alleged conflict between biology and religion later. It is sufficient here to note that if biology is the study of living matter, of living things, whether plants or animals, then it is not the study of God or gods. The study of living structures does not result in knowledge about something that is not studied, namely, a spiritual being or beings.

The mathematician, the physicist, and the biologist do not deal with subject matter that is relevant to the question as to whether or not all religions are subjective. That the sciences of mathematics, physics, and biology are simply irrelevant to religious questions will be shown in detail later. It is here necessary to note only that religion is not studied objectively when it is simply assumed that "no religion is objective." The various special fields of knowledge are not relevant to the point at issue. It is further evident that the psychologist, the sociologist, and the economist, *as such,* simply do not know whether religions are objective or not. Our refusal to consider such fields as psychology and sociology as relevant to the objectivity of all religions may be dismissed as arbitrary question-begging. The restriction that we would impose is required, however, by the very nature of our subject matter.

A proposition of psychology or of sociology could only be relevant to the subjective aspect of religion. Psychology deals with human beings—with their feelings, emotions,

15

and behavior; sociology deals with human groups—with man as he interacts with other men. Psychology and sociology do not examine the objective aspect of religions. The latter refers to what is non-human.

Certain religions are related to past events in such a way that the science of history is relevant to some of the statements that they make. The science of history is relevant to Judaism, Islam, and Christianity because some of their theological statements are false, unless certain historical propositions are true. Other world religions, such as Hinduism, cannot be tested by an appeal to historical events or to the testimony of eye witnesses.

If the various special sciences are not able to answer the question as to the truth of the proposition: "No religion has an objective basis," what then would be evidence as to its truth or falsity? The answer to our problem can be found by looking for premises which would justify the conclusion that "no religion has an objective basis." What propositions would have to be true in order for it to be true that "all religions are subjective"?

It is to be remembered that differences as to what religion is depend upon whether or not religion is considered to have an objective basis. Consequently, if we can disclose the reasons why people deny objectivity to religion, we shall have succeeded in giving a partial answer as to why there is disagreement with regard to the nature of religion. It will become increasingly clear that there is no single concept of religion.

From the standpoint of an individual's psychology, there are any number of feelings or emotions that may cause a person to be of the opinion that "no religion has an objective basis," but feelings are facts about people; they cannot serve as reasons why all statements of religion that are about a non-human objective aspect are false.

Religions would lack an objective basis if every proper religious statement that they made was false. When is a statement properly qualified by the adjective religious? At first glance it might appear that any statement dealing with a religious experience is a religious statement. Such statements as "John was converted," or "John believes in the efficacy of prayer" are statements about John's experience, not religious statements. Statements about John's religious experience may involve statements which are properly religious, but in so far as the reference is to an experience that John has, such a statement is not religious in any primary sense. In so far as statements deal with the feelings aroused by some aspect of human experience, such statements are a fitting object of study for the psychologist.

Instead of referring to feelings aroused by religious beliefs or attitudes, reference may be made to structural changes produced within a society, e.g., "The church seeks to control the state," or "Religious institutions are a threat to a free economy." Such expressions may involve statements which are properly religious, but in so far as the reference is to a social or economic structure of civilization, such a statement is the concern of a sociologist or economist and is not a religious statement in any primary sense.

There is still another group of statements which at first appear to be religious statements but which on closer scrutiny are not primarily religious, although they also may be used to support religious statements. For example, the statement: "Jesus turned water into wine at a wedding feast in Cana" is not a religious proposition. Its truth or falsity is in principle open to historical inquiry. Whether or not we are willing to consider such a proposition seriously will in part depend upon and in turn influence certain primary religious statements that we accept as true, but in itself the statement is not religious. Other statements of a similar nature such as "Jesus rose from the dead," are to be treated in the same manner, since their truth or falsity can in principle be ascertained without reference to proper religious statements.

What then is a proper religious statement? Let us propose a definition: A proper religious statement is a statement, the truth or falsity of which depends solely

17

upon the truth or falsity of other religious statements. To the degree that a statement is the subject matter of biology, psychology, sociology, the science of history, or any other science, such a statement is not religious. Such statements may be used in the service of a particular religion, they may even set its boundaries and mark off its limits; but they are not themselves the peculiar subject matter of religion, so they are, properly speaking, not religious statements.

Thus far we have stated what a religious statement is not. To state that "a proper religious statement is a statement, the truth or falsity of which depends solely upon the truth or falsity of other religious statements," would be helpful if we already knew what a religious statement was.

Let us try again: A proper religious statement is a statement which together with other proper religious statements describe the objective aspect of a religion. Proper religious statements refer to the objective, non-human building blocks of a religion. A proper religious statement is made about the objective aspect of religion. Its truth or falsity assumes the objective existence of what a particular religion holds to be the ultimate origin of the world, of ourselves, of what we are, and what we ought to become.

A further characteristic of a religious proposition is that its truth or falsity is not capable of being decided by a limited appeal to the senses. Statements used in support of religious statements may in principle be open to a direct and immediate test, but genuinely religious statements are not. For example, the apostle Paul mixes religious statements with historical statements. When Paul states that three days after his death Jesus "was seen of above five hundred brethren," Paul's statement can be checked in principle, but when he goes on to connect the death and resurrection of Jesus with the forgiveness of sin, and the final conquest of death, and when he elsewhere (Phil. 2) identifies Jesus with a pre-existent being who "being in the form of God, thought it not robbery to be equal with God" and who "was made in the likeness of men," then such

18

statements are, in principle, beyond what is immediately verifiable by any direct test.

A religious statement is true if the terms constituting it refer beyond themselves to a non-verbal state of affairs. The degree of correspondence between the normal signification of the words used, and the non-verbal state of affairs to which they refer in religious statements, is indicative of the literalness of the truth of such statements. Consequently, our question as to the objectivity of religion really asks whether there can really be any correspondence between genuine religious statements and non-verbal states of affairs. When it is asserted, for example, that "the world was created by God," or that "Jesus is God incarnate," what is the relation between the words used and what they designate? To hold that no religion is objectively true is to hold that the terms of any statement, which is a proper religious statement, fail to designate. That is, every genuine religious statement is false in the sense of *designational* falsity.

Whether or not a term designates objective states of affairs does not depend upon the whims or desires of a speaker, but it depends upon what is actually the case. "Unicorn" does not designate anything outside our minds, because there are no unicorns. To hold that "no religious statement has an objective basis" is to hold that religious statements are like statements about unicorns. Their key terms do not designate. To know whether a term designates requires knowledge about what is, and what is not, objectively real. Our knowledge of what is real has traditionally been called metaphysics. The denial of objectivity to religious statements thus depends upon metaphysical assumptions. It would be true that "all religion is subjective" if certain other metaphysical propositions were also true. If it is true that everything that is, is a part of an all-inclusive system of an impersonal nature, then there obviously is no room for intelligent, conscious non-human powers in nature, nor is there room for a God or gods beyond nature.

Naturalism, as a metaphysical position, has at least one reductionist thesis; namely, it reduces everything that is to a single, all-embracing system of things and events—a system that is explicable solely in terms of itself.

If naturalism is self-critical, it will seek to offer evidence to justify itself, but if its central thesis is simply assumed without evidence, it may be dogmatically set forth by its adherents as the very hall-mark of scientific objectivity. What is important for us to note is that it is simply uncritical to assume a metaphysical position without offering evidence and without at least making it clear that such a position has been assumed.

Definitions of religion that deny the very possibility of an objective basis to religion presuppose a basic naturalism in metaphysics; that is, they would be true if, and only if, naturalism is true. Naturalists usually agree that religion is to be defined in terms of some aspect of human nature. But there is no agreement as to precisely what it is that gives rise to man's religion. Many naturalistic definitions define religion in terms of a human motive, e.g., a desire to find meaning in life, a search for kindness, a help in times of stress, a form of enrichment. Religion then is caused by some basic insecurity. Man needs purpose; he needs comfort, happiness, peace of mind, a scale of values, something to look forward to; so out of his inner needs he creates a religion.[1]

Different attitudes may be expressed with regard to man's need for religion. Religion may be looked upon as a needless superstition, as an eternal hinderance to progress, as an immoral means of oppression, as something that will disappear as soon as man's fears are removed. Others may be inclined to regard religion as a stabilizing social force, as a sign of respectability, as something which may be utilized to instill the social and ethical norms of a society into the young. Whether the attitude of a naturalist is favorable or hostile, naturalists agree that statements ascribing existence to anything other than nature are false. Religious propositions may be useful in forming the right

20

attitude or in inculcating the right system of values, but they are never true in the sense that they claim to be.

A classic naturalistic explanation of religion is to be found in Ludwig Feuerbach's *The Essence of Christianity*. Feuerbach does not offer evidence that God does not exist; he simply assumes that he does not, and on the basis of this assumption, he then tries to show how religion arose, even though God does not exist.

Feuerbach claims to base his analysis of religion on objective facts, and the sole objective facts that he recognizes are material. Religion is the worship of man; he believes that human nature is divine. Religion simply mistakes a part of man's nature for something divine, whereas in fact there is no distinction between "the predicates of the divine and human nature, and consequently, no distinction between the divine and human subject."[2] Theology is, therefore, really anthropology. "Religion is the dream of the human mind." Man differs from animals in that he can conceive of himself; he is conscious of his own nature. And his religion is identical with the consciousness that man has of himself. The essential organ of religion is feeling, thus the nature of God is nothing except the expression of the nature of feeling.[3]

> Thou hast no other definition of God than this: God is pure, unlimited, free feeling. Every other God, whom thou supposest, is a God thrust upon thy feeling from without. Feeling is atheistic in the sense of the orthodox belief, which attaches religion to an external object; it denies an objective God—it is itself God.[4]

In religion man simply projects human qualities. Man knows what it is to love, to be wise, and to be kind, so he ascribes these qualities to God. Since man is a subject, he erroneously conceives of God as existing.[5] But God is in fact simply a feeling—the projection of human nature into objectivity. Man creates God and then regards himself as an object related to God, the subject.[6]

Feuerbach's analysis is plausible if religion has no objective basis. For if God does not exist, then in the beginning man created God in man's own image. If God

21

created man, man is then related to God as his creature; religion is then man's relation to God. However, if there is no God, the problem is simply to explain how the idea of God arose when in fact there is no objective basis for such an idea. Unless there is an objective aspect to religion, Feuerbach's position or some such alternative is inescapable.

On the other hand, if religion is conceived of as having an objective basis, this will give rise to an alternative definition of religion. But even when religion is conceived of as having an objective basis, there are still differences that must be taken into account. The objective aspect of religion may simply be identified with nature or with the universe. The divine may be regarded as impersonal or personal. The various parts of the universe may be thought of as separate gods that have partial control over the lives of men and things. The objective aspect may be conceived of as spirits that live in trees and in other natural objects, or it may consist of gods that have control over a phase of the cosmos. Not only are there different views of the nature of the objective aspect of religion, but also there is the further problem as to how man is related to this aspect, as well as the question as to how he knows what god is. Even among those who hold that there is an objective side to religion, i.e., a non-human aspect or object, there are still three possible areas where essential differences arise. There is the question as to what is the *nature* of the objective aspect, how is it *related* to man, and how is it *known*.

Many definitions of religion presuppose an objective basis for religion. Within the biblical tradition, religion denotes man's relation to God. "For it is He to whom we ought to be bound . . . ."[7] Special honor is due to God, since he is the first principle of all things. Religion is, therefore, a virtue, since it is a part of being good to render to God what we owe him.[8] Although it is impossible for man to pay God as much as he owes him, yet his whole life ought to be devoted to his honor. Thus, man's relation to God gives rise to certain acts, e.g., to devotion, where men subject themselves wholly to God; and to prayer, where man confesses his need of God and surrenders his mind to him. Religion is here more than worship; it is the service of God with one's whole being throughout the entire course of one's life. It is in this sense that the religious man's whole life is a prayer and an offering to God.

Our inquiry has shown that what religion is depends upon the nature of what is real. Different conceptions of religion are formed because people in fact have different views of the nature of the universe. Some conceive of our world as being all that there is. The world itself is "God"; it is what is ultimately real. To the degree that the world can be understood, it is intelligible to the natural sciences. Such a basic naturalism may be proclaimed as an article of faith in a way analogous to religious faith. Arguments in support of naturalism may be offered, but unless such arguments are metaphysical, they are irrelevant. If naturalism is true, all religions are subjective. Religion is reducible to feelings. It is incapable of being true or false.

An alternative view of religion recognizes that religion has an objective basis. Many differences may arise here, however, as to the nature of the objective aspect of religion. Nature or a part of nature may be deified and made the object of devotion, or God may be held to be above nature and not identical with it.

The most basic division that our analysis has disclosed thus far is that between the *subjectivists* and the *objectivists*. Furthermore, we have found no agreement as to what religion is. There is no single definition of religion that will suit everyone. Our examination of what religion is has thus brought us to an awareness of basic disagreements.

3. Can Religion be Examined Philosophically?

The purpose of our inquiry is to examine religion from a philosophical point of view. It is therefore necessary to ask what philosophy is. A philosophical inquiry requires consideration of both the objectivist and the subjectivist views as to the nature of religion. To dismiss either the one or the other is to betray an uncritical and dogmatic prejudice.

We have seen that there are two basic definitions of religion—the one subjective, the other objective. What does this have to do with philosophy? What is meant by a philosophical inquiry into the nature of religion? To answer this question, we must reach some agreement as to what philosophy is. Here, too, we encounter difficulties similar to those of the preceding section.

The term "philosophy" is today often used ambiguously, and many people have a very vague concept of philosophy. Some use the word to refer to whatever they regard as trivial and idle speculation. At best they regard it as an interesting hobby, or as poetry; it is a proper pastime for the impractical misfit, but it has nothing to do with the concrete world of dollars and cents. Many use the word to stand for an older way of looking at the world —a pre-scientific stage in man's development. To them it is a concession to tradition to have departments of philosophy in a university. They believe that those who teach philosophy simply teach the history of past ideas. The truth about man and the world is now to be found in the sciences. Philosophy is archaic; it belongs to the past. The history of philosophy thus becomes the history of ideas, ideas that are no longer relevant. Still others use the word to stand for a personal outlook, a way of life. For them philosophy lacks any objective meaning. It is simply the way in which a person meets his problems and adjusts to living. It lacks any justification in the nature of things and is simply a way of responding to one's social environment.

The situation is further complicated by the fact that philosophers themselves do not agree as to what philosophy is. Some hold that philosophy is primarily the study of first principles, of what is really real. Others deny that metaphysics is possible and hold that statements which purport to be metaphysical do not make sense. For some, the philosopher is able to use "reason" alone in a purely speculative way, so that whatever can be thought without contradiction is conceived of as existing. To gain knowledge, others would use "reason," together with sense experience. For still others, our knowledge not only begins in sense experience, it also ends there. And for others, it is the function of the philosopher to show that there is no philosophical knowledge. Philosophy is simply a mistake. Our knowledge is limited to what can be known through the sciences. A person may have beliefs in addition to what he "knows," but "philosophy" is not able to tell us what would otherwise be unknown. For others "philosophy" consists of ideas that are not necessarily true, but they may prove useful in reshaping society, in accomplishing some human purpose. It may serve as a weapon in some ideological task. Thus philosophers not only differ as to the nature of philosophy, but they also differ as to its relation to the special sciences, i.e., to physics, the science of history, etc.

Some hold that both philosophy and the sciences contain statements that are true only in the sense that they are useful. Others regard the statements of science as being useful, but not true, in the sense that scientific statements do not necessarily describe the world as it is. The truth about the world is left to philosophy, and it is in part the philosopher's task to clarify the sense in which the statements of the sciences are meaningful. Some philosophers regard philosophy and the sciences as being able to acquire genuine knowledge of the world, each working independently of the other; but some would either make philosophy dependent upon an autonomous science, or make science dependent upon an autonomous philosophy; while some regard science and philosophy as each depending upon the other.

25

To give a definition of philosophy that every philosopher will accept is not possible. However, it is necessary that we indicate what we consider philosophy to be, in order to show why this work claims to be a philosophical examination of religion. Either there is such a thing as philosophy or there is not. If the word "Philosophy" does not refer to what is distinct from other areas of human experience, then it is only confusing to use it as though it did. If philosophy is simply another name for poetry or one of the sciences, whether it be physics or theology, then why not call it poetry or theology?

Whatever philosophy may be, it is something. If it is worth knowing, it is worth knowing because at least some of its statements are true. Philosophers may differ as to which philosophical statements are true. They may hold to contradictory statements, both of which cannot be true, but it is hard to see how a person can regard himself as a philosopher, unless he holds that there are some true philosophical statements and that philosophy consists of the orderly, systematic arrangement of such statements.

To define philosophy as a discipline that is made up of true philosophical statements is illuminating only if we already know what a philosophical statement is. What is it that makes a statement philosophical?

To answer this question, it is not necessary that we scrutinize every possible philosophical statement, nor is it necessary to give an example of every possible type of philosophical statement. It is sufficient that we understand the general nature of a philosophical statement. The nature of the latter can be approached by first indicating what a philosophical statement is not.

A philosophical statement is not a statement that is made on the level of everyday common sense experience. On the level of common sense every person is aware of a world that exists independently of himself. This world is simply given as an indissoluble, unbreakable coherence. It is there and man did not make it. His knowing the world is not the same as his making the world. A theory about this basic naive experience may deny its trustworthy char-

26

acter, but on the level of common sense, the reality of the world is not a matter of theory; the world is accepted without further reflection. As long as the reality of the world is simply assumed without question, as long as the reality of the world is not made a problem, neither philosophy nor science has been born.

Philosophical statements about the nature of the world are made when what is taken for granted on the level of naive experience is made a problem. Philosophical thought is theoretical thought. It reflects upon the common experience of all men. It raises questions as to whether the world is what it appears to be. And when as a result of such reflection, statements are made about the world, such statements may be philosophical. Philosophy, however, is not the only discipline that reflects upon what is given in our naive everyday experience of the world. The various sciences also seek to know the world theoretically. In part, however, the difference between the sciences and philosophy is that each of the special sciences abstracts a particular aspect of the world as it is given to our naive common sense experience. For example, consider a concrete individual object such as a chair. The mathematician may abstract the numerical aspect of a chair and speak of it as a quantity, as one. The physicist may be concerned with its physical properties and discuss it in physical terms, e.g., in terms of electrons. The biologist may discuss it in terms of biological concepts, in terms of its organic structure, if it is made of stuff that was previously living. A psychologist may speak of its effect upon human feelings. The historian may be interested or uninterested in it, depending upon whether it was used by a person of historical note. The linguist may be concerned with its name; the sociologist with its function in society; the economist with its value in dollars and cents; the aesthetician with its style; the jurist may be interested in it as a piece of legal property; and the theologian may be interested in its relation to God as a part of a created or uncreated world.[9] In every case, however, it is the same chair that is the object of analysis. Each of the sciences abstracts a different

27

aspect of the chair, and the reality of the chair is not exhausted by any single perspective.

For a statement to be philosophical, it cannot be a statement *of* any one of the sciences. A statement is a statement *of* one of the sciences if the evidence that is relevant to its truth or falsity is also a statement *of* the particular science in question. The special sciences are each concerned with a single aspect of our experience. Philosophy is concerned with our experience as a whole. Its statements may be *about* a special science, or it may be *about* the interrelationships between the sciences. It is for this reason that philosophy is more concrete than any single science. The latter deals with a special aspect, whereas philosophy deals with every aspect. It is concerned with the whole of reality, with the totality of our experience.

Philosophy distinguishes the kinds of knowledge that each of the sciences discovers, and it seeks to show the relationship between the various kinds of knowledge. A philosophical statement may be either a statement *about* a special science, or it may be *about* the interrelationships between the sciences.

Traditionally, at least, the philosopher has not been satisfied to stop here. His concern has also been to determine the way in which the world of naive experience—the world investigated by the sciences—is related to its origin. Philosophers have never agreed as to what is the arché— the origin of all diversity and law within the world of immediate experience—but philosophers have traditionally sought to relate the world to whatever they held to be its ultimate source.

It is in this area that the philosopher has often entered into the same problems as the theologian. The relationship between philosophy and theology has often been the subject of intense debate. Some have maintained that neither philosophy nor theology, in the sense of the systematization of revealed truth, can provide knowledge about the ultimate ground of the universe. Others deny any claim to truth made by the theologian on the basis of revela-

28

tion but hold that the philosopher can at least show that God exists, while others base their knowledge of God on faith in revelation and deny that philosophy can furnish information even with respect to the existence of God. Still others assign an independent task to both philosophy and theology and assume that while philosophy (or natural theology) can show that God exists, it is only faith in revelation that provides an adequate knowledge of his nature. It is, however, not necessary for us to enter here more fully into this discussion.[10] It is not our concern to develop a systematic philosophy that includes every possible aspect of philosophical thought.

A philosophical examination of religion is concerned with a single aspect of human experience. The object that we would examine is religion, and we would determine the truth *about* religion as far as it is possible. Some say that man's religious experience is wholly subjective; others that it is objective. The most basic problem for the philosopher of religion is to determine the truth *about* religion. He must decide *what religion is?* But how is he to decide? We have already noted that as a man the philosopher is himself never wholly neutral with respect to religion, but the point has been made that this does not prevent him from examining the evidence. What we have called the objectivist and the subjectivist views of religion are mutually exclusive views *about* religion. Our task throughout the remainder of this book is to try to reach a decision based on evidence as to the truth or falsity of the propositions: "Religion is wholly subjective," or "Religion is based upon an objective relation to God."

It is self-evident that wherever religious beliefs are formulated into propositions that are contradictory, both statements cannot be true. For some religious propositions to be true, others must be false. It is also obvious that, if religious propositions are contradicted by statements that are derived from any of the sciences, either the latter are false or the religious propositions are false.

Not all religions deserve equal consideration on the part of the philosopher. For if the primary aim of a philosophical examination of religion is to determine what religion is on the basis of evidence, such an examination is primarily concerned with religious systems for which evidence is offered. In some instances, the conclusion reached will be that the particular religion in question lacks an objective foundation outside of human nature. It may prove to be the case, however, that in at least one instance there is sufficient ground to warrant the acceptance of certain religious propositions as true, although the evidence may not be conclusive in the sense of a formal demonstration.

The philosopher of religion is confronted with a variety of conflicting claims about the nature of the religious object, ranging from an identification of the world with God to a belief in a God that transcends the world.

The evidence that is offered in support of various beliefs about the object of religious worship may be divided into several main types. The first is individual and personal; it appeals to some private, immediate and direct human experience. Such experience may be indescribable and of significance only to the person that has had it; or it may be interpreted to others as also being meaningful, at least to the extent that it is communicable. Individual personal experience of the objective ground of religion, e.g., of God, may be thought to be the result of human initiative, of some human effort; or where God is held to be personal, it may be held to be the result of divine initiative, of an activity on the part of God, in which case such experience is a form of revelation, or divine self-disclosure. At times, such experience of God is alleged to have occurred to a single person, and at other times, more than one individual was involved. When the claim to such direct experience of God is made in the form of reports to others, whether in written or oral form, it becomes indirect evidence, and its reliability depends in part upon the trustworthy character of the witness. It is, of course, only meaningful to consider such testimony if there is some possibility that religion has an objective basis. The subjectivist may be so thoroughly convinced that religion is subjective that he will never consider the possibility of evidence to the contrary. It is dogmatic, however, to rule out the possibility of contrary evidence without first considering it.

In addition to claims to know God by some experience of him or of his activity, the attempt has also been made to demonstrate that God exists. If it can be shown that there are reasons to support the thesis that religion has an objective basis, this would increase the probability in favor of the actuality of the self-disclosure of such a being. It is, therefore, of interest to us to investigate how people support their beliefs by means of arguments.

Before we examine the arguments for the existence of God and the religions that purport to be based upon the revelation of a personal God, we shall look at certain forms of religion that seem to support the subjectivist view of religion. For it may well be that while not every religion is subjective, most of them are.

---

[1] Charles S. Braden, "Why People Are Religious," *Journal of Bible and Religion*, XV, No. 1 (January, 1947).

[2] Ludwig Feuerbach, *The Essence of Christianity* (New York: Harper & Brothers, 1957), p. XXXVII.

[3] *Ibid.*, p. 9.

[4] *Ibid.*, p. 11.

[5] *Ibid.*, p. 18.

[6] *Ibid.*, p. 30.

[7] Thomas Aquinas, *The Summa Theologica*, translated by The English Dominican Fathers (Burns Oates & Washbourne), Art. I, Q. 81; Vol. II, p. 9.

[8] *Ibid.*, Q. 81, Art. 2.

[9] For a further detailed analysis see Herman Dooyeweerd, *A New Critique of Theoretical Thought*, translated by David H. Freeman et al. (Philadelphia: Presbyterian and Reformed Publishing Co., 1957) Vol. I, Part 1.

[10] For a fuller treatment of this subject see David H. Freeman, *Recent Studies in Philosophy and Theology*, (Philadelphia: Presbyterian and Reformed Publishing Co., 1962).

CHAPTER II

NON-BIBLICAL RELIGIONS

1. *Religions of the Ancient Near East*

The view that religion is a subjective projection of the human fantasy is supported by the religions of the Ancient Near East and the religions of India. The Ancient Near East included Mesopotamia, Palestine, and Egypt, and there is evidence that Greece was also closely related to it.[1] The first literature in Asia was the Sumerian, written from about 3000 B.C. in Mesopotamia. It was replaced as a spoken language by Accadian, sometimes known as Babylonian or Assyrian. Hittite is included in Accadian. The most recent language to be deciphered is Ugaritic,[2] a branch of Canaanite. Some of the other languages to be found in this area of the world were Old Persian, Phoenician, Moabite, Aramaic, Egyptian, and of course Hebrew. For our study of the religions of the Ancient Near East we are fortunate in having a number of written sources available as well as numerous archeological remains.[3]

In Egyptian religion the origin of the gods is illustrated by an inscription carved inside of the pyramids of Mer-ne-Re and Nefer-Ka-Re of the Sixth Dynasty (24th century B.C.). The text was a part of a dedication ritual of a royal pyramid. It begins by evoking Atum-Kheprer, the God of Heliopolis, who was compounded of two phases of the sun. It recalls the first "creation," when the god Atum stood on a primeval hillock, arising out of the waters of chaos, and then brought the first gods into existence: Shu, the god of air, Tefnut, the goddess of moisture, Geb, god of earth, Nut, goddess of the sky, the gods Osiris, Isis, Seth, and the goddess Nepthys.

32

> O Atum-Kephrer, thou wast on high on the (primeval) hill; thou didst arise as the ben-bird . . . thou didst spit out what was Shu, thou didst sputter out what was Tefnut . . . O Great Ennead which is in Heliopolis, Atum, Shu, Tefnut, Geb, Nut, Osiris, Isis, Seth, and Nepthys whom Atum begot. . . .[4]

Another version which goes back to 2000 B.C. and is taken from the Book of the Dead begins with a speech of the Lord of all:

> I am Atum when I was alone in Nun (the waters of chaos, out of which life arose) ; I am Re in his (first) appearances, when he began to rule that which he had made.[5]

Atum is not eternal. In this text, he states simply that "I am the great god who came into being by himself."

When Atum-Re named the parts of his body, the other gods then came into being:

> . . . . Who is he? He is Re, who created the names of the parts of his body. That is how these gods who follow him came into being.[6]

The variations on this theme are numerous. Another version is found in a text employed for ritual and magical purposes. The ship of the sun god Re made a daily journey through the sky by day and through the skies below by night. Each evening Atum's ship is threatened with destruction by a dragon Apophis, a demon who lurks in the underworld.

> This spell is to be recited over Apophis drawn on a new sheet of Papyrus in green color and put inside a box on which his name is set. He being tied and bound and put on the fire every day, wiped out with thy left foot and spat upon four times in the course of every day. Thou shalt say as thou puttest him on the Fire: 'Re is triumphant over thee, O Apophis!—Four times, and Horus is triumphant over his enemy!—four times.'. . .[7]

This text is not only useful for dispelling dragons and thus repulsing the dangers that face the nation, but also it provides information about the all-Lord, Kephri, the morning sun-god, conceived as a scarab beetle. For the god tells us after he had come into being "many were the beings which came forth from my mouth."

> I planned in my own heart, and there came into being a multitude of forms of beings . . . . I was the one who copulated with my fist, I masturbated with my hand. Then I spewed with my own mouth: I spat out what was Shu (the air god), and I sputtered out what was Tefnut (the goddess of moisture).[8]

The text also provides information about the origin of man. For apparently Shu and Tefnut went out in search of Kephri's eye which had wandered off. He made a substitute eye to take its place. Shu and Tefnut brought his first eye back. In Kephri's own words:

> It was angry with me, after it returned and found out that I had made another in its place.

All was not lost, however, for the occasion was to cause man to be made. For as Kephri tells the story.

> After I had joined together my members, I wept over them. That is how men came into being from the tears which came from my Eye.[9]

On another occasion, however, mankind lost favor with Re.

> It happened that . . . Re, the God who came into being himself, when he was king of men and gods all together. Then mankind plotted something in the very presence of Re. Now then, his majesty was old . . . His bones were of silver, his flesh of gold.[10]

So he called together the other gods, including his eye, and asked Nun what he should do. For mankind had fled into the desert. The eye of the god was incapable, at least in its present form, of dealing with the situation. The goddess of destruction, Hathor, then set out to destroy mankind. After she had lessened their number, Re decided to spare the rest of mankind. With difficulty Re was able to trick the goddess Hathor, so that "she came back drunken without having perceived mankind,"[11] who was thus delivered from destruction.

34

The best preserved Sumerian account is that of Enki and Ninhursag. The text is based on a well-preserved six column tablet that has been excavated. It was inscribed sometime in the first half of the second millennium B.C.; the date of its original composition is unknown.

The plot of the story is complicated. Enki, the Sumerian water-god who dwells in Dilmun, a land where there is probably neither sickness nor death, impregnates the goddess Ninhursag or Ninter, who after nine days gave birth to Ninmu, who after sexual intercourse with her Father, Enki, also gave birth in nine days to the goddess Ninkurra. Enki then causes his granddaughter to become pregnant, and in nine days she gives birth to the goddess Utter. By this time the great-grandmother, Ninhursag, has had enough. The text is corrupted here and the next thing we know Enki obtains some cucumbers, apples, and grapes from a gardener which he brings to Utter who now receives his advances, but of this union no new goddess is born. Instead, eight plants are now brought into being. When Enki now proceeds to eat of the plants, he is cursed by Ninhursag and begins to pine away. At this point the fox comes to the rescue and succeeds in bringing Ninhursag back to the gods. She then seats Enki by or "in her vulva" and heals each of his sick members by creating eight new deities,[12] among whom was Ninkasi, the goddess of strong drink.

The chief Mesopotamian account of creation *Enuma Elish* ("when on high") in Accadian consists of seven tablets. The work was probably recast in its basic classical form in the first half of the second millennium B.C.[13] According to the account:

> Before the heaven had been named and before the firm ground below had been, there were not many at all; there was only the primordial sea god, Apsu, the begetter of other gods, and his wife Tiamat, the sea goddess.
>
> Then it was that the gods were formed within them ... Lahmu and Lahamu ... Anshar and Kisher ... Anu ... Nudimud (Ea, one of the names of the earth and water god) ...

The divine brothers banded together . . . they troubled
the mood of Tiamat[14] . . . Apsu also found them very
loathsome and noisy gods and wanted to destroy them
that quiet may be restored[15] . . . Tiamat, his wife the
Sea-goddess, was more kindly disposed. She pleaded
with her husband. 'What? Should we destroy that
which we have built? Their ways indeed are most
troublesome, but let us attend kindly. . . .'[16]

Instead of listening to his wife, Apsu listened to the
advice of Mummu, his vizier, and decided to destroy "the
gods, his sons," but when the gods heard this they were
astir or in tears until Ea, the All-wise, put Apsu to sleep
by casting a magic spell.

When Apsu he had made prone, drenched with sleep,
. . . he loosened his band, tore off his tiara, Removed
his halo (and) put it on himself. Having fettered
Apsu, he slew him![17]

The Babylonian god Apsu is dead! Tiamat now became very angry and with the aid of the god Kingu she
led a rebellion against the gods. For such an undertak-
ing she decided to make monsters.

Roaring dragons she has clothed with terror, has
crowned them with haloes, making them like gods. So,
that he who beholds them shall perish abjectly . . .
She set up the Viper, the Dragon, and the Sphinx,
The great-Lion, the Mad-dog, and the Scorpion-Man,
Mighty lion-demons, the Dragon-Fly, the Centaur.[18]

When the god Ea heard that Tiamat was girding for
battle, he took counsel with the other gods, who were of
course quite troubled. Who would not be afraid of "mon-
ster-serpents, sharp of tooth, unsparing of fang"?[19]
The only god that apparently had a chance against
Tiamat was "Marduk, the hero"; he alone could face Tiamat's roaring dragons and save the lives of the gods, who
"wailed in distress."[20] Marduk was made king among the
gods and was entrusted with the mission of killing Tiamat:

Go and cut off the life of Tiamat . . . Bow and quiver
he hung at his side. In front of him he set the lightning.[21] (What a sight it must have been.) With a
blazing flame he filled his body. He then made a net

to enfold Tiamat therein. The four winds he stationed that nothing of her might escape . . . He made seven more winds to assist him, and after mounting his terrifying storm chariot which he yoked to four poisonous steeds, he set forth to challenge Tiamat to single combat.[21]

When she heard Marduk's challenge, it was too much for the woman:

> She took leave of her senses. In fury Tiamat cried out aloud. To the roots of her legs shook both together. She recites a charm, keeps casting her spell, while the gods of battle sharpen their weapons.[22]

They began to fight. How terrifying. Tiamat and Marduk, the wisest of gods, locked in battle! Marduk kept trying to catch Tiamat in his net, and she tried to "open her mouth to consume him." That was her fatal mistake. For when Tiamat opened her mouth, Marduk let the evil wind, which followed behind, loose in her face.

> He drove in the Evil Wind that she close not her lips. As the fierce winds charged her belly, her body was distended and her mouth was wide open.[23]

Once having gotten Tiamat in this uncomfortable position, it required little marksmanship for the most honored of the great gods, Marduk, to shoot Tiamat with an arrow. This was more than the constitution of the goddess could stand. The arrow "tore her belly. It cut through her insides, splitting the heart."[24]

As a sign of victory the brave Marduk cast down the corpse of the now dead Tiamat and stood on it. This was too much for Tiamat's followers. They tried to get away, but Marduk caught them in his net and held them imprisoned, even though they cried to get out. Marduk then took the tablets of fate away from the god Kingu, for they were not rightfully his, and Marduk hung them on his own breast.

Marduk was not finished. The universe had not yet been made. Marduk decided to make it. What could be more suitable than the corpse of the dead goddess Tiamat? Marduk decided to use it.

> The lord trod on the legs of Tiamat, with his unsparing mace he crushed her skull. When the arteries of her blood he had severed, the North Wind bore it to places undisclosed.
> . . . Then the lord paused to view her dead body, that he might divide the monster and do artful works. He split her like a shellfish into two parts: Half of her he set up and ceiled it as sky . . . .[25]

He constructed stations for the gods, caused the moon to shine and to maintain a relationship to the sun. In short he made a world. But it was not complete. Man was still missing. The wise Marduk decided to make him too. He tells Ea, his father, of his plans:

> Blood I will mass and cause bones to be. I will establish a savage, man shall be his name. Verily, savage man I will create. He shall be charged with the service of the gods that they might be at ease.[26]

To make man Marduk needed some material. Since it was the god Kingu who had made Tiamat rebel in the first place, the gods decided to use him. Why not? They severed his blood vessels. "Out of his blood they fashioned mankind."[27] And that is how man was made, from a rebellious god.

That such accounts and such gods were taken seriously by the peoples of the Ancient Near East is attested to by numerous extant hymns, prayers, and rituals. For example, in the Ugaritic literature, the priests of Baal reenact on earth the deeds of their god as a part of their cultic practices. The puissant god Baal at times "desires a cow-calf . . . lies with her times seventy-seven . . . . She conceives . . . ."[28]

As Cyrus Gordon points out:

> Indeed the Hebrew view is to a great extent a conscious reaction against the Canaanite milieu. This is illustrated by the fact that bestiality, far from being looked at askance in Ugarit, was practiced by the adored Baal, who copulates with a heifer as is celebrated in the religious texts (67:V:17-12). If it be argued that Baal assumes the shape of a bull for the act, the same cannot be said for his priests who reenact his mythological career cultically.[29]

Much light has been shed upon the Old Testament from recent studies of the Ancient Near East. It is difficult, however, to see how anyone can accuse the Israelites of borrowing the idea of creation *ex nihilo* from any of the surrounding nations.

The religions of the Ancient Near East do in fact display certain formal similarities to that of the Old Testament. Both are concerned with the origin of man and with the origin of the present world. Both are concerned with man's relation to what is to be worshiped. The similarity ends with such formal agreement. With respect to content there are only striking contrasts. Similar language is used, but the concepts expressed are *essentially* different. To see the difference the text of the first chapters of Genesis need only be compared to the religious texts of the surrounding Ancient Near Eastern nations.

When the Israelites read their Scriptures they were made conscious of the difference between their faith and that of the nations. The Genesis account is the denial of the essential notions of non-biblical religions of the ancient world.

The gods of non-biblical religions have a beginning. They usually arise out of the waters of a primordial chaos. They are totally lacking in moral qualities. They kill, and are killed; they eat, drink, and engage in sexual intercourse. They literally display like passions with men. They are angry and afraid. They may in fact eat each other, as the god Mot eats puissant Baal.[30] They are deceitful and treacherous, engaging in plots and conspiracies. They are finite deities whose power and knowledge is limited. In fact such "supernatural" powers are more or less controlable by magic and ritual. The gods are neither eternal nor immortal, and they are in fact subordinate to the chaos out of which they arose. The gods had a beginning, but apparently the waters of chaos, out of which they arose, did not.[31]

The creative acts of Genesis refer to the acts of an omnipotent God. The phenomenal universe (heaven and earth) are brought into being (created) by him. The chaos

39

mentioned does not precede God, but God creates the chaos. All order, all law, all structures, the heavens and the earth, the sun, the moon, the stars, the world of plants, animals and the seas, in fact everything else, is not a god, but is a part of the created world which God alone has made.

In Genesis man occupies a special place. He is made in the image and likeness of God in holiness and righteousness, but he is not a part of God. He is neither the tears nor the blood of a slain deity. The world is not the body of a dead goddess; the cycles of drought and famine do not depend upon the death and re-living of Baal. Man need not fear the violence of the goddess Hathor who seeks to destroy him, for God is good. The world is not the abode of half-men and half-bulls; there are no gods who eat each other and rule the regions of the universe. There is no need to fear the dragon of the world below who each day threatens the sun with destruction. For all of nature is the creation of God and man has been given dominion over it. The animals are not incarnations of gods to be worshiped but they are to be controlled by man.

Man's present misery is not due to the whims of arbitrary deities. It is the result of his own willful transgression of God's holy law. There are no cruel deities that desire human sacrifice and arbitrarily threaten his destruction. For this is the world that God has made.

> Nothing is said as to how it was done, about process. This is important. Science is concerned with material and phenomenal things, with processes and changes, with differentiation and combination. This account does not deny process; it ignores it. It speaks in terms of a divine fiat, which can both use and dispense with process. Science deals with second causes: here the First Cause is the almighty Actor and second causes are ignored.[32]

It is impossible to examine every religion which seems to support the thesis that religion is the product of human fantasy. At this point the reader may be willing to grant that at least some religions are too fanciful to be more than myths and imaginative stories, of value solely for their literary and historical interest.

It is very unlikely that a reader today believes in such gods as Marduk, Ea, Re, in Osiris, or in Baal. Shu and Tefnut, Aspu and Tiamat, Atum, Nut, Isis, Seth, Nepthys, Enki, Ninhursag, Anu, Lahmu, Lahamu, Anshar and Kisher, and Kingu, and many others provoke smiles among those who belong to what is known as "Western civilization." What we are apt to forget is that one of the main reasons why we do not take such gods seriously is that our ancestors, whether Jews or Gentiles, came to believe in the first chapters of Genesis.

There are regions of the modern world where the great masses of people still live in a world like the religious world of antiquity. It is in such a setting that we discover the religions of India and the Orient. Many inhabitants of the East have broken with their past and have embraced the "new religion" of Marxism or some other form of secularism. Others have spiritualized the gods and treated them as symbols of a philosophical absolute. It is to this development that we shall now turn.

2. *Hinduism*

There are many affinities in the ancient religions and philosophical ideas of India and Persia.

> The process of god-making in the factory of man's mind cannot be seen so clearly anywhere else as in the Rig-Veda . . . .
>
> We may begin with the identification of the Vedic gods in some of their aspects with certain forces of nature, and point out how they were gradually raised to moral and superhuman beings . . . .
>
> The moon and the stars, the sea and the sky, the dawn and the nightfall were regarded as divine. This worship of nature as such is the earliest form of Vedic religion.[33]

India does not have a single religion, but there are combinations of related religions, based upon different phases of the Vedic tradition.[34] The texts are written in Sanskrit and constitute a vast body of material. The oldest Vedic texts are composed of four collections, known as

41.

the Vedas.[35]   Other literature based upon one of these
collections is also referred to as "Vedic" when the term
is used broadly. The four Vedas, the Sruti or "revelation,"
are the Rig-Veda, the Samaveda, the Yajurveda (of which
there are two recensions), and the Artharvaveda. In addition, certain prose treatises, the Brahmanas, that interpret Brahman; the Aranyakas or forest-teachings, and the
Upanishads belong to the Vedas.

Other Vedic documents are the Smrti which include
the Sutras, collections of aphorisms; the Dharmasastra, law
manuals; the Itihasas, or epic poems (the Bhagavagita is
also considered to be sacred); and the Puranas, ancient
traditional histories sometimes grouped with similar works
called Tantras.

The oldest document in Indian literature is the Rig-
Veda or verse-Veda.[36] It contains 1,017 hymns addressed
to the gods, covering about 10,600 stanzas. These prayers
are of importance for the understanding of Hinduism, since

they are the source of the later practices and philosophies of the Indo-Aryans, and a study of them is necessary for a proper understanding of subsequent
thought.[37]

It is not necessary for our purpose to enter into the
question as to the strata of development of the hymns.[38]
We can note that like the religions of the Ancient Near
East, they name and ascribe worship to many gods. The
most prominent is Indra, a deity of the thunderstorm, the
god of battle.

From the number of hymns addressed to him, Indra
is the most popular god of the Vedas.

To quote Radhakrishnan:

Indra is the god of the atmospheric phenomena, of
the blue sky. He is the Indian Zeus. His naturalistic
origin is clear. He is born of waters and the cloud.
He wields the thunder-bolt, and conquers darkness.
He brings us light and life, and gives us vigor and
freshness . . . Gradually Indra's connection with the
sky and the thunderstorms is forgotten. He becomes
the divine spirit, the ruler of all the world and all the
creatures, who sees and hears everything.[39]

42

Indra is

the hero-god who as soon as born shielded the gods, before whose might the two worlds shook—that, ye people, is Indra; who made fast the earth . . . who slew the serpent and freed the seven streams, rescued the cows, the pounder in battle . . . without whose aid ye never conquer.[40]

It is to be noted that like the other gods of antiquity, Indra himself came into being:

Him, verily, the moons, the mountains followed . . . Yearning with love both worlds approached, the waters waited on Indra when he first had being.[41]

In addition to Indra there are minor deities that represent the wind, Vata or Vayu, the terrible storm gods, the Maruts, and Rudra who later becomes Siva. There are also many goddesses.

Usas and Aditi are goddesses. The river Sindhu is celebrated as a goddess in one hymn (X.75.2,4,6), and Sarasvati, first the name of a river, gradually becomes the goddess of learning. Vak is the goddess of speech. Aranyani is the goddess of the forest.[42]

Other gods of importance in the hymns of the Rigveda are Agni, the god of fire; Varuna, chief of the gods of the natural and moral order; and Prajapati, the unknown God.

Second to Indra in the Rigveda is Agni to whom at least 200 hymns are addressed. Here we have an important phenomenon of nature raised to a deity:

Being born in the highest heaven Agni became visible to Matarisvan (a divine being) . . . His flames are fierce . . .

Preserve us, O Agni, never failing . . . (I.143).[43]

Agni became a supreme god, the mediator between gods and men, the helper of everyone.[44]

The god of fire unites the three parts of the universe: earth, heaven, and the atmosphere between.

O Agni, thou art the substance of young shoots . . . Innate in all things . . . The whole exists in thee . . . The all is reborn through thee.[45]

Other gods are also honored. Varuna, the god of the sky,[46] is the supreme God who others obey. In this he is like Marduk of the Babylonians.

Before the home of Varuna all the gods follow his decree . . . .[47]

He watches the world, the sun is his eye, the sky his garment. The universe follows his law.[48]

The law he determines is the Rta, the order of the world. It is difficult to see how Varuna is often thought to represent the beginnings of a monotheism that is in anyway comparable with the omnipotent creator of the heavens and earth in Genesis 1. Sin and forgiveness in the biblical world refer to the violation of the divine law and the pardon of a single, unique, holy, all-wise God. The notion of a high-god, who rules the gods, is entirely foreign to the biblical tradition, and strikes at the very heart of Israel's faith: "Hear O Israel, the Lord your God is one." The Rta or moral order of the world which the gods uphold is external to their nature. The notion that the Vedic conception of "sin" is analogous to the biblical view overlooks the very essence of sin in the biblical sense. For within the biblical tradition there is no moral standard apart from God. God's very nature is moral. His moral attributes are the expressions of his being. To sin in the biblical sense is not to violate some moral order, but to sin against God!

Some ten hymns are addressed to Surya, the sun, who in the form of Visnu supports all the worlds. Pusan is the god of wayfarers. The Asvins, the gods of dawn and dusk, are invoked in about fifty hymns. And Soma, the god of inspiration, the giver of life immortal, is not to be forgotten. It is impossible to list them all!

What is of significance is that the numerous high gods and minor deities, came into being like the gods of the Ancient Near East, the gods of Egypt, Babylon, and Greece.

. . . That which is earlier than this earth and heaven, before the Asuras (high-gods) and gods had being. What was the germ primeval which the waters received where all the gods were seen together? The waters, they received that germ primeval wherein the gods were gathered all together . . . .[49]

The hymn to the unknown God (Prajapti) (X.121) is sometimes said to be as purely monotheistic as a Psalm of David.[50] Such remarks, which are frequently made, fail to distinguish the essential from the superficial.

The following quotations from the hymn indicate that the god referred to came into being:

> As the golden Germ he arose in the beginning; when born he was the one Lord of the existent . . . whose command all the gods wait upon. . . . When the great waters came, bearing all as the Germ . . . then arose the one life-spirit of the gods . . . who through his greatness beheld the waters, that bore power and generated the sacrifice, who was the one God above the gods . . . .[51]

The theme that all that there is arose out of an unknown impersonal creative force, is found in Rigveda, X 129:

> Non-being then existed not nor being: there was no air, nor sky . . . . Death then existed not nor life immortal or neither night nor day was any token. By its inherent force the One breathed windless. No other thing than that beyond existed. Darkness there was at first by darkness hidden; without distinctive marks, this all was water . . . . That which, becoming, by the void was covered, That One by force of heat came into being . . . . Creative force was there, and fertile power . . . . Who knows for certain? . . . Whence was it born, and whence came this creation? The gods were born after this world's creation: Then who can know from whence it has arisen?[52]

The highest principle of the Rigveda is thus seen to be an impersonal, unknown "creative force." The gods to whom the hymns are addressed are secondary.

> The sages searching in their hearts with wisdom, found out the bond of being in non-being.[53]

Even the gods cannot know from whence came this creation. If they cannot know, then who can?

45

In any case no claim is here made that the highest principle is a personal, omnipotent being, who is infinite, eternal, and unchangeable, whose very nature is holy, just, and good, and who has revealed what men are to believe concerning himself, and what duties he requires of them.

The world of the Rigveda is the world of timeless myth; it is the world of subjective fantasy. From our point of view the Yajurveda, the Veda of the sacrificial formulas, the Samaveda, the Veda of melodies, and the nearly six thousand verses of the Atharvaveda, with its hymns and spells, contain nothing that is more than a projection of human feelings, hopes, and aspirations.

In the Yajurveda invocations are addressed not only to the gods, but even to cultic objects. It is filled with magical elements.

The Rigveda contains strange incantations and spells, charms and witchcraft, hymns to inanimate things, devils and demons, etc. There are charms of the robbers to lull the dwellers in a house to sleep, spells to prevent evil spirits causing women to miscarry, and charms to expel diseases. Such elements are incidental in the Rigveda, but they constitute the main theme of the Artharvaveda.[54]

> The religion of the Artharva-Veda is that of the primitive man, to whom the world is full of shapeless ghosts and spirits of death.[55]

It is a religion of snake and stone worship, a religion of goblins and gods, a world of scowling demons (Raksas) which are:

> objects of horror, whom the gods ward off and destroy; the divinities of the Atharva are regarded . . . with a kind of cringing fear, as powers whose wrath is to be deprecated and whose favour curried; it knows a whole host of imps and hobgoblins in ranks and classes, and addresses itself to them directly, offering them homage to induce them to abstain from doing harm . . .
>
> The most prominent feature of the Atharva is the multitude of incantations which it contains . . . . We find people sitting in the midst of five fires, standing on one leg, holding an arm above the head, all for the purpose of commanding the forces of nature and subduing the gods to their will.[56]

46

The Brahmanas and the Aranyakas, the forest treatises, also provide nothing that causes us to regard Hinduism as more than an example of a religion that is in fact a subjective projection. The former interpret Brahman by means of symbols. They contain cosmogonic legends, tales about the goddesses, and prescriptions for proper sacrifices. The latter are also filled with esoteric elements: words to be recited, verses about the horse sacrifice, human sacrifice, and the fire altar.[57]

The concluding portions of the Vedas are the Upanishads, the basis of Vedanta philosophy. There are over 200 although 108 are considered the traditional number, 10 of which are considered the most important.[58]

"The Upanishads belong to Sruti or revealed literature, and are the utterances of sages who spoke out of the fulness of their illumined experience . . . ."[59]

It is difficult to find a logical and coherent system of metaphysics in the Upanishads. They are an example of speculative metaphysics which serve a religious function. Different commentators find different beliefs in the Upanishads. Our concern, however, is not with the countless variations of beliefs and opinions that have arisen out of them. We shall examine certain central notions that are frequently found in them in order to illustrate their speculative character, and to show that they in no way claim to be the revelation of a personal God in the biblical sense. Indeed, it will become apparent that the highest principle that they reach is an impersonal absolute. The writings of the Hindus may be called "revelation" in the sense that they are the work of a lesser deity, of a goddess, Vak, the goddess of speech, or they may have "issued as breath from the self existent," but they do not claim to be the self-disclosure of a single conscious, omniscient sovereign God.

The highest principle of the Upanishads is impersonal. A man may become aware of Brahman, but Brahman is not aware of a man. Brahman is not aware of anything, for there are no "things." Brahman is, in highest wisdom, everything, and nothing. Brahman cannot be apprehended

47

by the mind. It is the one self-subsistent reality, beyond logical categories or linguistic symbols.

> The real which is at the heart of the universal is reflected in the infinite depths of the self. Brahman (the ultimate as discovered objectively) is Atman (the ultimate as discovered introspectively). *Tat tvam asi* (That art thou). Truth is within us.[60]

Within every being there is a portion of Brahman, the Atman.

> That which is the finest essence—this whole world has that as its soul. That is Reality. That is Atman (soul). That art thou . . . .[61]

According to Sankara, one of the greatest Hindu theologians, when we know that there is only one universal self, the practical view of the world is at an end. The eternal subject of everything is Brahman. "The distinction of objects known, knowers, acts of knowledge, etc. . . . is fictitiously created by Nescience."[62]

Brahman is like a primeval ocean, all things arise out of it and fade away again. Brahman is not a "he," not a person, but an "it."

> Brahman is hidden behind the diversity, behind the multiplicity of this world. Man is blinded by the latter, bewitched, and attracted until the moment he becomes tired of his senses and desires, and turns away from this multiplicity and sinks into himself. And then man has the greatest experience of his life, then he has a great surprise, because he begins to understand that the gaudy, bewitching world is only maya, ignorance, illusion, and that all the while Brahman, the deepest reality, the reality behind all realities, is present in stillness.[63]
>
> The self is not to be known as manifold, qualified by the universe of effects; you are rather to dissolve by true knowledge the universe of effects, which is the abode of Nescience, and to know that one Self, which is the general abode, as uniform.[64]

The individual soul is for Sankara one with the highest soul, although our nescience makes it appear otherwise. Just as in the dark a man may mistake a rope for a snake, so we may separate the individual self from the highest self. In truth, however, the individual self and the highest self differ, only in name. The manifold world does not exist apart from Brahman, although as long as knowledge of Brahman being the Self of all has not arisen, the world of phenomena is considered true, like the phantoms of a dream before the dreamer awakes.[65]

> The seers, absorbed in contemplation, saw within themselves the ultimate reality, the self-luminous being, the one God, who dwells as the self-conscious power in all creatures. He is One without a second . . . .
> This vast universe is a wheel. Upon it are all creatures that are subject to birth, death, and rebirth. Round and round it turns, and never stops. It is the wheel of Brahman. As long as the individual self thinks it is separate from Brahman, it revolves upon the wheel in bondage to the laws of birth, death, and rebirth.[66]

The ultimate aim of Hinduism is to overcome the illusion that the self is distinct from Brahman. Release (moksa) from error, from the wheel of rebirth, is attained by knowledge.

No adequate evidence is ever presented within the Upanishads that Brahman is the essence of all things. Nor is an explanation ever given as to how the subjective state of knowing can have consequences that effect the release of the soul from its constant bondage to the wheel of rebirth. That such is the case is simply asserted to be the case. The sages have come to this conclusion. How do we know they are right? There is no objective evidence, but we are invited to experience the oneness of all things in deep contemplation.

> The knowers of Brahman know him as the one reality behind all that seems. For this reason they are devoted to him. Absorbed in him, they attain freedom from the wheel of birth, death, and rebirth.
> . . . Know God, and all fetters will be loosed. Ignorance will vanish. Birth, death, and rebirth will be no more. Meditate upon him and transcend physical consciousness. Thus will you reach union with the lord of the universe . . . .

49

The truth is that you are always united with the Lord. But you must know this. Nothing further is there to know . . . .[67]

The one absolute, impersonal Existence, together with his inscrutable Maya, appears as the divine Lord, the personal God . . . . At the periods of creation and dissolution of the universe, he alone exists . . . .[68]

The many gods of the Vedas are subordinated to or are made a part of Brahman.

He (Brahman) is Brahma, he is Shiva, he is Indra, he is the supreme, the changeless reality. He is Vishnu, he is the primal energy . . . .[69]

This universe, before it was created, existed as Brahman. Brahman created out of himself priests, warriors, tradesmen and servants, among both gods and men.[70]

Brahman projected the universe, including the gods, out of himself. He is the subtle essence of everything.[71]

In fact this highest wisdom must also be learned by the gods, for they, too, obtain by their meditation all the worlds and all desires.[72]

Brahman makes himself in many forms.

This universe is a tree eternally existing, its root aloft, its branches spread below. The pure root of the tree is Brahman . . . .

. . . . The whole universe came forth from Brahman and moves in Brahman . . . . If a man fail to attain Brahman before he casts off his body, he must again put on a body in the world of created things.[73]

The gods themselves arose out of Brahman.

Out of the infinite ocean of existence arose Brahman,[74] first born and foremost among the gods. From him sprang the universe . . . .[75]

At death, the soul who knows Brahman escapes further incarnations and the "vital energy enters the cosmic source, the senses dissolve in their cause, and *karmas* and the individual soul are lost in Brahman, the pure, the changeless."[76]

There is nothing uncertain in human destiny, for it is governed by the causal law of *Karma*. Nothing is without its effect. Every act or thought produces its result, whether good or bad. One cannot escape the *karma* or retribution for his actions. We become what we think or do. Our present life is determined by what we did in our past life, and our future life depends upon what we do now.[77]

Our *karma* can be escaped only if we extinguish all thirst in the self for existence, so that we escape a new *karma*, which must in turn be fulfilled. Selfish action binds us to the chain of birth and rebirth. But we can break free by following a prescribed path. We can merge into Brahman, and gain release.

The concept of release or salvation in Brahmanism may be best understood in contrast to the concept of salvation within the biblical tradition. The word *"moksa"* may be translated as "salvation" but here the similarity ends. It is of course true that *moksa* is the goal of the Hindu sage, and that salvation is the goal of the biblical believer. *Moksa* and salvation thus have a comparable function from a formal point of view. Such *functional correspondence* lends itself to superficial comparisons. Hindus pray and Christians pray; Hindus offer sacrifice and the Israelites offer sacrifice; Hindus seek *moksa* and Christians seek *moksa;* therefore, so the argument runs, there is no difference between the major religions of the world.

Such a contention merely overlooks what is important, namely, the content and significance attached to prayer, sin, salvation, and sacrifice. From the fact that Hindus, Buddhists, and Christian all pray, the conclusion may be drawn that they are examples of what is usually understood by religion. When a Hindu prays, however, he may pray to any number of deities or if he is sophisticated he may regard "God" as a manifestation of one impersonal essence. When the Christian prays he prays to one God, who is infinite, eternal, and unchangeable.

> "God's" ego, the ultimate personal entity, will then be fundamentally as unreal as the human ego. To the ignorant, "God" may appear to have attributes, but this is self-deceit.

51

The Highest Being, as 'God,' is phenomenal—a majestic lordly face painted on the sublime blank of Brahman, true being, which is devoid of physiognomy as well as all other attributes and definitions.[78]

The biblical concept of salvation is concerned with the restoration of the proper relationship between a sinful man and a holy and just God.

It is possible for a Hindu to violate *Dharma,* a law of religious merit. That is to say, a Hindu may fail to fulfill the role assigned to him by *karma.* He may fail to obey the laws of universal harmony and follow the dictates of his own egoism. If he fails to fulfill his *Dharma,* the soul will not work off its residue of *karma,* and thus will not escape the endless round of rebirth. There is not one *Dharma* for everybody. Every person has his own individual *Dharma,* determined by race, caste, family, and private aspirations.[79]

This *Dharma* the Hindu may violate, but he cannot disobey or fail to conform to the law of a supreme, holy personal God, for such a being has no existence. *Karma* is an impersonal law of moral order:

> To obtain the experience which it lacks, the human soul, when called upon to live a new existence on earth, is placed in the most favorable conditions. If it fulfills the role assigned it by its *karma,* it obeys the laws of universal harmony. If it resists and simply follows the dictates of its own egoism, it wastes its efforts and has to suffer the consequences.[80]

There is here no personal God to show mercy to the sinner, to forgive his transgressions, and to punish his iniquities. The consequences of violating the impersonal moral law of a particular soul *(Dharma)* is punished by an impersonal law of retribution *(karma).* The soul is born and dies many times. Its life is a series of deaths and rebirths. "As a man lays aside outworn garments and takes others that are new, so the Body-Dweller puts away outworn bodies and goes to others that are new."[81]

Reincarnation is a necessity because the soul that has not secured release from the wheel of birth must return to work off its *karma.*

Several paths may be taken to secure release; the path of action, with its prayers, rites, pilgrimages; the path of initiation, with its ascetic practices and sacrifice; and the path of knowledge, the living of the spiritual experience of the Veda.[82]

> The aim *par excellence* of the Hindu religion is to help man to release, to liberation from samsara through the certainty of his identity as an individual with the absolute, that is to say, through his knowledge that the atman is a fragment of Brahman . . . to break the fatal chain of transmigration all desire must be extinguished in the self, for desire contains the seed and root of existence. Where desire no longer exists, the atman, delivered from terrestial bonds, returns to Brahman.[83]

The Hindu may violate *Dharma* but *he cannot sin,* not in the biblical sense. Where there is no sin, there is no forgiveness of sin; there is neither eternal punishment nor eternal reward.

Within the biblical tradition, salvation consists of the attainment of forgiveness of sin and the enjoyment of everlasting life. The redeemed in heaven will continue to be the same individual persons that they were on earth. They will never cease to be. In fact they shall not simply be disembodied souls, but they shall be persons—body-souls; the body of the believer is to be resurrected. Those who have attained salvation will live forever with God, but they shall *never* be God. Their personal identity is never at an end.

Within Hinduism "salvation," *moksa,* release, is the cessation of personal identity; it is not everlasting life, but everlasting death.

"The soul, being only Brahman, merges into Brahman" (Chandogya Up. VIII).

The individual ceases to be. In a sense he never *really* was, but in any case, now he is no more. He is Brahman. What is the essence of sin within the biblical tradition, i.e., to try to be God, is the essence of salvation in Hinduism, i.e., to be Brahman.

53

Within the biblical tradition, salvation depends upon the divine favor of God; it is God who takes the initiative in making a covenant with Abraham; it is God who delivers his people out of Egypt; it is God, in the person of the Son, who enters into human history and redeems his people by his death and resurrection. God here takes the initiative in the history of redemption.

Within Hinduism a man may accomplish his own "release" by following one of the paths, for which practical methods are prescribed. The discipline of Yoga may lead to release, to identification with the absolute, to freedom from the determinism of transmigration. There are many paths, many rules and observances, bodily postures, and forms of detachment, but the initiative lies in every case with man.[84]

Within Hinduism there is no conception of a unique person, distinct from every other person, with a single earthly life to live. The Hindu does not appeal to the evidence of unique historical events to support his "faith," for in a sense there are no unique events. What could an endless series of existences prove? There is nothing unique. A linear concept of history, with a beginning and end, is replaced by visions of cosmic cycles, divided into world ages. "The traditional texts allude only very seldom to the fact that the mythological events which they are describing take place again and again . . . every four billion three hundred and twenty million years."[85]

The duration of our world is limited; it ends and begins again:

All become resolved into the divine, primeval Substance. A state of total re-absorption then prevails for another Brahma century, after which the entire cycle of 311,040,000,000,000 human years begin anew.[86]

Our treatment of Hinduism is not meant to be complete; there are many sects, Vaisnavism, devoted to the worship of Visnu, incarnate as Krisna, Rama, and his other "avatars," with its Bhakti Yoga; there is the Pancaratra sect; the Bhagavatas, the Ramanujas, the Ramanandins, and numerous others, which modify to some extent the generalizations that we have made.[87] We have said nothing about the caste system, with its social consequences, nor have we discussed the practical ethical consequences of Hinduism. Our sole concern has been to examine a religion which, in its less sophisticated forms, makes its own gods, and in its more refined form, ends with a speculative metaphysical absolute.

The reader may judge whether Hinduism is an example of a religion that is in fact a subjective projection of human needs and feelings. Hinduism appeals to personal experience; it can make no appeal to historical evidence of an objective sort. It can not appeal to history, for in highest wisdom there is no history, nothing is unique. There is only one single reality. If such is the case, why not forget about it? But then we will continue on the wheel of birth, according to *karma*. How do we know there is *karma*? It is here that we encounter a basic religious conviction, one that is not readily shaken. The idea of *karma* and of *samsara*, the wheel of rebirth, is as we shall subsequently see, retained in Buddhism, even though the authority of the Vedas is repudiated.

There are no objective historical states of affairs that are relevant to the truth or falsity of Hinduism. Hinduism is not verifiable even in principle by an appeal to any objective non-personal experience. If the Christian faith is true, then everyone will know it, including the non-believer. He will know this after death, when he meets Christ as his judge. If, however, Hinduism is true, no one will know it for ultimately, there will be no one. Upon reabsorption into Brahman, the individual will no longer be conscious of himself. How then does reabsorption into Brahman differ from nothingness, from total annihilation? Would it make any difference to say that instead of Brahman being the essence of everything, that he was the non-essence of nothing? What would it be like if Brahman was not the essence of everything? Would anything be changed? What would be different? Would anyone know the difference?

Such questions cannot be answered. To the Hindu they betray a superficial outlook, one that looks upon the world of everyday experience as more than a cosmic illusion. The Christian and the materialist agree that the material world is not an "illusion." To the Christian, it is created; to the materialist it is eternal; to the Hindu it is not *really* there. Of course, it still *seems* to be there; but it *really* is not. The distinction may escape the reader, but then that may be because he is not a Hindu.

Hinduism has given rise to other movements, to Jainism, and the many forms of Buddhism. The latter is of special interest to us, for in its classic form it affords an example of a religion in which man projects his subjective feelings in the manner suggested by such subjectivists as Feuerbach.

3. *Buddhism*

Buddhism owes its origin, according to the accepted tradition, to Siddhartha Gautama. The date of his birth is around the middle of the sixth century B.C. Gautama Buddha, Gautama the enlightened one, as he is usually called, has been the source of inspiration to many different schools with a wide range of beliefs. Here, too, it is impossible to generalize. For some,

> Buddhism is not a religion in the sense in which that word is commonly understood, for it is not a system of faith and worship. In Buddhism, there is no such thing as belief in a Supreme Being, a creator of the universe, the reality of an immortal soul, a personal savior . . . .

> It is true that there are different types of devas or spiritual beings mentioned in Buddhism, but they are beings like ourselves, subject to the same natural law of cause and effect. They are not immortal, nor do they control the destiny of mankind. The Buddha does not ask us to accept belief in any supernatural agency or anything that cannot be tested by experience.[88]

Others have combined the original conceptions of Buddhism with belief in the popular gods.[89]

There is no unity in the Mahayana religion. It suffered religious superstitions gladly. Wherever it prevailed, India, China, Korea, Siam, Burma, and Japan, the indigeneous religions were tolerated . . . .[90]

Buddhism has spread beyond the borders of India throughout Asia. It has given rise to many traditions and conflicting schools and sects, the study of which lies beyond our present interest. In many forms it is a religion without God; it is a way of life, designed to give ethical guidance. In other forms, for all practical purposes, at least on the popular level, it simply makes Gautama, the Enlightened One, into a new god, the highest of the gods, to be sure, but one who differs little from the gods of the Hindu pantheon.

Bhikkhu Kashyup, a present-day Indian Buddhist scholar, applies the term Buddha to one who has attained the height of wisdom:

in numberless births during an incomprehensible length of time. A Buddha is not a person but is rather a personality evolved through the accumulation of spiritual qualities.

. . . He is a way-finder, a discoverer of the Path of Deliverance which will free men from the ills of the continuing migration through endless series of rebirths.[91]

Gautama was neither the first nor the last to become a Buddha. There have been others before him and there will be others after. Buddhas will appear to lead men to nirvana as long as beings need to be liberated from the wheel of rebirth.

Prior to his existence as the Buddha, Gautama, who was then Sumedha, met the Buddha of his day, Buddha Dipankara. Sumedha (who was to be born later on as Gautama) was greatly impressed. He, too, wanted to be a Buddha. It is not easy. But Sumedha was very compassionate; he felt sorry that so many miserable people were constantly dying and being born another time. Sumedha could have escaped from the suffering of worldly existence; instead he chose to sacrifice himself for "the welfare and deliverance of all beings. His genuine humanity made him vow at the feet of Buddha Dipankara to

57

become a supreme Buddha and solve the riddle of life for all beings, mundane and divine."[92]

Buddhism rejects the authority of the Vedas but it retains the notion of the wheel of birth. The purpose of the Buddha is to teach men to fulfill their duty *(Dharma)* so that they can enter nirvana, a state which is difficult to define, but which in any case means an end to the chain of temporal existence.

The Buddha-aspirant, a Bodhisattva, must undergo a long preparation; he must pass through numberless series of births, "sometimes as a god, sometimes as a human being, sometimes as an animal. It is a long and arduous training that evolves the personality to holiness, a gradual progress that rises in stages to Buddhahood, to Omniscence."[93] In any case, Siddhatha Gautama, the son of King Suddhodana, finally made it. He left his palace, renounced the world, and sought the ultimate deliverance of mankind.[94] After abandoning the practice of extreme asceticism, Gautama resolved to sit under a tree until enlightenment came. While sitting under the Bo tree, he was tempted by the god Kama-Mara (Desire and Death). By remaining immovable in introversion, the strength of his past perfections enabled him to resist temptation. The god who tempted him failed. The god then tried to destroy the Buddha, with storms, flaming rocks, and boiling mud. "But the future Buddha was not moved. The missiles became flowers as they entered the field of his concentration."[95]

Gautama became the Buddha that very night. For seven weeks, he shifted from tree to tree, spending a week at each, so delighted was he with his new found knowledge. It so happened that one of the trees under which he sat was the Mucalinda tree, where a great snake-king lived. Mucalinda was at home, and during an unexpected storm,

> issued Mucalinda, the serpent-king, from his abode, and enveloping the body of the Blessed one seven times with his folds, spread his great hood above his head, saying, "Let neither cold nor heat, nor gnats, flies, wind, sunshine, nor creeping creatures come near the Blessed One." Then, when seven days had elapsed,

and Mucalinda, the serpent-king, knew that the storm
had broken up, and that the clouds had gone, he un-
wound his coils from the body of the Blessed One. And
changing his natural appearance into that of a young
man, he stood before the Blessed One, and with his
joined hands to his forehead did reverence to the
Blessed One.[96]

The gods were afraid that the newly awakened Buddha
would keep his wisdom to himself, but Brahma then
descended and persuaded Buddha to teach. And this is
what he did:

> The Buddhas are not redeemers, messiahs, saviors,
> incarnations, or avatars—primarily the Buddhas
> are teachers who have discovered a great truth which,
> out of great compassion toward all beings, they teach.[97]

What did Gautama learn? He found out that ignorance
was the root of all evil. People suffer. Why? Because
they keep getting born. "They crave for pleasure and
they cause pain; when death destroys their individuality,
they find no peace; their thirst for existence abides and
their selfhood reappears in new births."[98]

What causes sorrow is that people go on living. If
there were no people then no one could be unhappy. The
way to end human misery is to get rid of humanity. Why
not just kill everyone? No! That will not work. For, if
at the time of death a person desires to live, he will just
return in a new birth. Some other way will have to be
found. Gautama diagnosed the difficulty and found the
way. That is why he is a Buddha. The trouble is that
there was in the beginning a "sea of ignorance," in which
awareness and feelings arose. "Feelings beget organisms
that live as individual beings."[99]

The latter then develop the five senses and the mind
(the six fields), which when brought into contact with
things create sensations, which in turn creates the thirst
of individualized being, and a cleaving to things. The latter is responsible for the growth and the continuation of
selfhood in renewed births. And, of course, the renewed
births end in old age, sickness and death, with its accom-
panying misery. This is the chain of dependent origin.

The solution is simple. Since ignorance is responsible for people, destroy ignorance, and you will get rid of people.

> The cause of all sorrow lies at the very beginning; it is hidden in the ignorance from which life grows. Remove ignorance and you will destroy the wrong appetences and you will wipe out the wrong perception that rises from them. Destroy wrong perception and there is an end of errors in individualized beings. Destroy errors in individualized beings and the illusions of the six fields will disappear. Destroy illusions and the contact with things will cease to beget misconception. Destroy misconception and you will do away with thirst. Destroy thirst and you will be free of all morbid cleaving. Remove the cleaving and you destroy the selfishness of selfhood. If the selfishness of selfhood is destroyed you will be above birth, old age, disease, and death, and you escape all suffering.[100]

The way to release is not to be found in either the extreme of self-indulgence or in the extreme of self-mortification. The middle path of the four noble truths, including the eightfold path is the key to becoming an Arahat, a person who dispells all ignorance and is freed from the bondage of the cycle of birth and death.

The end of cravings, nirvana, the extinction of self is attainable. Gautama taught; pupils listened, a brotherhood was formed. The law of *karma* could now be overcome. Good and bad acts leave their impressions, so that at death the process of a person's consciousness flow into another life. A bestial man may become an animal; the circle of life goes on; but now it can be broken. The doctrine, the *Dharma,* the religion taught by the Buddha enables us to know that all existence is impermanent. It is substanceless, in a state of constant flux. Our ignorance due to attachment causes us to accept the conventional view that things have identity. From the metaphysical point of view, things have no stability in them, and they can be of no solace to us. We must learn the true nature of existence, be rid of all desire, so that our actions no longer accumulate the potentiality of *karma,* and we then can escape birth and rebirth.

The understanding of the chain of dependent origin is essential to the enlightenment of the Buddha.

With the cessation of ignorance, *karma* formations cease, the moment of rebirth consciousness does not arise, psycho-physical existence, the organs of sense, contact, feelings, desire, grasping, the life process, birth, and old age, are at an end. Suffering ceases.[101]

The four noble truths are pronounced by the Buddha in the manner of a physician. He makes the diagnosis, not of the individual alone, but of all mankind, and he then prescribes the remedy.

The first truth: everything is suffering; all life is sorrowful. Suffering is a part of the very essence of existence. To live is to suffer. Happiness is unattainable as long as we have any desire or craving. Human suffering is not due to any voluntary disobedience or violation of the commandment of a holy and just God. It is rather a part of living. All suffering is evil; to live with desire is suffering; therefore, to live with desire is evil.

To the charge that such a view is pessimistic, the Buddhist may respond that we have missed the point. The second noble truth makes known the cause of the illness, and when the cause is known the remedy can frequently be found.

Buddhism is not pessimistic because the third noble truth tells us that the cure is possible. Suffering can be suppressed. The way to suppress it is found in the last noble truth: the eightfold path.[102]

Suffering is caused by craving. For our desires lead, according to the law of *karma,* to frustrations that bind us to further existence, the wheel of rebirth, the wheel of "re-dying." It is not only birth that we must escape, but it is also the ensuing sickness and death.

What originates is, however, subject to cessation. This is the note of optimism. This is the kingdom of righteousness established by the Buddha which caused gods, animals, and men to rejoice.[103]

Our ignorant craving, our misconception of the essence of the world, leads to our misery. Our misery will cease when our cravings cease. "With the cessation of birth, old age, death, sorrow, lamentation, pain, grief, and despair do not arise. Thus, the entire mass of suffering ceases."[104]

The middle path leads to the final cessation of all evil, to nirvana. The higher wisdom, the first two steps of the eightfold path, are right understanding and right mindedness.

The disciple who aspires to escape from suffering must have the proper theoretical understanding of the principles of Buddhism. He must have right understanding. The four noble truths, the principles of *karma* and the dependent origin of all things, as well as the impermanence, substanceless, and suffering of all things must be thoroughly kept in mind. To know these things theoretically is not enough, however. A disciple must also be rightminded, that is, he must exercise his will and renounce everything that stands in the way of the realization of his goal.

It is the recognition that it is not possible for one leading the household life to fulfill the pure life of holiness and that it is necessary to renounce worldly life and become a member of the Order. That renunciation is right-mindedness.[105]

The next three steps of the eightfold path are known as Ethical Disciplines: right speech, right action, right livelihood. The disciple is to refrain from lying; from murder, stealing, and sexual misconduct; he is to avoid dealing in weapons, intoxicants, in flesh, and in living beings. These maxims are more than ethical rules. They are a necessary part of the path to nirvana. If they are not kept, it will be impossible to attain the "concentration of mind which is necessary if the true wisdom is to dawn."[106]

The last three steps, known as mental discipline, right efforts, right mindfulness, and right concentration are based on pure conduct. By right effort the disciple seeks to prevent evil thoughts from arising, eliminates those that have arisen, cultivates the good thoughts that have not yet arisen, and conserves the good thoughts that have arisen.

By right mindfulness the disciple learns to develop a constant awareness of the states of his personality, i.e., the states of the body, the feelings, mind and of things. By paying attention to his bodily states and his feelings, the disciple attains the higher stage of mental discipline, equilibrium of mind, and is able to meditate upon the four noble truths and the impermanent nature of things, thereby preparing himself for the final stage of right concentration, in which he transcends normal discursive understanding and reaches the mystical state of *samadhi*. It is now that he intuitively realizes that all existence is impermanent, substanceless, and suffering. It is not worth pursuing. He then attains the passionless state of mind in which he is free from the bondage of all types of desire and thus attains nirvana.[107]

It is now that the disciple has reached his ultimate goal (nirvana) perfect peace, which is real and everlasting.[108] For now the process of becoming, the turning of the wheel of life, ceases. The cycle of birth and death is at an end. Ignorance is destroyed. Craving is annihilated; there will be no future birth and there is an end to the life process.[109]

Nirvana is thus attainable in this life through the enlightment or true wisdom that is reached by following the eightfold path.[110]

Those whose labors are unfinished merely go around the wheel of life and return again to labor toward fuller completion. Those who have followed the middle Path and finished their labors reach the state of Nirvana, the complete cessation of sorrow. To unmask the great illusion is the labor of man. To stand in equilibrium in the midst of worldly things is the way of the Buddha. To contemplate life but never to be enmeshed within worldly life is the law of the Buddha. To go forth out of worldly life is the advice of the Buddha. To be absorbed into what is real, permanent— into Nirvana—is the end of the Buddhist way of life, the path of the Buddha.[111]

Nirvana is the extinction of craving and attachment; it puts an end to *karma* formations, and delusion.[112] It is the absence of craving, the blowing out of the flame of desire.[113]

For some Buddhists the realization of the four truths occurs more than once. When the highest stage is reached, the person who attains becomes an *arahat;* he will never return.[114] "Nirvana is the only peace."[115]

To Lobsang Phuntsok Lhalungpa, a representative of Tibetan Buddhism, Nirvana is supreme enlightenment, the cessation of delusion.

> It is pure, eternal unchanging . . . It is emptiness but not nothingness . . . One has to realize it for one-self . . . it transcends the limits within which distinctions are made between elements and between space and time.
> . . . Empirical knowledge needs some tangible attributes to take hold of—but Nirvana has no such attributes. Transcendental intuition has only the void, essencelessness (sunyanta) for its object—consequently it cannot cognize Nirvana as being existence or nonexistence.[116]

Theravada Buddhism holds that monks should strive to attain Arahatship; they cannot become Buddhas, whereas in Mahayana Buddhism, everyone is entitled to become a Buddha finally. Nirvana, no matter how conceived is, however, the goal of all Buddhists.[117]

The state is indescribable, but for the Buddhist it is not simply annihilation.[118] What is it? It is nirvana, enlightenment; it's what you experience when you reach the final stage, the mystical goal of Buddhism.[119] Mahayana differs from Theravada in that it uses Sanskirt, rather than Pali sources, and emphasizes various Bodhisattvas rather than Gautama and the ideal of the *Arahat.*[120]

Buddhism is a religion in which man attains his own release from the bondage of ignorance. It has a vast literature in Sanskirt and Pali. Certain Buddhists do not worship images or pray to Buddha expecting any answer.

> The words they recite are meditations not prayers.[121] Prayers are meditations for purifying the mind in order that truth can be realized. According to Buddhism, the universe is governed by everlasting, unchangeable laws of righteousness—not by any god or any Supreme Being who can hear and answer prayers. These laws are so perfect that no one, no god or man can change them . . .[122]

64

Sin is the consequence of man's ignorance of these laws.

Things are born according to their karma energy on thirty-one planes of existence.[123] Many Buddhists do in fact worship deities and spirits.

> Buddhism, while clearly understood by the intelligent thinker to be atheistic, is taken by the general mass of the people to be a polytheistic religion.[124]

In Tibet, the Dalai Lama, the supreme temporal and spiritual power, is the incarnation of the Bodhisattva Avalokitesvara.[125] To install the right successor requires the efforts of men, gods, and Bodhivisattvas (a future Buddha).[126]

The monks of Tibet recite mantras, words that have spiritual power, by means of a prayer wheel, in the center of which thousands of mantras are written. To turn the wheel is the same as reciting the prayer.[127] Prayers may be offered to numerous deities, the deity of compassion, Avalokitesvara, of wisdom (Manjusri), of power (Vajorapari) to the goddesses Kurukulli, White Tara, to Parnasavari, and to hosts of others.[128] To the same Buddhists:

> all forms of existence in the six worlds—the worlds of hell, hungry demons, beasts, spirits, human beings, and gods—are indeed one's parents through their existence in previous births.[129]

One characteristic of Buddhism is its indifference to the gods of other religions. Many Hindu gods and goddesses have been incorporated into Buddhists' ceremonies; many Buddhists observe festivals associated with nature spirits. In China many Buddhist shrines are semi-Taoist; in Japan, the common people do not distinguish between Buddhist gods and Shinto gods.[130]

What is common to all the schools is the notion of Dharma, the path of enlightenment, with its various stages. Theravada Buddhism holds to the four stages that we have defined before a disciple becomes an Arahat. Mahayana Buddhism assumes many stages, varying in number with the different sects. Some Mahayanists skip many of the steps. Zen teaches that enlightenment can come by means of a direct intuition of one's own nature.

65

There is no conformity of teaching. The most widely accepted doctrines are that of universal suffering, to be overcome by the cessation of desire, usually by our own efforts, but in some instances with external help.[131]

The non-ego principle *(anatta)*, that life is a series of becomings and extinctions, the body being a composite of the five aggregates, rather than a being with a substantial soul, is also held throughout Buddhism.

The belief in rebirth, with some liberal exceptions, was taken over by the Buddhists from Hinduism. The principle of *karma,* that the individual is the result of a multitude of causes carried over from the past, and extending into the future, is believed in some form by all Buddhists. Theravada schools maintain that the state of a Bodhisattva depends upon the merits of his past lives, whereas Mahayana schools hold that a Bodhisattva is born because out of compassion he freely choses to be born.[132]

The chain of causation and the belief in dependent origination is accepted by all schools of Buddhism, but interpreted differently. Mahayana Buddhism finds in dependent origination the basis for its doctrine of the void, emptiness, *sunyata.* It holds that no existence is real, all things are but appearance.

> The void is all-inclusive; having no opposite, there is nothing which it excludes or opposes. It is living void, because all forms come out of it, and whoever realizes the void is filled with life and power and the Bodhisattva's love of all beings. Love is the moral equivalent of all-inclusiveness, which is nothing but the void.[133]

All Buddhists are in agreement that nirvana, enlightenment, is their goal, not a paradise or heavenly world. By following the right path, freedom from the bondage of existence can be gained.[134]

The universe in which Buddhists live, except where they have been educated in modern science, is shaped by belief in karma and rebirth. There are three planes or spheres into which people can be born according to their actions, the immaterial plane, where pure spirits live; the material plane, on which subtle bodies live; and the plane of desire, our natural world.[135]

On the plane of desire there are gods, men, spirits, animals, the damned, and sometimes demons. Man is actually better prepared for enlightenment than the gods; "they live much too long to have any appreciation for the doctrine of impermanence."[136]

Disagreement among Buddhists is most prevalent in their attitude toward their sacred writings. The latter differ essentially as we shall see, from the biblical concept of an authoritative word of a personal, supreme, omnipotent, creator God. Within Buddhism there is "no one scripture which is accepted as having the same authority for everyone who calls himself a Buddhist."[137]

The Zen sect emphasizes direct insight and pays little attention to the writings; Theravada Buddhism accepts Pali writings as authoritative, but rejects the Mahayana writings.[138]

The second major point of difference between Mahayana and Theravada Buddhism concerns the Buddha. The Pali writings speak of Seven Buddhas, including Gautama, and some of the books mention twenty-four Buddhas, although Gautama (also known as Sakyamuni) is the most popular. Pure realm Buddhism prefers Amitabha Buddha to Gautama.

The main difference between Theravada and Mahayana Buddhism is that the former holds to the historical Buddha, whereas the latter introduces the notion of the eternal Buddha and regards the earthly form of Gautama as quite temporary.

There are innumerable Buddhas in Mahayna Buddhism; there were many in the past, are many now, and there will be many more in the future. Every Buddha shows compassion for the suffering and helps them along the path to nirvana usually by bringing the disciple to a heaven where he can hear the preaching of the doctrine that leads to enlightenment.[139]

Professor Nakamura, of the University of Tokyo, correctly observes that—

Even though there is a distinct difference between Theravada and Mahayana in their beliefs concerning the Buddha, there never has been a belief that a Buddha is the creator of the universe. Buddhism has never believed in a creator-Buddha or a creator God.[140]

To the non-Buddhists, in spite of protests to the contrary by Buddhists, Buddhism is a nihilistic renunciation of the world and of life. The assumptions that it makes concerning suffering, the substanceless character and impermanence of all things, rebirth, *karma*, dependent origin, the role of the Buddhas, and Nirvana, are made without argument or evidence.

Buddhism reject the Vedas, the caste system, and extreme asceticism. It makes its own gods celestial beings on different subtle planes of existence, where they are born, live, and die. It is a religion that proceeds solely from man's own experience. Its sacred writings are to be studied, practiced, and realized, but they are not the self-disclosure of a creator-God. There is no creator-God; in fact there is no substantial world. What arises as the world of appearance is due to ignorance that is to be overcome by following the path of the Buddha. What would happen if everyone followed the path at once, and attained Nirvana together? There would be no more suffering. What would there be? Nothing! The Buddhist may not like the answer. He does not like to be called a nihilist, but what alternative is there? Suzuki points out with respect to Zen Buddhism:

> Zen is one thing and logic another. When we fail to make this distinction and expect Zen to give us something logically consistent and intellectually illuminating, we altogether misinterpret the signification of Zen.[141]

What Suzuki says of Zen holds for Buddhism in general. It is beyond logic. A is at once A and not A.

Buddhism is not a guide for attaining eternal life; it is rather a guide to no life at all; it is a guide to nirvana. On its own principles Buddhism can exist only as long as it is unsuccessful, for if everyone were to follow the path, then there would only be nirvana, and no one really knows what that is like. If ignorance ceased at once, the cause of the world would cease; rebirth would end, and we would be left with nothing enjoying nothing. The illusion of the self would end! There would then be no more Buddhists.

There are certain superficial comparisons that can be drawn between Buddha and Jesus Christ, and between Buddhism and Christianity. Comparative religion may be helpful, but only if a comparison is really made. To pass over essential differences as though they did not exist, does not do justice to either religion. In what sense is Christianity like Buddhism? Only in the superficial sense that both are usually regarded as religions. The former believes in a creator-God, the latter does not. Christianity believes in a non-illusory created world-order, in the everlasting existence of persons, Buddhism does not. When the Christian uses the word "sin" he means disobedience to the supreme being who has revealed himself in the Old and New Testament. For Buddhists, existence itself is evil; to desire to be is, therefore, "sinful."

A comparison between the many Buddhas of Buddhism and the Christian conception of the unique person of Jesus, the second person of the Trinity, the Messiah, again as in the case of Hinduism, results in superficial functional similarities and in essential contrasts. The many Buddhas are of importance to Buddhism but Jesus is essential to Christianity. The Buddhas are the subject of Buddhism, but Jesus is also the object of Christian faith. Jesus is called the savior, and the Buddhas are compassionate. Jesus had followers and the Buddhas had followers. Jesus taught and the Buddhas taught. The difference, however, is that for Buddhists anyone or many can become a Buddha but no Christian can become a Christ. Buddha wants to make other Buddhas. Jesus did set a moral example by keeping the moral law perfectly, he was without sin. The Christian is to be like him in this respect, but he is never to become the second person of the Trinity.

As the savior, Jesus sacrifices himself as the substitute offering for sin to satisfy divine justice. The repentant believing Christian is pardoned of his disobedience

69

and accepted as righteous in God's sight solely because of the righteousness of Christ, which is received by faith alone. The Christian is saved from sin and its consequences. At death he is not reborn nor does he enter into a state of nirvana, but he is made perfect in holiness. At the resurrection he does not cease to exist, but is made perfectly blessed. He does not become God, nor does he lose his personal identity in a cosmic soup. He lives forever as a person in the full enjoyment of God. Jesus' love for man is a sacrificial love for real men, not simply a compassion for non-real men who suffer because they are deluded by their ignorance, and pass through endless cycles of non-real existence. Jesus is not a god among gods; he is God and man, in two distinct natures, and one person. He is unique. There can be no other Christ; there can be many Buddhas.

The subjectivists' definition of religion, as exemplified by Feuerbach, is apparently a true account of the nature of Hinduism, Buddhism, and the religions of the Ancient Near East. To this list we would add Shinto and the host of primitive religions with their many gods and goddesses. Such religions may satisfy the psychological need for security and may relieve anxiety and despair, but they are hardly credible to anyone that demands logical consistency and some evidence for what is believed.

Because some religions are subjective, it does not follow that all religions are subjective. We still need to examine religions that claim to be based upon the revelation of a supreme personal God, but before we proceed to a discussion of Judaism, Christianity, and Islam, it is necessary to understand why people believe in the existence of God and what is meant by revelation.

---

[1] See Gordon, Cyrus, *The World of the Old Testament,* 2nd ed. Doubleday, N. Y., 1958, pp. 15ff; especially pp. 20-21.

[2] *Ibid.*

[3] See *Ancient Near Eastern Texts, Relating to the Old Testament,* Edited by James B. Pritchard, Princeton University Press, Princeton, N. J., 1955.

[4] *Ibid.,* p. 3.

[5] *Ibid.*

[6] *Ibid.*, p. 4.

[7] *Ibid.*, p. 6.

[8] *Ibid.*

[9] *Ibid.*

[10] *Ibid.*, p. 11.

[11] *Ibid.*

[12] *Ibid.*, pp. 37-40.

[13] See Cyrus Gordon, *op. cit.*, p. 45.

[14] Pritchard, *op. cit.*, p. 61.

[15] *Ibid.*

[16] *Ibid.*

[17] *Ibid.*

[18] *Ibid.*, p. 62.

[19] *Ibid.*, p. 63.

[20] *Ibid.*, p. 65.

[21] *Ibid.*, p. 66.

[22] *Ibid.*

[23] *Ibid.*, p. 67.

[24] *Ibid.*

[25] *Ibid.*

[26] *Ibid.*, p. 68.

[27] *Ibid.*

[28] *Ibid.*, p. 139.

[29] Gordon, Cyrus, *op. cit.*, p. 99.

[30] Pritchard, *Ancient Near Eastern Texts*, p. 140.

[31] The reader may be struck by the similarity between the chaos out of which the gods arose and the *apeiron* of Anaximander, as well as Thales' fascination with water. This is not surprising if we remember Ancient Greece is a part of the same civilization. Cf. Cyrus Gordon on "Homer and the Ancient East" in *op. cit.*, pp. 101 and 112.

[32] Allis, Oswald T., *God Spake by Moses*, Presbyterian and Reformed Publishing Co., Philadelphia, Pa., 1951, p. 10. The problem of the relation between science and religion will be treated in chapter six. It is well to note here that the word "day" is used in the biblical Scriptures in various senses.

[33] Radhakrishnan, *Indian Philosophy* (N. Y.: MacMillan Co., 1956), pp. 73-75.

[34] See Lemaitre, Solange, *Hinduism* (N. Y.: Hawthorn Books, 1959), p. 9.

[35] For our account of the Vedic texts we are indebted to the description given by Solange Lemaitre, Chargee de Mission at the Louvre and at the Guimet Museum. Cf. *Hinduism* pp. 14-57, and to Radhakrishnan, *Indian Philosophy*, Vol. I.

[36] There is no agreement as to exactly how old the hymns are. Radhakrishnan assigns them to the fifteenth century B.C. See *Indian Philosophy*, Vol. I, p. 67.

[37] Intro. by Radhakrishnan in *A Source Book in Indian Philosophy* (Princeton, N. J.: Princeton Univ. Press, 1957), p. 3.

[38] There is no agreement among scholars as to the spirit of these hymns. They are regarded as childlike naive prayer, as primitive monotheism, as allegorical representations of the attributes of the supreme deity, as entirely allegorical or as naturalistic interpretations of the gods. Radhakrishnan does not find these diverse views to be antagonistic. They simply point to the heterogeneous nature of the collection. "It is a work representing the thought of successive generations of thinkers, and so contains within its different strata of thought. In the main, we may say that the Rig-Veda represents the religion of an unsophisticated age. The great mass of the hymns are simple and naive, expressing the religious consciousness of a mind yet free from the later sophistication." *Indian Philosophy*, Vol. I, p. 69.

[39] *Indian Philosophy*, Volume I, p. 86.

[40] Rigveda, ii. 12, quoted by Radhakrishnan, in *Indian Philosophy*, Vol. I, p. 86.

[41] Rigveda X. 89 in *A Source Book in Indian Philosophy* edit. by Radhakrishnan and Moore, Princeton University Press, p. 7.

[42] Radhakrishnan, *Indian Philosophy*, Vol. I, p. 89.

[43] *Source Book in Indian Philosophy*, p. 9.

[44] Radhakrishnan, *Indian Philosophy*, Vol. I, p. 83

[45] Quoted in Solange Lemaitre, *op. cit.* p. 60.

[46] Radhakrishnan believes Varuna is identical with the Greek Ouranos. His companion is Mitra.

[47] *A Source Book in Indian Philosophy*, (VIII. 41) p. 17.

[48] Radhakrishnan, *Indian Philosophy*, Vol. I, pp. 77ff.

[49] *A Source Book in Indian Philosophy* (X. 82) p. 18.

[50] See the remarks of Epiphanus Wilson, in his introduction to *Sacred Books of the East* (New York: Wiley Book Co., 1945), p. 4.

[51] *A Source Book in Indian Philosophy*, p. 24.

[52] *Ibid.*, p. 23.

[53] *Ibid.*.

[54] See Radhakrishnan, *Indian Philosophy*, Vol. I, pp. 117-118.

[55] *Ibid.*, p. 119.

[56] *Ibid.*, pp. 120-121.

[57] See Solange Lemaitre, *op. cit.*, pp. 24:25.

[58] See Radhakrishnan, *A Source Book in Indian Philosophy*.

[59] *Ibid.*

[60] *Ibid.*, p. 38.

[61] *Chand. Up.* VI. 13. 1-111, quoted by LeMaitre, *op. cit.*, p. 27.

[62] See Sankara, *Readings in the Philosophy of Religion*, edit. by John A. Mourant (Thomas Y. Crowell Co., 1959), p. 87.

[63] J. H. Bavinck, *An Introduction to the Science of Missions*, trans. by David H. Freeman, (Phila.: Presbyterian and Reformed Publ. Co., 1961), p. 267.

[64] Sankara, *loc. cit.*, p. 88.

[65] *Ibid.*.

[66] *The Upanishads*, trans. by Sivarni Prabhavananda and Frederick Manchester (N. Y.: New American Library (Mentor) 1961), p. 118.

[67] *Ibid.*, p. 119.

[68] *Ibid.*, p. 121.

[69] *Ibid.*, p. 115.

[70] *Ibid.*, p. 81.

[71] *Ibid.*, p. 68.

[72] *Ibid.*, *Chandogya*, p. 78.

[73] *Ibid.*, *Katha*, p. 23.

[74] Brahma, the God, is not to be confused here with Brahman, the ultimate reality, nor with the Brahmins, the priestly caste.

[75] *Upanishads*, Mund., *loc. cit.*, p. 43.

[76] *Ibid.* p. 48.

[77] See Solange Lemaitre, *Hinduism*, pp. 73ff.

[78] Heinrich Zimmer, *Philosophies of India*, (N. Y.: Meridian Books, Inc., 1960), p. 427.

[79] See Solange Lemaitre, *op. cit.*, pp. 73-78.

[80] *Ibid.*, p. 76.

[81] L. D. Barnett trans. *Bhagavigita*, II, 22, quoted by Solange Lemaitre, *op. cit.*, p. 74.

[82] See Solange Lemaitre, *op. cit.*, p. 78.

[83] *Ibid.*, p. 77.

[84] Cf. for a brief but comprehensive description of Yoga, Solange Lemaitre, *op. cit.*, pp. 79-85.

[85] Heinrich Zimmer, *Myths and Symbols in Indian Art, Readings in Philosophy of Religion*, p. 449.

[86] *Ibid.*

[87] See Solange Lemaitre, *op. cit.*, Chapter XI, "The Sects."

[88] U. Thittila, "The Fundamental Principles of Theravada Buddhism," in *The Path of the Buddha, Buddhism Interpreted by Buddhists*, edit. by Kenneth W. Morgan, The Ronald Press Co. N. Y. 1956, p. 71.

[89] *Ibid.*, pp. 282-285.

[90] Radhakrishnan, *Indian Philosophy*, Vol. I, p. 596.

[91] J. Kashyap, "Origin and Expansion of Buddhism," in *The Path of the Buddha*, p. 3. Our exposition on Buddhism does not pretend to be exhaustive nor does it apply to every school. It will however be representative of one of the main streams of Buddhism, and where possible our interpretation will conform to the interpretation of contemporary Buddhists.

[92] *Ibid.*, p. 4.

[93] *Ibid.*, pp. 4-5.

[94] See *Ibid.*, pp. 7ff., for much of our treatment of the origin and expansion of Buddhism.

[95] Heinrich Zimmer, *Philosophies of India*, pp. 206.

[96] *Mahavagga*, quoted by Zimmer, *op. cit.*, p. 206.

[97] *The Path of the Buddah*, p. 9.

[98] "The Gospel of Buddha," in *Readings in the Philosophy of Religion*, edit. by John A. Mourant, p. 242.

[99] *Ibid.*

[100] *Ibid.*

[101] *The Path of the Buddha*, p. 26.

[102] Cf. Zimmer, *op. cit.*, pp. 467-469.

[103] Cf. *The Path of the Buddha*, p. 28.

[104] *Ibid.*, p. 26.

[105] *Ibid.*, p. 29; Kashyap, the author of this quotation is a representative of Theravada Buddhism.

[106] *Ibid.*

[107] *Ibid.*, p. 32.

[108] *Ibid.*, p. 75.

[109] *Ibid.*, 81.

[110] *Ibid.*, p. 99.

[111] *Ibid.*, p. 101.

[112] *Ibid.*, p. 103.

[113] *Ibid.*, pp. 111-112.

[114] *Ibid.*, pp. 151-2.

[115] *Ibid.*, p. 289.

[116] *Ibid.*, p. 305.

[117] *Ibid.*, p. 382.

[118] *Ibid.*, p. 414.

[119] It is beyond our purpose to discuss the many schools and sects that have arisen throughout the world. Our exposition is largly that of Theravada (Hinayana) Buddhism. Certain forms of Buddhism, for example, in Tibet, have numberless deities (*Path of the Buddha* pp. 283ff). Their role is secondary to that of the attainment of nirvana. Zen Buddhism in which there has been a great deal of recent interest in the West, is simply one of the many schools of Buddhism. See D. T. Suzuki, *Zen Buddhism*, Anchor Book, N. Y. 1956, p. 56. The two major schools of Buddhism, are Theravada, found mainly in Ceylon, Burma, Thailand, Cambodia, and Laos; and Mahayana, found mainly in China, Tibet, and Japan. Tantrayana is a third type, not a separate school (See, *The Path of Buddha*, p. 39). The number of people who are Buddhists today is estimated at from 100 to 500 million. 150 million is the widely accepted figure (*ibid.*, p. 364).

[120] *Ibid.*, p. 46.

[121] *Ibid.*, p. 75.

[122] *Ibid.*, p. 76.

[123] *Ibid.*, p. 78.

[124] *Ibid.*, p. 228.

[125] *Ibid.*, p. 255.

[126] The Buddhists of Tibet believe that the Buddha has continued to function in the world even after his passing into nirvana . . . he will appear in inumerable worlds in order to help and to liberate living beings (*ibid.*, p. 260).

[127] *Ibid.*, p. 266.

[128] *Ibid.*, p. 283.

[129] *Ibid.*, p. 318.

[130] *Ibid.*, p. 370.

[131] *Ibid.*, p. 377.

[132] *Ibid.*, p. 379.

[133] *Ibid.*, p. 381.

[134] *Ibid.*, 135.

[135] *Ibid.*, p. 383.

[136] *Ibid.*, p. 384.

[137] *Ibid.*, p. 391.

[138] According to Hajime Nakamura some of the most important Mahayana writings are: Amidu Sutra, Amitayurdhyana Sutra, Mahavairocana Sutra, Mulamadhyamaka Sastra, Prajnaparamitahridaya Sutra, Saddharma Pundarika Sutra, Sukharativyuha Sutra, Vijnaptimatratasiddhi, and Vimalakirtinirdesa Sutra (*ibid.*, p. 392).

[139] *Ibid.*, p. 394. Pure Realm Buddhism is an exception. To be born in the pure realm is to attain nirvana.

[140] *Ibid.*, p. 395.

[141] *Zen Buddhism*, p. 19.

CHAPTER III

ARGUMENTS FOR THE EXISTENCE OF A SUPREME BEING

There is no single definition of religion that is acceptable to everyone. Definitions of religion differ because of real disputes concerning the nature of the object of religious beliefs. Many hold that there is no religion which has an objective basis outside of the mind of the believer, i.e., that all religions are subjective.

Whether or not at least one religion has an objective basis depends upon whether there is something outside the mind that is designated by the term "God." If it could be shown that our concept of God intends a non-mental state of affairs, that God is a being outside of our mind, that he is like we conceive him to be, even though our conception of him may be inadequate, then the conflict between the objectivists and the subjectivists would be resolved in favor of the former.

Either the subjectivist view of religion or the objectivist view of religion is the correct one; they cannot both be correct. If an objectivist were able to prove that his own position is correct, then he would at the same time prove that the subjectivist view is incorrect, and conversely. It does not follow, however, that the failure of the subjectivist to prove that religion has no basis outside of human fantasy amounts to disproof of the subjectivist's position and a proof of the truth of the assertion that God exists. Nor does the inadequacy of a demonstration of the existence of God amount to a demonstration that God does not exist.

Questions of what is and what is not true are different from questions as to what can be proved to be true. Presumably, micro-organisms existed before it was possible to demonstrate that they existed. Whether or not such and

76

such *is* the case is a different question from why we believe that such and such is the case. When challenged to give evidence, to answer the question as to why he thinks a particular religion is objective, the objectivist may simply confess his faith and express his conviction that God exists. If he is a Christian, he may appeal to the testimony of Scripture. He may also appeal to his own experience, to what he calls the inner testimony of the Holy Spirit. Some objectivists do not seek to prove by arguments that there is a God. Others, and it is with these that we are concerned in this chapter, offer arguments to provide conclusive evidence that there is a supreme being or God.

Some objectivists limit their religious assertions about God to what they can demonstrate to be true of him and exclude revelation as a source of further knowledge about God. For them religion is restricted to what can be demonstrated. Others accept some statements about God as true because they have been revealed but insist that the existence of God is knowable apart from revelation. They believe that man is endowed with the ability to arrive at the conclusion that God exists by a process of reasoning without the support of revelation.

Demonstrations or arguments in support of the existence of God have traditionally fallen into two classes—those that begin with an analysis of the nature of God and those that seek to infer his existence indirectly from our experience of his effects.

Before we examine both types of arguments we should note that neither type of argument purports to be "scientific" in the same sense as this term is used in the natural sciences.

Those who hold that the scientific method of observation and experiment is the only method of arriving at true propositions about matters of fact will reject the very attempt to demonstrate what is not ascertainable by the scientific method. To assume that what is in principle observable is, however, not an assumption which is verifiable in terms of any appeal to the scientific method. Such a presupposition begs the question. Its truth depends upon

77

the assumption that everything is of such a nature that it can be reduced to the concepts of the natural sciences. Naturalistic materialists may make such an assumption.

To postulate a basic naturalism without argument is an uncritical dogmatism. The scientific method is undoubtedly successful in doing what it sets out to do. It can, moreover, be successfully utilized by believer and non-believer alike. The question as to whether the world is all that there is, is not a question that can be answered by noting how the world looks when we look at it. The subjectivist and the objectivist in religion can agree as to how the world looks. The issue is whether the world is explicable solely in terms of itself, i.e., is the world itself ultimate, or is there a being other than the world to which the world is related?

1. *The Ontological Argument*

The arguments for the existence of God seek to offer evidence to prove conclusively that the world is not God. The first type of argument, as formulated by Anselm, is known as the ontological argument. The argument takes the form of indirect proof. The conclusion to be proved is that God exists objectively. Instead of proving it directly, Anselm proposes that we assume that God does not exist, and he then seeks to show that the assumption that God does not exist leads to a contradiction or to an absurdity. Contradictions are impossible; consequently, the assumption that God does not exist must be rejected as false. If it is false that God does not exist, then he exists and the desired conclusion is reached. But to discover the nature of the alleged contradiction that is involved in assuming that God does not exist, it is necessary to examine the argument in more detail.

The fool says in his heart there is no God. How can he do so, if it is impossible to think of God as not existing? Anselm's answer is that he does so simply because he is a fool. Can anything be said in behalf of the fool? Apparently not, says Anselm, for even the fool understands

78

what he hears when he hears the name God, that is, he understands a being than which nothing greater can be conceived. And since he understands what he hears, God exists at least in his understanding. Because he is a fool, however, he is too dull to see that a being than which nothing greater can be conceived cannot exist solely in his understanding. For if it did, if God does not exist both in and outside the mind, then we could still think of something greater, namely, that which does exist both in and outside of the mind. It is impossible, and it is contradictory, to think of a being than which nothing greater can be conceived and not to think of the greatest conceivable thing. If that, than which nothing greater can be conceived, exists in the understanding alone, the very being, than which nothing greater can be conceived, is one than which a greater can be conceived. But obviously this is impossible." Why? Because it is contradictory.

The argument is not meant to apply to any being other than God, for God alone is the being than which nothing greater can be conceived. To conceive of such a being is to ascribe every perfection to him, and since to exist outside of the mind is a perfection, God cannot be thought of as being perfect in every way and yet lacking in existence. Everything other than God can be thought of as not existing; but God, the being whose very nature is to exist, cannot even be thought of as not existing.

What can be said concerning the validity of the argument? It has been both severely criticized and strongly defended. The assumptions that it makes are obvious and have frequently been pointed out. Is it in fact the case that everyone understands by the term "God" a being than which nothing greater can be conceived? Are there not those who think, not of one God, but of many beings, beings that do not have all perfections as a part of their nature? And is there any ground for holding that to exist outside the mind is greater than to exist in the mind alone? How could one answer the assertion that what exists in the mind is greater than what exists in and outside the mind? Most people might agree, but how can it be demonstrated that non-mental existence is more perfect than mental existence? Such questions certainly pose difficulties for any proponent of the ontological argument. It may be the case that it belongs to God's nature to exist, that existence is his essence, but in the order of knowing, we could only know this to be the case if we first knew that God exists.

The crux of the difficulty with Anselm's argument is that he passes from the conceptual realm to the non-conceptual realm, from the mental world to the non-mental world. It is difficult to see how premises based upon an analysis of concepts can reach conclusions about actual non-conceptual states of affairs.

If Anselm's argument proves anything at all, then it proves only that if one conceives of God as a being than which nothing greater can be conceived, and if one's concept of the greatest conceivable being includes the notion of non-mental existence, then one cannot conceive of such a being unless one conceives of such a being as having non-mental existence. But whether such a being actually has non-mental existence is precisely the point in question.

The error in Anselm's reasoning can be shown if we reformulate his argument. Instead of its being of the form "if P then Q, and not Q, therefore not P," it is really of the form "if P then Q, and not Q, therefore R." In the first premise "if P then Q," P is equivalent to "God is thought of as not existing," and Q is equivalent to a contradiction: the greatest being is thought of and is not thought of. To deny the consequent Q is to deny that one *can* think of the greatest being and one *cannot* think of the greatest being. The conclusion that can properly be drawn is that P is false, namely, that one cannot think of God as not existing. The conclusion that Anselm would draw is that it is false that God *actually* does not exist, that is, God *actually* exists. The notion that God actually exists is thus deduced from premises that simply refer to what we conceive of as existing. Whether or not something is the case in fact is not determined by an analysis of a concept of what we mean. It begs the question to assume

80

that the order and connection between our concepts corresponds to the order and connection between things outside of our mind.

Our concepts may be able to grasp the essential properties of things that we experience and to draw inferences based upon such abstractions, but it is difficult to see how our analysis of our own meanings can ever reach a conclusion about a matter of fact outside of our own mind. It may be that the existence of God is demonstrable through his effects, but to begin with an analysis of the nature of God, with his essence, is to presuppose the very point in question, namely, that there is a being whose very nature is to exist. It is precisely this point that the subjectivist is unwilling to admit. He does not deny that men think of God as existing. But thinking does not make it so.

2. *Thomas Aquinas*

The second type of argument, which indirectly infers the existence of God from his effects, received its classic Christian formulation in Thomas Aquinas. The existence of God, as well as his perfections, are knowable to reason apart from any divine revelation. The existence of God is not self-evident; it is not known *a priori,* nor is it an article of faith. The famous five ways of Aquinas in fact constitute a single argument based upon causality. The first way begins with our experience of motion. When something moves, it is moved by something else. It is, moreover, impossible to proceed to infinity with respect to movers and things moved, for then an infinite number of bodies would move in a finite time. God, the supreme desirable, is the first mover, moved by no other. If there were no first mover, there would be no present motion, but since there is motion, there must also be a first mover.

That the world has a beginning in time is not what is here demonstrated. The proof remains the same if the world is regarded as eternal rather than as created, for it is not some past motion that is needed to start things moving. God is not a cosmic push. It is the present, actually given motion, which requires a first mover to be intelligible.

Thomas' argument presupposes a hierarchical order of causes. To be moved in the physical universe requires that the thing moved be moved by a moving cause superior to it. Within a species a particular moving cause cannot be the primary source of its motion. The sufficient reason must be sought outside the species, and ultimately every instrumental cause must be related to a first cause. To explain motion "it is necessary to arrive at a first mover, moved by no other; and this everyone understands to be God." God is thus needed if cosmic motion is to be explained.

A second aspect of divine causality is disclosed by the order of efficient causes in the world. It is impossible for a thing to be prior to itself, so nothing can be the efficient cause of itself. It is, moreover, not possible in efficient causes to go on to infinity. For, in the order of efficient causes, the first is the cause of the intermediate, and the intermediate the cause of the last. To remove the first cause is to remove the intermediate and the last, since the removal of a cause implies the removal of the effect. The absence of a first efficient cause would mean the absence of any other efficient causes. The argument takes the form of a condition. If it were possible to go on to infinity, there would be no first efficient cause, nor ultimate effect, nor any intermediate efficient causes. The consequence is denied, for there are effects and intermediate efficient causes. There is something, and not nothing, so the antecedent of the condition is false, that is, it is impossible to proceed to infinity, so that it is necessary to admit a first efficient cause, to which everyone gives the name God.

The point that Thomas would make is not that one cannot conceive of an infinite series on the same level of causation, but rather that each such series of efficient causes itself requires an explanation. Consequently, if the various series of causes are to be explained at all, they require the positing of a first efficient cause which is not

82

a part of any series. To keep going back on the same level of causation is simply to fail to find a sufficient reason, a sufficient explanatory principle. When Aquinas says you cannot go back to infinity, he means that this will not give any explanation whatsoever.

Suppose, for example, that two men were placed in the middle of a long suspension bridge without knowing its nature. They might see the cables overhead and imagine the bridge was suspended by an infinite cable. It may even be possible to conceive of a cable extending to infinity, but this does not satisfy the men on the bridge. For even if a cable extends to infinity, an infinite cable hanging in the air requires some explanation. What holds up the infinitely extended cable? A very, very long cable suspended in mid-air is just as puzzling, if not more so, than a short cable. The two men could, of course, imagine that the cable they saw was suspended by a second cable, and that by a third, and so on, never stopping, but each cable would in turn require just as much explanation as the first. A cable is not the sort of thing that hangs by itself. It requires an explanation in terms of something that does not hang in the air. It is in a similar argument that Aquinas denies that one can proceed to infinity in efficient causes. Of course one can keep going back and back, but one cannot go on to infinity if one is to find an answer to one's question. If reason is to find an answer, if experience is to be explained, a first cause must be posited. A person may be too dull, too preoccupied, or too lazy to look for causes, to seek to find God by reason, but if he will but look around (and this brings us to the third way), he will become aware that there is nothing in his world of experience that has as a part of its nature the wherewithal to be. There is nothing that is the cause of its own motion, nor the cause of its own existence; all that we experience is contingent, that is, it is possible for it to be and not to be. If there were nothing whose nature it was to be, if there were no necessary being, there would now be nothing. There is something, however, not nothing; therefore, not all being is contingent. There must be some being

83

having of itself its own necessity, which it does not get from another, but rather "causing in others their necessity. This all men speak of as God." God, the efficient and moving cause, is also necessary being. If everything were contingent, at one time nothing was in existence, and if this were the case nothing would now exist. God is, therefore, necessary being. His existence depends upon nothing outside of his own being.

The fourth and fifth parts of Aquinas' argument note, respectively, that we find a gradation in things, so that there must be something which is the cause of the perfection of things, and the fact that things achieve their end by design is explicable on the hypothesis that there is an intelligent being that directs things to their end. Natural bodies, while themselves lacking intelligence, still seek to obtain the best result, by acting purposively, designedly toward an end. What lacks intelligence cannot act intelligently, if it is not directed by some intelligent being, and this being we call God.

Each of Thomas' ways purports to be based upon a fact of experience, that there is motion, reciprocal action in things, beings that are born and die, more or less perfect things, and that there is order and design in things. Each way appeals to a principle of causality to infer that God is the sole cause of sensible experience. The phenomena of sense are thus held to be intelligible if and only if a cause is posited on an explanatory level higher than that of scientific explanation. The positive sciences cannot give the why of things, their *raison d'être*. The principle of causality employed by Thomas presupposes as self-evident the principle that nothing exists unless it has a sufficient reason to exist. It is not contradictory to conceive of an infinite multitude or of a succession without beginning or end, providing such an infinite series is on the same level of causation. The causes to which Thomas refers do not merely disclose a temporal succession; they are logically subordinate to each other. They are causes on different levels; each accounts for the nature or determination in

being of the following. The line of intelligible condition-
ing leads vertically to a transcendent cause.

Thomas believes that the existence of a first cause is
demonstrated by his five ways, and he also believes it
possible to demonstrate that certain attributes belong to
the first cause. It is impossible to comprehend the essence
of God but it is possible to know what God is not. By
removing what is not proper to him, the divine attributes
can be deduced. Since God is self-subsisting being, he is
distinct from the world. The world is composite; God is
not composite, he is simple. God is not a body, since he
is not moved by anything else; he is devoid of potentiality,
and is the most noble of things.

God is distinct from every finite being, because he
alone has existence as belonging to his nature. There is
no accident in God, since he is without potentiality. The
perfection of God is realized by eliminating all possible
imperfections. God is perfect because he is self-subsisting
being. By pre-supposing that God is a pure act-of-being
we can infer that a pure act of being is absolute perfection,
and since perfection is to lack no good, to be perfect is to
be the good. For God to exist is for God to be good.
Infinity is also a mode of perfection. God is the cause of
the being of creatures, not only at their creation, but
throughout their duration. God is the act of existing of
whatever exists, causing all things to be.

Knowledge of God's nature is found by utilizing notions
found in things and applying them to God without limitation or imperfection. Such a procedure presupposes that
the human intelligence is in no way limited to the sensory,
but is rather ordinated to the perception of being concretiz-
ed in sensible things, and is able to draw, from material
things, a conceptual object beyond the visible, and thus to
conceive of being freed from sensory limitations. In the
realm of being, human intelligence is able to seek the reasons
for the concrete manifestation of being. Human nature is
thus able to ascend above the human, and to know God, not
in his essence, but in such transcendental perfections which
are analogically common to the divine and the created.

It is not our purpose here to give a detailed treatment of the position of Thomas Aquinas.[1] The case of the objectivist has been stated fully enough to permit us to examine the reasons why the subjectivist remains unconvinced.

3. *Hume and Kant*

Let us first look at David Hume, and then at Immanuel Kant. David Hume's *Dialogues Concerning Natural Religion* subjects all such efforts to a critical analysis. The existence of God is, on the surface at least, not here called into question by Hume. Any effort, however, to infer what God is, either by rational argument or by inference drawn from sense experience, is subjected to criticism.

The choice of a dialogue form makes it difficult to ascertain Hume's own position with certainty. The three principal characters in the dialogue, *Demea, Cleanthes, and Philo* respectively represent orthodox rationalism, empirical evidence for a supreme designer, and Humean scepticism. That Philo's principles are more probable than those of Demea, and that those of Cleanthes are even nearer to the truth is the conclusion of Pamphilus, the narrator of the dialogue. Whether David Hume chose Philo or Cleanthes to be the winner of the argument is of historical interest; the subsequent importance and significance of the dialogue largely rests upon the fact that many have since declared Philo to be the victor.

The *Dialogues Concerning Natural Religion,* together with Immanuel Kant's *Critique of Pure Reason,* have led some to abandon natural theology altogether and others to seek to reformulate their arguments. Among those who abandon natural theology, the subjectivist seeks to get rid of God entirely, while others regard Humean scepticism as an ally which enables them to appeal unabashedly to revelation. No matter which course is followed, it is in any case evident that no serious student of philosophical theology can neglect Hume's *Dialogues.*

Demea and Philo agree verbally in their opposition to Cleanthes' attempt to draw inferences about the nature of God from the nature of the world. Philo and Cleanthes agree in their opposition to Demea's *a priori* argument to establish the infinity and unity of the Deity. The main debate takes place between Philo and Cleanthes. It reaches its culmination in Part XI when Philo abandons his mere cavils against design and draws attention to the presence of natural and moral evil within the world.

Demea, the representative of orthodox rationalism, is opposed by Cleanthes and supported by Philo in his insistence upon the incomprehensibility of the divine nature. Demea's distrust of arguments based upon experience and probability does not stem from scepticism, but springs from the conviction that it is impious to pry into the nature and essence of God. To reach conclusions which represent the Deity as similar to the human mind and understanding is to make ourselves the model of the whole universe. We cannot legitimately make inferences from ourselves to God. Human modes of thinking, ideas, and sentiments do not resemble the Deity. By reading a human author, a reader enters into the author's mind, but the order of the world, the book of nature, contains an inexplicable riddle. God's ways are not man's ways. Human reason is changing, whereas the incomprehensible nature of God is immutable and simple. There is no acquisition, diminution, change, or succession in God. To argue *a posteriori* from the world to God is to forget that a finite effect can never prove an infinite cause.

The infinity of the divine attributes and the unity of the supreme being can be demonstrated with absolute certainty by the following *a priori* argument. Granted that everything has a cause and nothing can be the cause of itself, either there is an infinite succession of causes and effects or there is an ultimate cause that is necessarily existent. The first disjunct is false. Therefore, there is an ultimate necessarily existent cause.

Why is it false to suppose that there is an infinite succession of causes and effects? Because each effect within the infinite chain of causes and effects exists by reason of the immediately preceding cause. The chain, however, requires a cause or reason as much as any member of the series. For why did this particular succession of causes exist from eternity and not some other series, or no series at all? Why is there something and not nothing? Why did this particular possibility become actual and not some other? If there is no necessarily existent being, every supposition is equally possible. The consequence of this condition is, however, false, for there is just this particular possibility that has been actualized. To deny the consequence of a condition is to deny the antecedent. There is, therefore, a necessary existent being who carries the reason of his existence in himself, and who cannot be supposed not to exist without a contradiction.

Cleanthes attacks Demea's *a priori* argument as illgrounded and of little consequence to piety and religion. A cause implies a priority in time and a beginning of existence. What exists from eternity has no beginning and therefore cannot have a cause. The material universe could have some unknown qualities which make it noncontingent, necessarily existent being, except that the expression "necessary existence" has no meaning. For if God is thought of as an existent being, that is, if his existence is taken to be a matter of fact, then his existence is not demonstrable. For if "God exists" is demonstrable, "God does not exist" implies a contradiction, since nothing is demonstrable unless a contradiction is implied by its contrary. However, if we can clearly conceive of God as existing, we can also conceive of him as not existing, since whatever we can conceive of as existent can also be thought of as non-existent. Consequently, since God can be conceived of as not existing without implying a contradiction, "God exists" is not demonstrable. No matter of fact, no existent, is ever demonstrable or necessary.

Cleanthes' attack on Demea is not prompted by scepticism. Complete scepticism makes survival impossible and is belied by the sceptic's reliance upon the maxims of science, ethics, and prudence in his daily conduct. Cleanthes admits that God possesses many powers and attributes which are incomprehensible but unless our ideas are true as far as they go, then the name "God" lacks meaning. Demea's pious utterances are in fact more dangerous than Philo's scepticism. For Philo's scepticism, like Descartes', is methodological, as he himself admits in Part XII when he states: ". . . a purpose, an intention, a design strikes everywhere the most careless, the most stupid thinker; and no man can be so hardened in absurd systems as at all times to reject it . . . ."[2] Demea's insistence that there is no analogy between the human mind and the divine mind, between the nature of the world and the nature of God, is virtually identical with an atheism which asserts that a first cause is unknown and unintelligible. A totally simple and immutable mind is no mind at all. It makes no sense to use the word "God" unless something is known about his nature. Such knowledge is attainable. The nature of God can be inferred from the nature of the world. The similarity of the world to a giant machine composed of an infinite number of little machines indicates the adaptation of means to ends throughout nature, and such adaptation, analogous to human design, permits the ascription of intelligence, thought, and wisdom to the Deity. A rational cause is needed to account for the works of nature.

Philo's attack on Cleanthes originates in a methodological scepticism which presupposes the insufficiency of human reason to attain theoretical certainty with regard to the first principles of any system. His doubts do not arise on the practical level, for in the final section of the *Dialogue* (part XII) Philo acknowledges that he is deeply religious and in spite of his arguments against design, he concedes that no man can be so hardened in absurd systems as at all times to reject it. He permits natural theology to conclude that the cause or causes of order in the universe probably bear some remote analogy to human intelligence, although such a conclusion does not provide the basis for any inferences that affect human life.

Philo does not object to Cleanthes' appeal to experience, but insists that our ideas cannot go beyond experience.

89

We may call the original cause of the universe God, but the attributes of the divine being are incomprehensible, since there is no reason to hold that the perfections of the Deity bear any analogy to the perfections of human creatures. We have no experience of the whole of the world, nor do we experience the origin of worlds. To suppose that the material world requires a mental cause is to forget that the mental world would itself require a cause. If the material world is dependent upon an ideal world, why not trace that ideal world into another, and so on *ad infinitum?* If it is possible to stop at all, why not stop at the very beginning with the material world? For by supposing it to contain the principle of its order within itself, we in effect assert it to be God.

Even if we ascribe the material world to a Mind like the human mind, there is still no reason to ascribe perfection or unity to the Deity. The world may be the product of trial and error, or the work of many finite gods who came into being and are themselves corporeal.

Since there is an absence of data for the formulation of any system of cosmology, and since there are no rules to follow, the world can be regarded as an animal with a deity for its soul. The world may contain its own eternal principle of order, attended by continual upheavals and changes. Its origin may be attributed to vegetation or to generation rather than to reason and design; its resemblance to a plant or animal is greater than its likeness to a machine.

The present order of the world need not be explained in terms of design. For by supposing a finite number of particles, capable of finite transpositions, and given an infinite duration, every possible order or position must be tried an infinite number of times.

At the end of Part X, Philo admits that such objections to intelligence and design are forced, based upon dodges, subterfuges, cavils and sophisms. His more serious arguments seek to show that the existence of a cause, bearing some similarity to human intelligence, does not warrant the ascription of moral attributes to the deity. The issue is not whether misery is fleeting and momentary, nor whether it is outweighed by happiness, but why is there misery at all?

The present situation in which man finds himself might be compatible with the antecedent conviction that the world is the effect of a finite deity, but the world provides no basis for the inference that there is a supreme, benevolent, powerful intelligence.

The presence of pain, the uniform course of events, the frugality with which creatures are endowed with powers and faculties, and the inaccurate workmanship of the machine of nature preclude the inference that the Deity has moral attributes, although if we had *a priori* knowledge of the moral qualities of the Deity, the circumstances of the world could be harmonized with them. From the phenomena of the world, it appears that the original source of all things is morally indifferent.

It is absurd to think that the Deity has human passions and is concerned with our vices and follies. A rational religion can be beneficial to a society, but the religion of the masses often ends in superstition and is detrimental. Remote promises and threats of future rewards and punishments are not as effective in promoting a stable social order as is man's inclination to honesty and benevolence.

Again it is not our purpose to decide here as to the merits of Hume's arguments. It is an historical fact that Hume's line of reasoning has been accepted by many as being valid, and if God is totally unconcerned with our vices and follies, it is not difficult to disperse with God altogether.

Kant's criticism is of a different and more technical nature. Kant does not simply reject the ontological argument, but rather he holds that the cosmological argument of Thomas Aquinas is equally deceptive, since it reasons from the unconditioned necessity of some being to the unlimited reality of that being. It holds that if anything exists, an absolutely necessary being also exists, and since I at least exist, the desired conclusion is reached.

Experience is in fact used by the cosmological proof only to conclude to the existence of a supreme being, the properties of which cannot be determined by experience, so that in effect the cosmological proof presupposes the ontological proof. Otherwise it could not infer that the concept of an *ens realissimum* is the only concept appropriate and adequate to necessary existence. Experience is unable to demonstrate that absolute necessity belongs to any determinate thing.

Moreover, the proposition that every necessary being is the most real of all beings, when converted, implies, according to Kant, that every *ens realissimum* is a necessary being. And such is determined solely from the fact that the concept *ens realissimum* implies its absolute necessity, which could be the case only if the ontological proof were valid, an assertion not admitted by the cosmological argument.

The contingent can have meaning solely in the sensible world, and the principle of causality is meaningless when extended beyond the latter. And even within the world of experience there is no justification for the assertion that the impossibility of an infinite series of causes implies a first cause. It is illegitimate, on the ground that we can think of nothing further, to remove all conditions which make the concept of necessity possible, and then to complete the concept of the series. The cosmological proof confuses logical possibility with actuality.

The existence of an all-sufficient being can be postulated as an admissable hypothesis, but it cannot be said with absolute certainty that such a being necessarily exists. The idea of a supreme being is only a regulative principle of reason. And the concept of necessity is a formal condition of thought, not a material condition of existence.

The only other possible rational demonstration of the existence of God can also, according to Kant, be shown to be unsatisfactory. Such an alleged proof, designated by the term "physico-theological," proceeds on the basis of a determinate experience of the constitution and order of things within the world to a supreme being. But the very idea of a necessary and all-sufficient being is so far above anything empirical, that the latter can never be expected to provide a sufficient basis for such an inference.

All laws pertaining to cause and effect, all synthesis and extension of our knowledge, refer to possible experience, to objects of the sensible world. Consequently, reason is unable to bridge the gap between a series of natural causes and a transcendent intelligible being.

The physico-theological proof is based on our experience of order in accord with a determinate purpose believed to be alien to the things themselves, so that such order is explicable in terms of an intelligent cause, the unity of which can be inferred from the unity of the reciprocal relations existing between the parts of the world. Thus the order and purposiveness of the world presupposes the existence of a cause proportioned to it, a being possessing all the perfection proper to an all sufficient being.

The difficulty is, however, that physico-theology is unable to give any determinate concept of the supreme cause of the world, since empirical analysis can never lead to an absolute totality beyond the sensible world, so that the gap can only be filled by the ontological argument.[3]

Those who reject an Aristotelian-Thomist conception of knowledge reject Thomas' proofs of the existence of God. The Thomistic arguments presuppose that the principle of causality is known by an intuition; it is a metaphysical axiom. Those who either deny causality or make it a category of the mind are unwilling to go beyond the sensible realm to a cause that is not sensible.

In other words, the arguments of Thomas depend upon a principle of causality which to some subjectivists is itself as questionable as the existence of God.

The Thomist holds that the principle of causality is known by an intuition bearing on the primary aspects of being, although it may be provoked in the mind by a sensible example. It is a metaphysical axiom of which every philosopher ought immediately to be aware, an axiom which reasoning itself presupposes.

The principle of causality is intellectually seen. It imposes itself with absolute necessity, by force of the notion of being itself. It is rooted in intelligible, not in sensible, appearances.

The principle of causality, as a metaphysical principle, belongs to a perfect form of knowledge. It is a part of a true science. It belongs to the world of the supra-universal, to a sphere of intelligibility having its determination in itself. Thus metaphysics reaches above time, and grasps a world of eternal truths, a world which does not need the verification of the senses.

The principle of causality by which God is known does not arise from an analysis of the sensible but from necessities which are intuitively grasped in being. When given a diversity of things which do not suffice for their own existence, we know immediately that they depend upon a cause sufficient for their existence.

The principle of causality is therefore pregnant with ontological meaning. It is an ontological principle which is not derived from experience, but which applies to the latter.

The principle of causality may be dispensed with in the sphere of phenomena, but it is indispensable in the sphere of being. For as soon as the existence of a contingent being is admitted, the existence of necessary being is implied. Thus a philosopher cannot think of the non-sufficiency of his thought without knowing that it depends on supra-thought, which guarantees its actuality and its being as thought. An infinite series is impossible here since it is a reason of being which is here sought, and an infinite series is not a reason of being. My act of thought is caused by an absolute uncaused thought. And it is after I know that such a thought is an existing reality that I deduce his infinite perfections. Real existence is not here deduced from the idea of total perfection. But without recourse to the ontological argument, it is known that being *a se* exists, and that the notion of aseity includes total perfection.

To demonstrate the existence of God is, however, not to subject him to our grasp. The concepts and names which describe God's perfections, although fully realized in God, do not delimit divine reality. The divine perfections are identical in God, and the Deity is above everything which circumscribes the idea of being. Yet metaphysics demonstrably knows that the divine essence subsists in itself.

To many critics, Thomas' identification of the first cause, the unmoved mover, with the God of Christianity appears to be unwarranted. To others, the arguments, when regarded as syllogisms, appear to be invalid in that their premises speak of finite existence and their conclusions speak of God's existence. To speak of God's existence and the world's existence, for example, is to speak analogically, so that any argument in which existence is predicated of both God and the world, uses the term in two different ways. Aquinas' arguments are thus accused of being invalid, since they violate one of the rules of a syllogism by containing four terms, instead of three.

E. L. Mascall, a neo-Thomist, admits that it is in no way evident that each of the five ways ends with the same God. The five ways disclose to us that finite being does not explain its own existence. They are not so much syllogistic arguments as discussions that enable us to grasp that finite being is finite.

> Considered as proofs they may well seem to be circular. Anyone who cannot see that the essence of finite beings does not involve their existence is hardly likely to admit that they are contingent in the precise way the Third Way requires . . . .
>
> The existence of being in which essence and existence are really distinct does not *logically* imply the existence of a being in which essence and existence are really identical . . . .[4]

In answer to the objections of Kant, critics point out that an erroneous theory of existence is involved in Kant's view of a concept and a judgment. Kant was correct in pointing out the weakness of the ontological argument. A purely analytical process cannot reach existence itself without presupposing any datum of experience. But Kant wrongly concluded that the concept of existence adds nothing to a subject and is not a predicate. Existence has a content, an intelligible value. It is a predicate with reference to a perfection, the actuality of every act.

When reason establishes the existence of God, it starts with data of experience where existence is apprehended, and under the compulsion of intuitively grasped first principles, it compounds the notion of a first supreme cause with that of existence, so that reason does not need to employ the ontological argument, for reason knows the existence of a first cause from experience itself.

Kant fails to see the radical difference between conception and assertion, between simple apprehension and judgment. Kant argued that to demonstrate the existence of God by his effects is to establish the existence of an absolutely necessary being, starting from contingent existence, and to conclude that such a being is God, since the absolutely necessary being is supremely perfect. The ontological argument is thus presupposed by the cosmological argument since the proposition "the absolutely necessary being is supremely perfect" is the major premise of the ontological argument "the supremely perfect being is absolutely necessary." But the question has been raised as to what constitutes the heart of the ontological argument. Does it identify necessary existence and supreme perfection, or does it pass from supreme perfection conceived to necessary existence affirmed?

If the two theses: "any supremely perfect being is absolutely necessary" and "any absolutely necessary being is supremely perfect" are taken as equivalent, the first holds that "any supremely perfect being merely represented exists necessarily in effect," and the second holds that "any absolutely necessary being merely represented exists effectively with complete perfection." Aquinas would begin by establishing that an absolutely necessary being exists, and he then would feel justified in concluding that this being, of which he knows that it exists, possesses a supreme perfection which also exists.

The pitfalls of the ontological argument are avoided if one merely affirms that if it exists, every supremely perfect being exists with an absolute necessity, or if it exists, any absolutely necessary being is supremely perfect. Thomas does not begin with a concept but with experience. He first establishes the existence of a primary cause or intelligence, and it is only after the question of existence has been decided, that he concludes that such a being is pure act and infinite perfection. Thus Thomas does not pass from the ideal to the real but from the real to the real.

The proofs of the existence of God presuppose a critical realism, an Aristotelian-Thomist conception of knowledge. And it is precisely this that Hume and Kant refused to admit. The critical problem is not how it is possible to pass from *percepi* to *esse*. For the intellect deals first of all with being, and it discovers the principle of identity in its very apprehension of it. Epistemology is itself a part of metaphysics, and it has no existence apart from the latter; consequently, Kant is unable to refute the Thomistic proofs of the existence of God by means of an epistemological analysis of pure phenomena. For it suffices for things to exist independently of the mind for God to become inevitable.

The arguments of Thomas Aquinas help some objectivists to justify the reasonableness of their position and also to convince some subjectivists that they are in error. Others remain unconvinced. The evidence in support of the objectivist view of religion does not end here, for many objectivists appeal to revelation to support their beliefs.

------

[1] For a further discussion see David H. Freeman, *Recent Studies In Philosophy and Theology*, (Philadelphia: Presbyterian and Reformed Publishing Co., 1962).

[2] *Hume's Dialogues Concerning Natural Religion*, edited by Norman Kemp Smith, (New York: Thomas Nelson and Sons, LTD, 1947), p. 214.

[3] For a Neo-Thomist answer to this argument, see Freeman, *op. cit.*

[4] E. L. Mascall, *Existence and Analogy*, (London: Longmans, Green and Co., 1949), p. 78.

CHAPTER IV

THE PROBLEM OF REVELATION

The orthodox adherents of Christianity, Islam and what is called modern Judaism not only agree that religion has an objective basis, but also they share the belief that man can know the nature of God because God himself has taken the initiative to make himself known.

The question as to whether or not there is revelation is not identical with the question as to where revelation is to be found. It is possible to grant that there is revelation and to differ as to its extent and nature. Christians, Moslems, and many modern Jews differ as to where God has revealed himself, but they agree that he has revealed himself. The present chapter is primarily concerned with the problem as to whether or not there is revelation.[1]

Anyone who holds that religion has an objective basis cannot intelligently refrain from considering what is known about the nature of God. It became apparent in the preceding chapter that even some of those who would demonstrate that God is, depend upon revelation, not reason, for their fullest knowledge of God.

The question as to whether there is revelation is a meaningful question, at least in the sense that it is readily understood, even by most of those that answer it negatively. Of course, those who hold that God exists are apt to be more interested in the question than those who do not. Interest, however, is a personal matter; it has nothing to do with the importance of an issue.

1. *The Importance of the Problem*

The question of revelation may be of tremendous importance, even though genuine interest in it may frequently be hard to find.

There are many reasons why people lose interest in a question. If the answer is already known, there is little point in further inquiry. One reason why many people no longer concern themselves with the problem of revelation is that they live under the illusion that they have already solved it. It is somehow thought that only a negative answer is possible.

A truly critical attitude, however, calls for a careful investigation before giving an answer. It is quite possible to reach a negative answer as to whether or not there is revelation, even after the question has received careful consideration. It is, however, dogmatic either to ignore the question or to dismiss it in any arbitrary manner.

The reader who has never considered the question of revelation might reflect upon the historical fact that for hundreds of years learned men held to the common conviction that men could and did have knowledge of God that was the result of the initiative of God. What fact or facts have since been discovered that demonstrate that such initiative was never taken? Does the reader have any firsthand evidence that Augustine, Maimonides, and Avicena were wrong in their beliefs?

Interest in the question of revelation may be reawakened by considering certain historical developments within the Western world. For centuries revelation and reason were both accepted as means by which God was known. At times a greater emphasis was placed upon one rather than the other. The assumption was commonly held, however, that when properly interpreted revealed truth and truths of reason were never in conflict.

This state of harmony did not last forever. With the dawn of modern times, the certainty that there could be no conflict between the truth of revelation and that of reason vanished. The harmony was broken. Some chose the side of reason, others of revelation. Some held to revelation, but limited its voice, ascribing to reason alone the task of constructing a picture of the world. Man now ascribed to his own personality the free sovereign creative power that he previously had ascribed to God. With mathematics as his model, he proceeded to create his own world, a world which later seemed to have little room for his new found freedom, since his own personality was ever threatened by the alleged scientific view of the world that he himself was in the process of creating.

The 17th century in general did not deny the fact of revelation. It simply made it unimportant. Reason was all that was really needed. But in the 18th century revelation came under direct attack. God and morality were to be retained only to the extent that they were compatible with reason. Toward the end of the 18th century Kant put an end to reason. What began with a rejection of the importance of revelation in the name of reason, ended in a rejection of both reason and revelation.

The rejection of a revealed God ended in the rejection of the God of reason. Whether this process was accidental or causal may be a question. But it is clear that something has happened in what has been called our post-modern, post-Christian era. The story is not complete. There is a correlation between what a man thinks of God and what he thinks of himself. When man believed that God was the creator, he regarded himself as a creature.

As long as man believed in a revealed God, he could turn to what was revealed about God and learn about himself. He could learn what he should do to glorify God, and since God was believed to be holy and just, his own conduct was prescribed by the very nature of God. His conduct was determined for him by God's holy law, found for both Christians and Jews in the Decalogue.

At first, even when a revealed God was rejected, it was still thought that man had a nature, and that certain rights were guaranteed to him by the author of his nature. The God of reason remained, and standards of conduct

100

could still be read by understanding what conduct would complete or perfect man's nature.

The situation remained unchanged from a practical point of view even after Feuerbach, and others, rejected the existence of God, since it was still held that man had a nature and that there are unchanging moral standards. It was not until the end of the 19th century that human nature and moral standards together with the notion of a revealed God were discarded. Man now derived his nature from the group to which he belonged. He became a part of the herd, or one of the leaders. His nature and his conduct now depended upon the group to which he belonged, upon his purposes, upon the "values" that he adopted. There was no longer any agreement as to what man is, and there was no agreement as to what he should do, as to how he should behave. Some would have him do whatever the majority want to do. Others would subordinate his interests to those of the state or a party. Some simply wait gloomily for the giant mushroom cloud that may put an end to further debate within the Western world. Some remember the gas chambers of Hitler. Others have forgotten. And some, perhaps even some of the readers of this book, have again become interested in the question of revelation.

It is difficult, if not impossible, to become interested in something that is intrinsically absurd. There would not be much point in asking whether or not there is revelation, if such a question were nonsense like "Cat no six," or if such a question were like asking whether or not there are round squares, or holes that are both empty and filled to the brim with concrete.

If an intelligible meaning can be ascribed to the words "God has revealed himself," then it might at least be worth while to ask whether the proposition expressed by the combination of words is a true proposition.

The accusation that religious utterances are nonsense is dealt with in Chapter 7. If the reader is unwilling to admit that it is possible to use the word "God" in any meaningful way, he may refer to that chapter. If he still

101

remains unconvinced, perhaps he will continue to read anyway, in the hope that while what follows may be non-sense, perhaps it is important nonsense, at least it is the kind that people keep right on talking even after they have been repeatedly told that they cannot say what in fact they do say.

For those who are willing to proceed further, the proposition "God has revealed himself" will be true under certain conditions and false under others.

There are several conditions that would render the above proposition false. It would be false if the concept of God referred to by the word "God" failed to designate anything outside of the world of concepts. If God has no objective existence, the statement "God reveals" cannot mean what it means for the orthodox believers of the religions under discussion. If there is no being capable of revealing, then the statement that such a being reveals is simply false. It is then false for the same reason that the statement "Leprachauns drink milk" is false (as there are no Leprachauns).

There is a second reason why the proposition "God has revealed himself" could be false. It might be held that although God exists there is something about the nature of God that makes it impossible for God to reveal himself, or it might be held that although he could, if he wanted to, there is, however, no evidence that he has done so. In short, the proposition is false simply because God has not revealed himself, at least not in the special way maintained by orthodox Christians.

Of course, some may even be willing to concede that given the existence of God, there is a certain sense in which it can be said that God reveals. If one simply means that God's existence is somehow evident within his mind or from the nature of the external world, then in this general sense God may be said to reveal. However, if one means more than that, the proposition is false. The proposition "God reveals himself" would thus be equivalent in meaning to the proposition "Man is aware of God."

102

2. *The Meaning of Revelation*

It is evident that the words "reveal" and "revelation" can refer to different concepts. What the orthodox religious believer means when he says God reveals himself is that it is God who is active. The word "reveal" here refers to something that God does and not simply to a human awareness of God. Before answering the question as to whether the proposition "God has revealed himself" is a true proposition, it is first necessary to clarify what is comprehended in the concept of revealing. What does the orthodox believer mean?

But first what is ordinarily understood by an act of revealing under circumstances other than religious ones? There are certain necessary conditions without which an act of revealing does not take place. One prerequisite for such an act is *ignorance*. In order for X to reveal something to Y, Y must first be ignorant of what X reveals. If Y already knows what X says then X simply tells Y what Y already knows and X then does not reveal anything to Y. Ignorance on the part of Y is thus a necessary, although not a sufficient, condition for an act of revealing to take place. Before there can be an act of revealing there must be some person or persons that are related in some way to Y. Unless there is an X with whom Y is in contact, there can be no act of revealing. X reveals S (something) to Y. But this still does not exhaust what is ordinarily meant by the word "reveal." On occasion Y may learn something from X by accident. And the word "reveal" is sometimes used in this somewhat restricted sense: that X discloses something to Y unintentionally. There is a stronger usage, however, and it is this stronger sense that is of importance to our problem. In a somewhat stronger sense X is said to reveal something to Y when X does so intentionally, that is when X has a purpose P. It is, moreover, not to be overlooked that when X reveals something to Y for purpose P he does so at a particular time and place T by certain means M. In this strong sense then, an act of revealing takes place solely between persons, for persons alone

103

are capable of having conscious purposes, at least on a high level of complexity.

An act of revealing thus takes place when X reveals S to Y for purpose P by means of M at time T. What is thus transmitted to Y may then be referred to as the revelation of X to Y. It is this strong usage of the word "reveal" that is in question when orthodox Christians, for example, utter the statement God has revealed himself. And for this proposition to be true one must be able to assign an intelligible meaning to X, S, Y, P, M, and T. If one of the conditions is not met, the proposition "God has revealed himself" cannot be a true proposition in the strong sense of revealed.

Let us continue our analysis in more detail. God can be truly said to have revealed himself if, and only if, there is a God, our previous X. But the mere fact that God exists does not constitute an act of revealing. It is presumed by theologians that God was before the existence of the world, before there was any person or being to whom he could reveal himself. God can only be said to reveal himself to some one. And if God has revealed himself to Y, in this case to some human beings, then God has revealed something to Y, something which Y did not know before. And since accidental behavior is hardly to be ascribed to what men understand by "God," it is to be assumed that whatever God does is purposive. It is equally obvious that if God is to reveal himself to men he must do so at a certain time and place, by means that are intelligible to Y. If all such conditions have in fact been met, then it can be truly said that "God has revealed himself." The expression "the special revelation of God" can then be used to refer to all such acts of revealing that satisfy the conditions X, S, Y, P, M, and T. Stated in a more formal way, one can say that there is divine revelation if, and only if, all the conditions X, S, Y, P, M, and T are satisfied where X refers to God, S to what is made known, Y to those persons to whom S is made known, P to the purpose X has in making S known to Y, M to the means used by X to make

104

S known to Y, and T to the time and place where X made S known to Y by means of M for purpose P.

The question as to whether God has in fact revealed himself is distinct from the question as to whether it is possible that God could have revealed himself. The possibility of revelation might be granted, while the actuality of revelation might be denied. It is also to be remembered that even if it is granted that God could and did reveal himself, this still would not decide the question as to where and when such actual revelation occurred. It is obvious, however, that if one knew where and when such acts of revelation actually occurred, one would of course know that revelation is possible. Whatever is actual must be possible, but if something is possible it is not necessarily actual. Of course, if something is impossible, then it can never be actual.

We have already noted the widespread tendency to assume that revelation is impossible. Are there any reasons for this assumption? Is this simply an *a priori* of faith, a dogmatic postulate, an unproven assumption from which one can deduce that all claims to the contrary are false? Or are there any grounds for this assumption? What would someone need to know in order to assert with certainty the proposition "Revelation is impossible"? Remember that this proposition not only denies the actuality of revelation, but it also denies the very possibility of it, thereby precluding further investigations into all claims that revelation is actual.

We have seen what conditions would need to be met to establish the actuality of revelation. From our analysis it is readily evident that revelation would be impossible if in fact there was no God (X) who knows something (S) and has purposes (P) and is capable of employing means (M) at a certain time and place (T) to make S known to man (Y).

Whatever is impossible is absurd, and whatever is absurd is impossible. What is it that makes something absurd? Something is absurd if, and only if, it is intrinsically contradictory. Such a situation is reached when

105

the same proposition is simultaneously asserted to be true and to be false. It would be absurd to assert that God exists and God does not exist. It would be absurd to assert that God knows something and God does not know something. To assert that God has the means and the purpose to make something known to man and that God has no means and no purpose to make something known to man is absurd. And whatever is absurd is impossible, and vice versa. Revelation, in our sense of the term, would be impossible and therefore absurd if either God did not exist, or he had no purposes, or he did not have the means or the knowledge to disclose to man.

The person who asserts that "revelation is impossible" either knows what he asserts or he does not know it. The word "know" may be used in a way that is synonomous with faith. We may say we know something when what we mean is that we believe it with psychological certainty. If, when someone asserts that he knows revelation to be impossible, he simply means that he is psychologically convinced that revelation is impossible then he is doing little more than disclosing something about his own personal state of mind. He is confessing his faith.[2] However, "know" may be used to stand for what one holds to be true on the basis of conclusive evidence. Now what type of evidence would a person have to have in order to "know" that revelation is impossible in this second stronger sense? If someone knew that God did not exist then he would know that revelation is impossible. But what conclusive evidence is there that God does not exist? A person may believe whatever he wishes but what a person believes and what he knows are not necessarily identical.

Propositions that have God as their subject are religious and/or metaphysical propositions. To assert that God exists or to deny that God exists is to assert a religious and/or a metaphysical assertion. The evidence that is relevant to the establishment of the truth or falsity of such assertions must, therefore, be religious and/or metaphysical assertions. It will be shown in Chapter 6 that the truth or falsity of a genuine scientific proposition is simply

106

irrelevant to the truth or falsity of a metaphysical proposition. In any case it ought to be evident here that to know that revelation is impossible is not easy. Anyone who thinks he knows this in the strong sense of "know" thinks that he knows quite a bit. For he claims to know the very nature of the universe. He also knows that all claims that people have made that such disclosures have taken place are in fact false claims.

Revelation is admittedly impossible unless there is a God that is capable of knowing and of having purposes. Frequently what lies behind the tacit assumption that revelation is impossible is the assumption that a personal God is impossible.

Many people today still use the term "God" but they use it to refer to the totality of things that constitute what is ordinarily called the material world. "God" is used synonymously with "nature." The term "God" may also be used to stand for the sum total of human ideals. It then becomes apparent to many that while man becomes aware of nature or of his own ideals, his ideals do not become aware of him. An act of revealing can take place solely between persons, so if within the universe man alone is capable of purposive behavior, then man alone is capable of revealing.

The rejection of revelation here rests upon the metaphysical assumption that everything other than man is impersonal. The extension of the concept of a person is limited to man alone.

When it is said that man is a person, what is meant, among other things, is that man is capable of conscious, purposive, intelligent behavior. To be a man is to be a person. It is to be aware of one's self and to be aware of others. A person is conscious of himself and of the world in which he lives. He functions in every aspect of his world. A person lives under the same physical conditions as does a stone. The concepts of the physicist can be applied to both man and the stone. But this does not imply that men are stones or that stones are men. The difference between man and a stone is partly expressed by the term "person."

The biologist is also able to describe man and animals in certain common terms. They share certain functions from a strictly biological point of view. Because men share certain biological functions with animals it does not follow either that animals are men or that men are animals. Men defecate and animals defecate, but this does not mean that men are animals. And what makes man different from the animal is partly expressed by the term "person." It is precisely the fact that man is a personal being that enables him to state that he is an animal. We know of no animals that have claimed to be men.

What makes man a person is not that he has such feelings as pleasure and pain, but that he is aware of such feelings; he can study them, form concepts about them, and subordinate them to his plans and purposes. What makes man a personal being is that he can freely transform his physical environment into a civilization, constituted by government, art, science, language, law, religion, and a wide variety of groups and purposive associations.

In brief, to conceive of man as a person is to conceive of a wide variety of free, conscious, purposive behavior. It includes man's knowing, planning, conceiving, and many other aspects of his nature. The essential characteristic, however, is the element of self-conscious, purposive activity, i.e., when someone acts as a person he is aware of himself when he acts, and in general he knows why he acts. He has a purpose.

Now when it is said that God is a personal being what is meant, in part, is that God acts in a personal way, so that while God cannot act in a way that would be contradictory to his own nature, he can act in a conscious, purposive manner.

It is precisely at this point that the objection might be made that what makes revelation impossible is the fact that personal beings alone are capable of performing acts of revealing. And since God is not a personal being, God is not capable of performing acts of revealing. We have argued in support of the major premise, that personal beings alone are capable of revealing. And if the minor premise is granted: that God is not a personal being, the argument would be sound. It is precisely the minor premise, however, that begs the question. That "God is not a personal being" is the very point of contention.

In support of the minor premise it might be argued that the very notion of a personal being is derived from human experience and is to speak of God in human form. While it may be acknowledged that there is some power or force in the universe that may be called "God," yet to speak of God as a personal being is to ascribe human traits to what is admittedly infinite and beyond all human limitations.

The preceding argument undoubtedly objects to the tendency of many to conceive of God in terms similar to Michelangelo's painting, i.e., as an old man with a beard. Those who would conceive of God as a force, however, often forget that the notion of a force or power also originates in human experience. There is the danger of thinking of God as an old man, but there is also an equal danger that one might begin to thing of God as electricity. What purports to be a more modern sophisticated view simply becomes the deification of nature. There is certainly nothing new and modern in this procedure.

There are many reasons for the widespread acceptance of the premise that God is not a personal being. It is probable that the rise of secular education has produced the phenomenon that many otherwise well-educated people are childish in their understanding of what theologians have said, and are saying. It is not uncommon to meet a person who has distinguished himself in a non-theological specialty, who rejects or accepts religious beliefs on the level of comprehension possible to a bright eight-year-old child.

There is no difference between the view of the child and the view of the adult in such a case. However, there is frequently a difference between their respective attitudes. The child is bright and alert; he knows that he is growing up, and is therefore inquisitive and open to new interpretations. He is filled with questions. But the adult with childish religious beliefs in other respects acts like an adult.

He is psychologically as certain of his childish beliefs as he is of his mature judgments, and he is often completely unaware that there are those who have gone beyond the level of a child in religious matters. The rejection or acceptance of a personal God is immature if a person does not understand what it is that he is asked to accept or to reject.

Few, if any, biblical theologians have ever conceived of God in a crude, literal fashion. There is something peculiar about religious language. For example, the reader may remember the Old Testament account of the occasion when Samuel appeared before King Saul to rebuke him for his disobedience. In I Samuel 15, verses 10 and 11, we read, "Then came the word of the Lord unto Samuel saying, It repenteth me that I have set up Saul to be king," and in verse 35, we read, "and the Lord repented that he had made Saul king over Israel." And yet just a few verses before, in verse 29, we read, "And also the strength of Israel will not lie nor repent: for he is not a man, that he should repent."

It would be easy to dismiss these verses as hopeless contradictions. Anyone unfamiliar with biblical exegesis might simply hold that the author here affirms that God repents and God does not repent. It is, however, reasonable to ascribe as much intelligence to the author of such a narrative as we would like to have ascribed to our own efforts at communication. The simple and obvious explanation is that the word "repent" is being used in more than one sense. The negative statement—God does not repent because he is not a man that he should repent—is meant to be literal. As we shall see in detail it fits in with the Old Testament portrayal of God. The statements that the Lord "repented" that he made Saul king are more difficult to understand. They are, however, not to be taken univocally, i.e., the writer is not here ascribing human emotions to God in a strictly literal sense.

The popular misconception that the God of the Old Testament is a crude tribal deity who is vengeful, fickle, and fearsome, while the God of the New Testament is a God who is meek and mild, is in part due to a failure to give due consideration to the nature of the language used within the biblical text.

All language that man uses is human language. And when man speaks of God, he must speak as man. Likewise, if it is the case that God has in fact revealed himself to man, the means that he uses must be such that man could understand what God would have him understand.

It is not necessary to go into all the implications and exegetical difficulties in the statement that the Lord repented that he made Saul king over Israel. Verse 29 makes it obvious that Samuel clearly does not intend to ascribe any activity to God that is contrary to the divine nature. Repentance when ascribed to God differs from human repentance as the divine nature differs from human nature. Samuel may be saying no more than that Saul's behavior is contrary to what God would have him do, and that the consequence of his disobedience was to be his downfall. Much more may be implied. In any case Saul knew more about God after Samuel left him than he did before.

Many modern intellectuals erroneously feel that they are in the grip of the following dilemma. If a person speaks of God literally, then the result is a crude primitive theology that is absurd. If a person does not speak literally about God, the result is a scepticism that entails the rejection of a personal, revealed being. And since a person must either speak of God literally or not speak of God literally, he must either accept an absurd primitive theology, or he must accept a scepticism that entails the rejection of a personal, revealed being.

The force of this dilemma lies in its formal validity, but it can readily be rebutted by an equally valid counter-dilemma: If a person speaks literally about God then this will not lead to scepticism, and if a person does not speak literally then this will not lead to absurdity. And since we must either speak literally or not speak literally of God, we either do not end in absurdity or we do not end in scepticism. The choice between speaking literally and speaking analogically may not be quite so simple as the preceding dilemma supposes. It may be that what is said of God is

111

not always meant to be entirely literal, nor is it meant to be wholly non-literal. It may be that sometimes when a person speaks about God there is an element in what he says that is literal and an element that is also analogical in a proper non-metaphorical sense.

It might then be argued that sometimes when a person speaks literally and analogically about God, he does not speak absurdly. But what is meant by speaking analogically? There is much that could here be said and there are many distinctions that could be made.[3] Suppose, for example, one were to say that the lion is to the beasts of the field as the king of England is to the people of England. Such an ascription of kingship or dominion to a lion is hardly to be taken literally. There is no sense in which a lion is really a king. And yet the metaphorical use of kingship, when applied to a lion, gives some indication of his strength, grace, and beauty. Nevertheless, there is not much likeness between a lion and the king of England.

Suppose, however, one were to say that a chair has arms and a man has arms. In what sense could one then speak of the ascription of arms to a chair and the ascription of arms to a man as being analogical? Obviously the arms of a chair are not the same as the arms of a man. And yet something is literally asserted about a chair when it is said that a chair has arms. Let us imagine a situation in which someone who had never seen a chair before was told what a chair was and that it had arms. Do you suppose that when confronted with a chair he would confuse the arms of the chair with its legs? Probably not, at least not if he knew what human arms were. There is some recognizable similarity between human arms and the arms of certain chairs. But of course the difference is tremendous. The arms of the chair are to the chair as the arms of a man are to a man. And insofar as men differ from chairs, chair arms differ from human arms. It might make sense to ask whether the average arms of a chair are longer than the average arms of a man, but it would be rather odd to ask: which requires more blood transfusions at the loss of an arm, a chair or a man? At times non-literal,

112

rather than literal, statements about God appear to end in absurdity. For example, Samuel's statement that "God will not lie nor repent: for he is not a man, that he should repent," is certainly meant literally and when so understood precludes views of God that would otherwise lead to absurdity.

When it is said, however, that God is a personal being and man is a personal being, the concept of a personal being need not be ascribed to man and to God in a univocal sense. What is affirmed with respect to God is both literal and analogical. To speak of God as a personal being is not to ascribe to him every trait and characteristic that is ascribed to a man. Nor is it entirely different. The sense in which God is a personal being is not wholly other than the sense in which man is a personal being. "Personal being" is not ascribed to God in a purely equivocal manner. Something is literally asserted about God when it is said that he is personal. Among other things what is meant is that God is not an unconscious force, but he is a conscious, intelligent being capable of purposive action.

To say that God is a personal being is not to ascribe human weaknesses and defects to God. Perhaps the following chart will help to clarify what is meant.

A—MAN IS A PERSONAL BEING

B—GOD IS A PERSONAL BEING

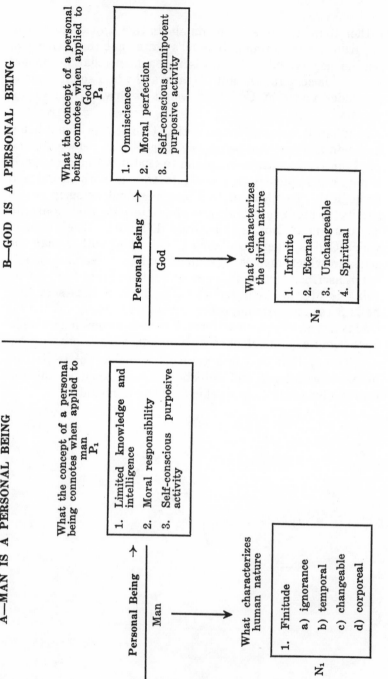

B—GOD IS A PERSONAL BEING

What the concept of a personal being connotes when applied to God
P_2

1. Omniscience
2. Moral perfection
3. Self-conscious omnipotent purposive activity

Personal Being →

God

What characterizes the divine nature

1. Infinite
2. Eternal
3. Unchangeable
4. Spiritual

N_2

A—MAN IS A PERSONAL BEING

What the concept of a personal being connotes when applied to man
P_1

1. Limited knowledge and intelligence
2. Moral responsibility
3. Self-conscious purposive activity

Personal Being →

Man

What characterizes human nature

1. Finitude
   a) ignorance
   b) temporal
   c) changeable
   d) corporeal

N_1

114

Under heading A the reader will find a partial description of what is meant by "Man is a personal being." What is included under P_1 is a partial description of what is comprehended in the concept of a personal being on the human level, while N_1 contains a partial description of what characterizes human nature. B contains a partial description of what is meant by "God is a personal being." P_2 delineates the partial comprehension of the concept of a personal being on the divine level, and N_2 gives a partial description of the divine nature.

"Man is a personal being" and "God is a personal being" differs in meaning as P_1 differs from P_2, and P_1 differs from P_2 as N_1 differs from N_2.

The statement "Man is a personal being" literally asserts that the concept "man" designates a being that has a nature which includes what is described in N_1 and which also has the properties included in P_1.

The statement "God is a personal being" literally asserts that the concept "God" designates a being that has a nature which includes what is described in N_2 and which also has the properties included in P_2.

The personal character of a man is to the nature of man as the personal character of God is to the nature of God. Whatever is ascribed to man and to God differ as the nature of man differs from the nature of God. The limitations and imperfections are to be found on the side of man (A), while there is no limitation or imperfection that is to be ascribed to God (B).

No attempt has been made to demonstrate by the preceding discussion of what is meant by saying that "God is a personal being" that there is in fact such a being. It should be apparent, however, that to conceive of God as a personal being does not necessarily imply a lack of sophistication.

Moreover, a second point, which is of far greater importance than being sophisticated, whatever that may mean, is that to grant that God is a personal being is to grant the possibility, if not the actuality, of revelation.

Among the suppressed premises of one who denies the possibility of revelation is to be found the denial that God is a personal being. To grant that God is personal is to grant the possibility of revelation. To deny that God is personal is to deny the possibility of revelation. The admission of a personal God is equivalent to the admission of the possibility of revelation. The rejection of a personal God is equivalent to the rejection of revelation. There can be revelation if, and only if, there is a personal God.

It is absurd to hold to the possibility of revelation if, and only if, the prior denial of the existence of a personal God has been made. Otherwise, the question of the actuality of divine revelation remains an open question.

We have now reached the point in our discussion where it is clear that anyone who holds to the existence of a personal God must allow for the possibility of revelation. The problem remains, however, as to how one moves from the notion that there is a God, to the notion that God is personal, and from there to the notion that God has revealed himself.

Anyone who accepts the validity of the arguments put forth in the last chapter holds that the existence of God is demonstrable. Such a person may be psychologically more willing to identify the God of reason with a revealed, personal God, and yet he, too, must admit that although he is committed to the existential identity of the God of reason and the God of revelation, the way that he knows the one from the other, differs as faith differs from rational demonstration.

The person who accepts the statement "God has revealed himself" as being true, will, when challenged, usually refer to what he calls his faith.

3. *The Meaning of Faith*

Why do people believe that God has revealed himself? It is here well to remind ourselves of our overall aim. The philosopher is concerned with the truth about religion. He

116

should analyze the evidence in support of both the objectivist and the subjectivist view of religion. Our current interest is to examine the way faith in revelation is used to strengthen the objectivist point of view.

The words "faith" and "belief" are used in different senses. When used in its weakest sense the word "faith" refers to such beliefs that are little more than guesses, opinions, or weak convictions that are readily abandoned. Such transitory beliefs lack any psychological certainty and usually concern matters of little or no consequence. The evidence in favor of such beliefs is either wholly lacking or it is too meager to produce more than a very faint glimmer of certainty and conviction. Such weak beliefs and opinions seldom characterize what is meant by faith in religious matters.

A second usage of the word "faith" is to be found in connection with beliefs of some importance and marked by varying degrees of psychological certitude. Such beliefs are usually retained for some time by the believer and may also concern religious matters. This second type of faith (F_2) shares with faith (F_1), described in the preceding paragraph, the characteristic that both F_1 and F_2 refer to beliefs for which evidence is wholly lacking, or if such evidence exists, the believer is unaware of it. They differ in that the beliefs included in F_1 are transitory, trivial, and unaccompanied by any high degree of conviction, whereas the beliefs referred to by F_2 may be more or less permanent, important, and marked by greater psychological conviction.

The term "faith" is used in a third sense (F_3) when it refers to beliefs concerning matters of importance, for which there is evidence sufficient to produce a degree of certainty that scarcely admits any doubt or wavering. F_3 differs from F_1 and F_2 in that the believer who has faith in this third sense bases his convictions upon evidence of which he is aware and which he deems adequate. Faith in this last sense is usually restricted to matters of great importance, and it is frequently such faith that is to be found among religious believers.

117

A fourth sense of the word "faith" (F_4) does not refer to any particular set of beliefs, but it refers to the phenomenon that human experience is never free from acts of belief in the sense of F_1, F_2, and F_3. There is no area of human experience which is free of beliefs and convictions. Faith here refers to the fact that unless faith F_1, F_2, and F_3 are held, knowledge would be impossible. It is necessary to believe in order to know. F_4 refers to that aspect of human experience which makes F_1, F_2, and F_3 necessary for all experience.

The universality and necessity of the faith referred to by the term F_4 may become evident to the reader if he notes that unless he "believes" in such things as the identity of his own person, the general reliability of his memory, and in the general trustworthiness of his senses, he will be unable to read this page.

Within the area of religion the very subject matter requires the exercise of faith, and there is a sense in which no one can avoid a certain religious *a priori*. There is a sense in which all men make implicit, if not explicit, assumptions about themselves and whatever they hold to be the origin of themselves and of their world, with its many structures and laws.

The object of religion need not be an objective supernatural being; it can be a part of nature, or it can be man himself that is taken to be the origin of all purpose and meaning within our world and our experience. But whatever it is, in the last analysis, the choice that is made, at least in part, is due to the faith that one has.[4]

Such a faith is usually not solely an individual matter; it is shared by many others. At a given time within a certain community certain common beliefs are held by its members with such conviction that they are never questioned. The acceptance of such commonly held beliefs are often necessary prerequisites for belonging to the community.

What we are saying here is that the subjectivists and the objectivists both constitute a community of believers. In the last analysis, at least part of their reasons for looking at religion the way they do depends upon their basic faith and commitments, and such faith may be supported by evidence or it may be held in the absence of evidence.

---

[1] Much of this material has previously appeared in *Recent Studies in Philosophy and Theology.*

[2] It will subsequently become clear that the term "faith" is used in more than one way. It sometimes stands for what we believe in the absence of evidence, the weaker sensc, and at other times it stands for what is believed on the basis of partial although *adequate* evidence. We are here using the term in its weaker sense.

[3] For a more extensive discussion of the problems that are involved here, the reader might consult E. L. Mascall, *Existence and Analogy,* (London: Longmans, Green and Co., 1949).

[4] For an extensive argument in support of this essentially Augustinian thesis, the reader is referred to H. Dooyeweerd, *A New Critque of Theoretical Thought,* Vol. I, Presbyterian and Reformed Publishing Co. 1957.

CHAPTER V

THE RELIGIONS OF REVELATION

Few of the religions of the world claim to be religions of revelation. By revelation in the religious sense is meant the disclosure of a message to men from the personal, true, and living God. This message is mediated through men and takes the form of a written word which from the time it was given to the end of time remains the word of God. This word of God is the source of all knowledge of the Deity and provides the pattern for man's life in this world and furnishes men the way of converse with and acceptance by God.

In some religions which do not fall into the category of revelatory religions men still claim to believe in the existence of an absolute and ascribe to it attributes which transcend men. But such religions lay no claim to having received from God a written document that discloses his being and mind. They rely upon man's own powers to discover what the ultimate is and what is required of men. Man's own reason and insight furnish all that is necessary for an understanding of himself, the gods, and the world.

The purpose here is not to vindicate the religions of revelation as over against religions which derive from man's powers. To say the least, the objectivist point of view is intellectually respectable and reasonable. This has been shown in previous pages. Religion is from God or it is not from God. And if the claim is that it is from God, it must be verifiable by some objective data, if the claim is to be substantiated. A written, transmitted word in the form of a book, upon which the religions of revelation rely for their knowledge of God, is common to the religions of Islam, Judaism, and Christianity.

1. *Islam*

There was a day when Moslem armies stormed the gates of Western Europe. They subjugated Spain and penetrated into the heart of France but were decisively defeated by Charles Martel at the Battle of Tours (A.D. 732). We might speculate as to what might have been the course of European history if they had conquered and overrun the Western World. But what might have been nobody knows. However, in any event today Islam is the religion of a vast number in the Near and Far East. It has gained adherents also in Europe and on the American continent. The year of its beginning dates from the flight of Mohammed to Mecca known as the Hegira (A.D. 570). Mohammed, the founder of this religion, was born about A.D. 621 at Mecca. Not much is known of his early life. Certain scholars believe that the young Mohammed suffered from fits,[1] but in any case he was prone to fasting and secluded meditation in caves. It was in a cave that his first "revelation" came to him at about the age of forty-five. At first he feared that he was possessed by a Jinn, but he soon began to propound divine revelations with frequency.

The Koran, the "revelation" of the Moslem, was spoken by the Prophet Mohammed, retained in the memory of his close associates, and "written down by such as were able to write. . . ."[2] The orthodox Moslem regards the Koran as the supernatural dictation of God. The Old Testament and the New Testament are also regarded as revelation but their teaching have been distorted by Jews and Christians. The Koran is the definitive form of revelation.

Mohammedanism like Judaism and Christianity claims to be a religion of revelation. And this revelation, purportedly from God, written in the Arabic language, is the Koran. The sources upon which the Koran draws are recognized by non-Moslems to be pre-Islam Arabian religion, Talmudic Judaism, and Oriental Christianity.

Basic to any religion is its view of God. For Islam the seven words which form its basic creed and reveals its

121

view of God are: *La ilaha illa Allah, Mohammed rasul Allah*—There is no god but Allah (and) Mohammed is the prophet (or apostle) of Allah. This creed is known as the *Kalimet*. With regard to it, it is well to remember a traditional saying of Mohammed, "God said to Moses, if you were to put the whole universe on one side of the scale-pans and the words *La ilaha illa Allah* on the other this would outweigh that."

The Koran constantly reiterates this formula. It is understood to be a great enunciation of God's unity. The name Allah is derived from the Semitic *El* (great God, *ho Theos*) which name designates in the religions of the Ancient Near East the most high god. In the religions outside of Israel, he is the chief god of the pantheon. The name Illah is pre-Islamic for any god and by using it with the definite article it came to denote *"the* god" or the supreme god above all the others. Polytheistic religions single out one god as supreme and as the main object of worship and religious attention. Mohammed has precursors who led the way for his insistence upon one absolute God.

In Islam there is great insistence on the unity of God. This is the cornerstone of Mohammedan belief. The unity of God is proved from creation in the following Surahs (divisions): 6:96-100; 16:3-22; 21:31-36; 27:60-65, as well as elsewhere. The statement is also made that polytheism and atheism are contrary to reason (Surah 23:119) and that dualism is self-destructive (Surah 21:22). In Surah 71:23 we find that Noah and Mohammed agree in condemning the idols of the anti-diluvian polytheists. Yet the fundamental conception of Allah or God is impersonal and negative. He is a vast monad that has no resemblance to anything known or to any creature. Mohammed says in Surah 112, "There is not to him a single equal." A popular song puts it this way: "Whatsoever your mind can conceive, That Allah is not you may believe."

122

The absolute precept of love, Thou shalt love the Lord thy God with thy whole soul, is not formulated in the Koran. What is brought out is, first of all the inscrutable sovereignty of God and then, total and blind surrender.[3]

God is so different from his creatures that very little can be postulated of him.

The Koran says much about the attributes of God. These are God's excellent names (Surah 7:179). According to tradition it is believed Mohammed said, "Verily, there are ninety-nine names of God and whoever recites them shall enter Paradise." It is the custom of many pious Moslems to employ in their devotions a rosary of ninety-nine beads to represent these names. Thirty-six names in the Koran describe Mohammed's ideas of Allah's power, pride, and absolute sovereignty (see Surahs 3,7,8,9,10,15, 20-97). There are five attributes which describe Allah's hurting and avenging (Surahs 22,25,80,90,91), for Allah leads astray and works harm. Yet Allah is also holy and truthful (Surahs 4,29,51,85).

The passages in the Koran that deal with sin are the following: Surahs 4:30; 2:80; 4:46; 14:39; 2:284-286; 9:116; 69:35; 86:9; 70:19-25; and 47:2,3. From these we learn that sin is a willful violation of known law. Sins of ignorance are not crimes and smaller and lighter offences will be forgiven. It is the greater sins which are to be shunned.

In the Koran, nothing is right or wrong by nature, but becomes such by the fiat of Allah. What he forbids is sin even if it appears right and good to us. If Allah allows it, it cannot be sin at the time he allows it, though it may have been sinful before and after.

There is the recognition of moral and ceremonial law but the distinction between them is blurred. The Koran holds that it is as great an offence to pray with unwashed hands as to tell a lie. The breach of a ceremony is worse than moral turpitude. What matters is the repetition of the creed. Reformation of character is insignificant compared to this. Just to repeat the *Kalimet,* "There is no god but Allah and Mohammed is the prophet of God" *ipso facto* constitutes one a true believer and opens the door into the religion of Mohammed.

The moral law is subject to change, according to times and circumstances. Allah himself is not subject to an absolute standard of rectitude but can do what he pleases. If he so pleases Allah can mock, deceive, and plot in which activities he is most proficient. According to Mohammed God is the proud, the slayer, the indulgent, and the harmful.

"As he wills it" recurs very frequently in the Koran, Allah's will is divorced from reason and love. Allah is, according to the Koran, the author of evil (Surah 113:2) but good also comes from him. In twenty passages of the Koran, Allah is said to lead men astray, and is ever ready to punish and to ruin. Men are not to be in doubt that Allah's cunning and pride are above theirs.

Man is what God makes him, be he good or evil. The Koran makes no attempt to harmonize divine sovereignty and human freedom. It is well to note the view of predestination in the Koran. The word used in the Koran is *kadar*, "to measure out," "to order beforehand." (See Surahs 54:59, 3:139; 8:17; 9:51; 14:4.) Surah 76:29, 30 states: "This truly is a warning, and who so willeth taketh the way of his Lord; but will it ye shall not unless God will it, for God is knowing, wise." *Kadar* in the Koran amounts to a doctrine of inevitable necessity in the nature of things. This is fatalism even if an omnipotent, sovereign power is implied. The will of Allah is an irresistible force. It is equated with fate. There can be no responsibility, and God becomes the author of evil. In twenty passages of the Koran Allah is said "to lead men astray." Adam was created with sinful desires which made his fall inevitable.

In the Koran there can be no prayer for God's will to be done. To the Moslem, Allah reveals his will in accomplishing it, and all that man can do is submit. He must bow to inevitable necessity. Fate binds him in fetters from which he cannot extricate himself. He is in a dungeon without exits. The phrase *El-Hamdu-lillah* ("the praise is to God") expresses submission, passivity, and fatalism.

124

Islam offers a way of salvation without forgiveness of sin. The latter is not necessary since transgressions of the moral law, as recorded in the Koran, are not really sinful. Slight faults are permitted (Surahs 7:10-17; 38:20-24). God is so merciful that what appears to be sinful in his favored ones is not really sinful. The way of pardon and acceptance by God is by his abrogating his law and passing over guilt without penalty. In Islam God is not absolutely unchangeable and just. His law is not the expression of his moral nature but of his arbitrary will.

> The Moslem God can best be understood in the desert. Its vastness, majesty, ruthlessness and mystery—and the resultant sense of the utter insignificance of man—call forth man's worship and submission but scarcely prompt his love or suggest God's . . .[4]

A second article of orthodox Moslem faith is a belief in angels. It was the angel Gabriel that brought the Koran to Mohammed. Every person is accompanied by two recording angels who record his good and bad deeds. Two other angels Nakir and Munkar quiz every newly buried corpse on the faith. They first make the corpse sit up. If the corpse acknowledges the prophet, it is let alone; otherwise it is beaten severely, and although mortals cannot hear its cries, animals can. Some say it is beaten until the resurrection.

There are many intermediary creatures between men and angels. These are called Jinn.

> These are created of smokeless flame, eat and drink, propagate their species, and are capable of both belief and unbelief. Mohammed was sent to them as well as to men, and good Jinn now perform all the religious duties of Moslems (See Surrah 62:1,2,15,16).
> The Jinn often appear as animals, reptiles, etc., or in human form.[5]

The revelation of God has been given to man, to the prophets, but the Jews and Christians have distorted the writings. Jesus is not the Son of God. "Allah forbid that he should have a son."[6] The Jews did not kill Jesus, "nor did they crucify him, but they thought they did."[7] At the day of judgment:

125

All men will then be raised; the books kept by the recording angels will be opened; and God as judge will weigh each man's deeds in the balances. Some will be admitted to Paradise, where they will recline on soft couches quaffing cups of wine handed them by the Huris, or maidens of paradise, of whom each may marry as many as he pleases: others will be consigned to the torments of hell. Almost all, it would seem, will have to enter the fire temporarily, but no true Moslem will remain there forever. Other traditions picture a bridge as sharp as a sword over the pit, from which infidels' feet will slip so that they fall into the fire, while the feet of Moslems will stand firm.[8]

The religious observances and social practices of Islam may be briefly noted. The creed, the Kalimah, is to be recited, ritual prayer five times a day is required, as well as congregational prayer at noon on Fridays. During the ninth month of the Moslem year, Ramadan, with the exception of the incapacitated, Moslems are required to fast from dawn to sunset. Legal alms are also to be given, and when possible, at least once in a lifetime a pilgrimage to Mecca is enjoined upon the faithful.[9]

It is these Five Pillars, and particularly the profession of the Creed and the performance of prayer and fasting, which chiefly make up the practice of Islam to the average Moslem. He who acknowledges the Unity and Transcendence of God, pays him his due in prayer and fast, and accepts Mohammed as the last and greatest of the prophets, may well, indeed, have to taste the fire, but hopes that he will not, like the infidel, remain in it forever—through the timely intercession of the prophet.[10]

It is of interest to note that the true believer is also enjoined to "fight for the cause of Allah."[11] "Fighting is obligatory for you."[12] "If you do not fight He will punish you. . . ."[13] "Mohammed is Allah's apostle. Those who follow him are ruthless to the unbelievers but merciful to one another."[14] "Allah loves those who fight for his cause."[15]

Every Moslem is enjoined to answer any legally valid summons to war against infidels. This duty of Jihad or Holy War is not limited to the inception of Islam, for Islam

126

is to be spread by the sword. The world where Islam does not reign supreme is *Dar al Harb*, "the abode of war."

As to ethical practices, Moslems are enjoined to marry no more than four legal wives at one time, "and he may also cohabit with as many slave concubines as he may possess."[16] Married women are forbidden to the Moslem unless they are slaves. A Moslem may divorce his wife at any time, for any reason, but women can never divorce their husbands.

> Islam sanctions slavery and the slave trade, and the unlimited right of concubinage . . . with female slaves.[17]

Of course many of these practices, while sanctioned in the Koran, are disappearing in modern Islam. And yet the thief may still have his right hand cut off, and the adulterer may be stoned.

It is beyond our present concern to deal with the many sects and modern modifications of orthodox Islam. We shall now turn to Judaism and Christianity, of which Islam, at least to the non-Moslem, is a perversion.

2. *The Religion of Judaism*

The source material for Judaism is contained in the Hebrew Bible. Since the time of its completion in antiquity, the Hebrews or Jews have carefully guarded their Scriptures from interpolation and changes. They have, however, added other books of religious import which are of significance for their religious profession.

Judaism is a religion which claims to be a revelation from God. The Old Testament is regarded as that revelation. The Old Testament ought to be allowed to speak for itself. Any attempt to get behind what is said by conjecture and emendation, when the words plainly declare their meaning, is an unwarranted imposition which springs from a prejudicial view of the biblical content.

127

The Jews regarded their Bible as worthy of close study and obedience because it claimed to be from God. No book or words were given a place equal to it. In the Hebrew Bible God claims to direct the Israelites or Jews to the Bible itself. "This book of the law shall not depart out of thy mouth; but thou shalt meditate therein day and night, that thou mayest observe to do according to all that is written therein: for then thou shalt make thy way prosperous, and then thou shalt have good success" (Joshua 1:8). God here claims to have given the words of the book. This is corroborated by this statement made by God to Moses: "I will raise them up a Prophet from among their brethren, like unto thee, and will put my words in his mouth; and he shall speak unto them all that I shall command him" (Deut. 18:18).

Again and again the expressions "Thus saith the Lord," "Hear the word of the Lord," and words of like import are found in the Old Testament. Many passages may be cited. "The Lord spake also unto me again saying" (Is. 8:11; cf. vs. 11). "For thus hath the Lord spoken unto me" (Is. 31:4). "The Lord said also unto me in the days of Josiah the king" (Jer. 3:6, cf. 13:11). "And the word of the Lord came unto me, saying" (Ezek. 21:1; cf. 25:1). "Thus saith the Lord" (2:1). "Hear this word that the Lord hath spoken against you, O children of Israel" (3:1). Wherever we turn we are confronted with statements which claim that the words of the Old Testament are the words given to the people of Israel by God himself.

It is needless to multiply quotations from the Old Testament to the effect that words of the Old Testament are regarded by the Old Testament itself as of divine origin and authority. When a prophet spoke he claimed that though it was he who was speaking yet the words were the words of God. The following statement by Jeremiah who was commanded by God himself to speak can have no other meaning: "Hear ye the word of the Lord, O kings of Judah, and inhabitants of Jerusalem; Thus said the Lord of hosts, the God of Israel" (Jer. 19:3); "Hear ye the word which the Lord speaketh unto you, O house of Israel"

128

(10:1). Also in times of national and religious crises God intervened and spoke to rulers through men chosen by God as the following: "But the word of God came unto Shemaiah the man of God, saying, Speak unto Rehoboam" (I Kings 12:22, 23); "The word of God came to Nathan, saying, Go and tell David my servant, Thus saith the Lord" (I Chron. 17:3,4).

In the Psalms there is the following: "The law of the Lord is perfect, converting the soul: the testimony of the Lord is sure, making wise the simple. The statutes of the Lord are right, rejoining the heart; the commandment of the Lord is pure, enlightening the eyes" (Ps. 19:7,8); "The words of the Lord are pure words" (Ps. 12:6).

That the Jews from ancient times believed their Scriptures according to its own witness to itself is plainly indicated throughout their history. For many Jews today, Scripture still is what the Old Testament claims to be, the true and authoritative word of God.

A curse is pronounced upon all who disobey its precepts and a blessing is declared to all who observe its commandments: "Behold I set before you this day a blessing and a curse; a blessing, if ye obey the commandments of the Lord your God, which I command you this day: and a curse, if ye will not obey the commandments of the Lord your God, but turn aside out of the way which I command you this day to go after other gods, which ye have not known" (Deut. 11:26-28; cf. 27:26, 28:15; Josh. 8:34). And among the devout Israelites there was expressed the desire to keep the words of God: "For I have kept the ways of the Lord, and have not wickedly departed from my God" (Ps. 18:21). "The statutes of the Lord are right, rejoicing the heart: the commandment of the Lord is pure, enlightening the eyes. The fear of the Lord is clean, enduring forever: the judgments of the Lord are true and righteous altogether. More to be desired are they than gold, yea, than much fine gold: sweeter also than honey and the honeycomb" (Ps. 19:8-10). "O how love I thy law! it is my meditation all the day" (Ps. 119:97). Thus subjectively and objectively, the religion of Israel was devotion to God

expressed in the observance of the written, divinely inspired word. Their well-being in this world and in the
next was bound up with this adherence to Scripture.

What is it that the Jews believed? What was the
religion of ancient Israel which was established by their
belief in the divine origin and authority of the revelation
contained in the Old Testament? What conception of God
is found in the Hebrew Scriptures? The Old Testament
attributes to God distinct existence and personal identity.
He is apart from all that is and cannot be equated with
mere force or power. As a personal being he has the attributes of a person, namely, thought, feeling, and volition.
He shows favor and kindness but also displays wrath. He
speaks in the first person and men address him in the
second. He is worshiped and loved by men and he speaks
to men with authority and also with love. While these
attributes of a person belong to men, in God they are
possessed in perfection and without any limitation. To the
Jews this was not a way of conceiving God drawn out of the
human consciousness. The Old Testament God knows,
feels, and acts independently of men. We find God speaking to Adam (Gen. 1:29; 2:16; 3:9, 13, 17), revealing himself and speaking to Noah, (Gen. 6:8, 13), entering into
covenant with Abraham (Gen. 12:1, 7; 15:1), and con-
versing with Moses as a friend with a friend. To prophets
chosen by himself he declares his mind with the commission
that as he instructed them they should instruct the people
(Deut. 18:18; Amos 1:1; 7:1). Such actions can be true
only of a person.

A personal, living God to whom men are morally related is the only one which the Old Testament knows. He
is not a fabrication which grew out of man's need for a
unifying principle.

From earliest times men have fabricated legends to
account for the world. But the Old Testament data bearing
upon the origin of the world is written in the vein of sober
narrative.

The first statement of the Hebrew Bible asserts, "In
the beginning God created the heaven and the earth" and

then in narrative form, purporting to tell what happened, this ancient text gives in concise and unambiguous language the fiats of God by which he brought the world that we know into existence.[18] The following are some of the expressions used: "And the Spirit of God moved upon the face of the waters." "And God said, Let there be light: and there was light"; "Let there be a firmament in the midst of the waters"; "Let the waters under the heaven be gathered together unto one place"; "Let the earth bring forth grass"; "Let there be lights in the firmament of the heaven"; "And God made two great lights; the greater light to rule the day, and the lesser to rule the night: he made the stars also"; "And God made the beast of the earth after his kind"; "And God said, Let us make man in our image"; "So God created man in his own image; in the image of God created he him, male and female created he them"; "And God saw everything that he had made, and, behold it was very good."

And so the book of Genesis in the early chapters continues to tell us of the way in which the creative fiats operated in the world of God's making. The fact of the creation of man is given without embellishment.

To this personal God is attributed self-existence without beginning or end. He is in no way identified with the world. He stands apart from it and is its cause. In no way is the world confused with God's being. He is a personal being distinct from the world and upholds it and all that is in it. The pantheistic notion that God is identifiable with the world is alien to the Jewish thought of the Old Testament as is clearly seen in the following words of king David: "Before the mountains were brought forth or even thou hadst formed the earth and the world, even from everlasting to everlasting, thou art God" (Ps. 90:2). "The heavens declare the glory of God; and the firmament showeth his handiwork" (Ps. 19:1).

In Judaism there is the claim to a revelation of the God who created, sustains, and rules the world. This God is regarded as the only, the true, and the living God. "Hear, O Israel: The Lord our God is one Lord" (Deut. 6:4).

131

"But the Lord is the true God, he is the living God, and an everlasting king" (Jer. 10:10), "I am the Almighty God" (Gen. 17:1), "And God said unto Moses, I AM THAT I AM" (Ex. 3:14). The peoples of the ancient biblical world claimed the superiority of the gods of their own nation or tribe, but they also recognized the existence of the other gods. The Bible however denies the existence of the gods of the other nations. The statement in the Ten Commandments (Ex. 20:1-17) "Thou shalt have no other gods before me," cannot be construed as implying the existence of other gods, because in the immediate context the God of the Bible declares himself to be the sole creator of heaven and earth: "For in six days the Lord made heaven and earth, the sea and all that in them is" (vs. 11). There is no allowance for another creator. When other gods are referred to they are looked upon as imaginary beings, or if allowance is made for the possibility of their existence as "spirits," they do not have attributes which belong to God, namely, power and wisdom. Statements like the following are found in the Hebrew Bible: "Behold, they are all vanity; their works are nothing: their molten images are wind and confusion" (Is. 41:29). "But where are thy gods that thou hast made thee? let them arise, if they can save thee in the time of thy trouble: for according to the number of thy cities are thy gods, O Judah" (Jer. 2:28). "They shall be turned back, they shall be greatly ashamed, that trust in graven images, that say to the molten images, Ye are our gods" (Is. 42:17).

The Jews of Bible times who regarded their Scriptures as divine revelation were humble when it came to expressing themselves as to what God is in himself. They acknowledged that as creatures of God they were finite and therefore could not fully comprehend the infinite God. They did not seek to undertake a philosophical inquiry to determine the nature of God. This was beyond the ability of limited men. A query put by the Old Testament is, "Canst thou by searching find out God? Canst thou find out the Almighty unto perfection?" This does not mean that though God was incomprehensible he was wholly un-

132

known. Indeed they claimed to know much about God, but for this they were dependent upon God's self-revelation.

When, as we have seen, God is believed to be *One*, in Deuteronomy 6:4 it must not be inferred that God exists as a monad, or as a unitary substance. There are indications that point to multiplicity or more than one person in the being of God. In the book of Genesis the name of God is in the plural form (*Elohim*) and the personal pronouns are often in the first person plural ("Let us make man in our image.") Although this is not conclusive because it may indicate the plural of majesty, yet when taken with other revelant material there is good ground for the contention that the Old Testament self-disclosure of God is pluralistic, that is, the one God exists in more than one person. There appears the Angel of the Lord who is distinguished from God and yet divine attributes are accorded him and divine worship rendered to him (Gen. 16:7,13; 21:17; 18:3, 13,14; Judges 5:11,14; 13:13,22; I Chron. 21:16,17; cf. Ps. 34:7.) Beside this data pertaining to an Angel who exercises the prerogatives of God, who is called God, and who is honored and worshiped as God, there is the further disclosure of a divine Messiah. To this person is ascribed a superhuman nature and superhuman powers.

The Psalmist speaks of one who is fairer than the children of men whom God has blessed. To him is ascribed might and majesty. Not only does this infer a divine being but also he is actually called God: "Thy throne, O God, is forever and ever: the sceptre of thy kingdom is a right sceptre. Thou lovest righteousness, and hatest wickedness: therefore God, thy God, hath anointed thee with the oil of gladness above thy fellows" (Ps. 45:6,7). This is not an isolated passage in the Psalms, for a divine being is evident in Ps. 2:7 and 110:1 "I will declare the decree: the Lord hath said unto me, Thou art my son; this day have I begotten thee," "The Lord said unto my Lord, Sit thou at my right hand, until I make thine enemies thy footstool" (Ps. 110:1) (cf. Ps. 116:11-13). And in Isaiah 9:6 the following is noteworthy: "For unto us a child is born, unto us a son is given: and the government shall be upon his

133

shoulder: and his name shall be called Wonderful, Counsellor, The mighty God, The everlasting Father, The Prince of Peace." One should also compare Micah 5:2 in which a coming ruler is predicted "whose goings forth have been from of old from everlasting," and in Jeremiah 23:6 this coming one is called "The Lord our Righteousness." (Particular attention also should be given to Zech. 13:7, Dan. 7:13, and Mal. 3:1.) But these are not the only references to a divine Messiah. He is referred to as the ruler over the peoples (Gen. 49:10; Ps. 72:11) to the ends of the earth (Deut. 33:17-19); who shall destroy the enemies of God (Num. 24:17) and finally save God's people (Zech. 9:9; Ps. 72:4,12) and usher in universal peace (Gen. 49:11, 12, Is. 7:15; 11:4,9; Micah 4:4; Zech. 3:9, 10; 9:10). It must be borne in mind that this disclosure of a divine Messiah or a person having the attributes of God is within the framework of belief in the Oneness or Unity of God. So also is there in the Old Testament a being called the Spirit of God. He is represented as the source of all intelligence, order, and life in the created universe (Gen. 1:2), and throughout the history of the Jews he appears as the inspirer of their prophets, the giver of wisdom and strength, the teacher of the pious, and as one who can be sinned against and grieved (Psa. 104: 29,30; Isa. 32:14,15; Job 33:4; Ps. 139:7; Ex. 31:2,3; Num. 27:18; Judges 3:10; I Sam. 16:13,14; Is. 42:1; Is. 11:1,2; Micah 3:8, Ps. 51:11). Thus in the faith of the jews as given in the source of their religious ideas, God is One but existing not as a monad but in separate and distinct persons without even verging on polytheism. There is no formula to explicate this data but it nevertheless entered into their belief in the One God. As already indicated this purports to be God's own disclosure of himself since man has no way of knowing what God is in himself. "Touching the Almighty, we cannot find him out: he is excellent in power, and in judgment, and in plenty of justice" (Job 37:23).

Since man is seen as a creature and therefore finite, and since God is the Creator and therefore infinite, the question arises, can God be known by man. The Old Testament recognizes the vast gulf between God and man and is fully aware of man's necessary limitation. Nevertheless, it declares unmistakably that man can know God his creator. In the garden of Eden, God communicated with Adam and Eve and they with God; there is direct address between God and man: "And the Lord God commanded the man, saying, Of every tree of the garden thou mayest freely eat: But of the tree of the knowledge of good and evil, thou shalt not eat of it: for in the day that thou eatest thereof thou shalt surely die" (Gen. 2:16,17). "And the Lord God called unto Adam, and said unto him, Where art thou? and he said, I heard thy voice in the garden, and I was afraid .... And the Lord God said unto the woman, What is this that thou hast done? And the woman said, The serpent beguiled me, and I did eat" (Gen. 3:9,10,13). To Cain God spoke directly, "And the Lord said unto Cain, Why art thou wroth? and why is thy countenance fallen?" (Gen. 4:6). These communications between God and man are not rare. In fact we find constant verbal intercourse between God and man, indicative of close personal relationship. He spoke to the patriarchs, with Moses he talked intimately, and to prophets he revealed his will (Gen. 12,15,17,22,26, 35; Ex. 3ff.; see the Psalms and the books of the prophets).

The knowledge which man has of God is only partial. There is no claim to comprehend fully the infinite God. He is past finding out. The Almighty cannot be understood to perfection. Nevertheless, the knowledge of God as determined by his self-revelation is true knowledge. The Israelites knew nothing of an unknown God, neither did they speak of God as simple being, or as a mere abstraction, a name for the moral order of the universe, or as the unknown and unknowable cause of all things. To them God was a person whom man resembles, for man was created in the image of God. That which has absorbed the attention of man from earliest times, as seen in the most ancient literature of the Near East, is the origin, purpose and end of man: how did man come into being? why death, and is there a life after death? The Old Testament deals with these basic questions and answers them in a matter of fact fashion.

God created man. There was no question or dispute on this point. No attempt is made to mythologize or to allegorize the early chapters of the book of Genesis which contains the account of beginnings. The record narrates that man was created by God. "And the Lord God formed man of the dust of the ground, and breathed into his nostrils the breath of life; and man became a living soul" (Gen. 2:7). And he was created perfect; "And God said, Let us make man in our image, after our likeness: . . . So God created man in his own image, in the image of God created he them, male and female created he them . . . and God saw everything that he had made, and behold it was very good" (Gen. 1:26,27,31). In making man after God's image man is distinguished from all other inhabitants of the world and given a place immeasurably above them. He was made a rational and moral being and thereby enabled to communicate with his maker. Old Testament religion constantly exhibits communication on the part of man with God. He was bound to obey God. So we read: "And the Lord God commanded the man, saying, Of every tree of the garden thou mayest freely eat: But of the tree of the knowledge of good and evil, thou shalt not eat: for in the day that thou eatest thereof thou shalt surely die" (Gen. 2:16,17). This leads to the consideration of what is called sin in the Jewish Bible. Sin is in simple language disobedience to God. In disobeying the command of God the first pair in the garden of Eden sinned; "She took of the fruit thereof and did eat, and gave also unto her husband with her, and he did eat" (Gen. 3:6). The result of this act of transgression was woe and death, both physical and spiritual. Man's body became subject to dissolution and he was cast out from God's presence (Gen. 3:14-24).

This Genesis account, when contrasted with the mythological tales of antiquity, presents apparent differences. The former is simple and intelligible while the tales of the nations surrounding Israel are crudely speculative. The Bible account is an integral part of a book which purports to be historical and factual. It is the first of the ten divisions into which Genesis is divided and is an integral part of the entire book. The rest of the Old Testament would be meaningless, if man had not sinned. For the burden of man is his sin against God and the consequent loss of favor. The question—How can man be right with God?—is ever present.

The return to acceptance by God is, however, provided for. How this was accomplished occupies the attention of the Israelite. The initiative was taken by God. When man disobeyed and thus forfeited the good pleasure of God, man was sought by God in the Garden of Eden, "And the Lord God called unto Adam, and said unto him, Where art thou?" (Gen. 3:9). The way of salvation was by the offering of a sacrifice for sin. Here we come to material that is prevalent in the Old Testament. The sacrifices and their meanings occupy a considerable part of the Jewish Bible. An animal was slain with religious ceremony. The innocent victim died in the stead of the sinner (Lev. 4:20,26; Num. 6:11; Lev. 16:6). However appraised, this method of reconciling men to God enters into the warp and woof of the religion of Israel. To propitiate God's wrath, the death of a vicarious substitute instead of the actual offender did not carry with it the notion that God was a tyrant who needed to be appeased. Sacrifice for sin takes into account the gravity of man's offence and provides forgiveness before a holy and just God. That which separates this procedure from the sacrifices outside of the Bible is that the sacrifice to God was commanded by God himself. It was his own provision for receiving man and not a device of man to placate God. It was demanded and necessary to satisfy the just God (Lev. 17:10; Ex. 30:12-16; Is. 53).

Substitutionary sacrifice, as the way for man's forgiveness, entered vitally into the religious thinking of the Jews who were nurtured on the Old Testament. In the matter of man's sin the coming Messiah is depicted as the sufferer and victim for the sins of men. The death of an animal was inadequate to pay the price of man's redemption and presupposed the death of the Messiah who was to suffer and die in man's place (Is. 53).

137

The insistence upon external sacrificial rites did not make the religion of Israel perfunctory and legalistic, for there is something unique in the emphasis placed upon these rites. They had deep personal religious significance and involvement for the individual as well as the nation. They were never designed to be detached from personal commitment and love to God himself. In the performance of rites the Israelite was indoctrinated in his proper relation to God as his creator and redeemer. Underlying the commandments of the Decalogue, as well as all other statutes and ceremonies, was the requirement of love; "and thou shalt love the Lord thy God with all thine heart, and with all thy soul, and with all thy might"; therefore thou shalt love the Lord thy God, and keep his charge, and his statutes, and his judgments, and his commandments, always (Deut. 6:5; 11:1; cf. Josh. 22:5; Ps. 31:23; Dan. 9:4). The Israelite was continually reminded that love and obedience were basic to his approach to God in the ritual. This is in sharp contrast to the cultic practices of the surrounding nations.

A question of paramount importance was ever before the mind of the Israelite in this requirement of spiritual religious devotion. How was the observer of the rites to acquire the requisite love? This was a pertinent question in view of his complete separation from God because of sin. The Bible view of the effects of sin is the complete estrangement from God which leaves man unable to effect a reconciliation. The answer lies in the quickening, revivifying, converting power of God by his Spirit. God recreated and man turned in response with faith in and love to God (Ps. 51; Ezek. 36:26,27; Jer. 31:18).

Old Testament religion was not an end in itself. Involved in personal commitment to God were ethical implications. The godly man, as he was called, was constantly reminded of the tremendous importance of the here and now. This world was the stage of his activity and here duties and obligations devolved upon him. His neighbors' well being and interests were to be sacred to him, and the concerns of the nation were to be his own. Interest in his own good was never to be to the exclusion of the good of those near and far. (See Ex. 20:12-17 for an epitome of man's duties to man.)

But it must not be inferred that though a tremendous concern for this life is emphasized in biblical Judaism that the interest of religion was preoccupied with this world alone. Patriarch and prophet looked beyond to a life after death. It would seem strange that amidst nations that sought desperately to give meaning to life and to provide some future for their dead, that Israel should show no concern for this ever recurring and vexing problem. And since Israel claimed a revelation from God, it would be difficult to perceive that there should not be revelation on this matter.

We find that God's abode is declared to be in heaven: "hear thou in heaven thy dwelling place" (I Kings. 8:30); "but our God is in the heavens: he hath done whatsoever he hath pleased" (Ps. 115:3). "Unto thee lift I up mine eyes, O thou that dwellest in the heavens" (Ps. 123:1). "Thus saith the Lord, The heaven is my throne, and the earth is my footstool" (Is. 66:1). This language in no way is at variance with God's omniscience and omnipresence. Since God is a personal being, he has an abode. And the hope held out to the people who are devoted to God is to be with God: "Thou wilt shew me the path of life: in thy presence is fulness of joy; at thy right hand there are pleasures for evermore" (Ps. 16:11). "As for me, I will behold thy face in righteousness: I shall be satisfied, when I awake, with thy likeness' (Ps. 17:15). Not only was the entrance into God's abode looked for at death but there was the belief in the resurrection of the body. "Thy dead men shall live, together with my dead body shall they arise. Awake and sing, ye that dwell in the dust: for thy dew is as the dew of herbs, and the earth shall cast out the dead" (Is. 26:19). "For I know that my redeemer liveth, and that he shall stand at the latter day upon the earth: and though after my skin *worms* destroy this body, yet in my flesh shall I see God" (Job 19:25, 26). In this hope of eternal life with God the Israelite lived and died.

139

God being the living God, it followed that he was the God of the living.

Thus no superficial sentimentality is pictured among the pious of the Old Testament. They had a piety that was profound and deep. It rested on God's revelation of himself.

A religion like this did not produce in its adherents despair and futility. God is holy and righteous and must in justice execute judgment and bring wrath upon man the sinner; therefore he was to be feared, yet he is also the God of unbounded mercy and loving-kindness. His mercy goes to the extent of redeeming the unworthy and bringing them to his own abode in heaven. And this tended to serenity, confidence and hope here and now.

Neither did the Israelites keep their faith to themselves. They did not confine it within the nation. Their God was not a tribal God but the God of all flesh; therefore; their religion received from God was to be proclaimed to peoples near and far. There was always before the pious of the nation that the knowledge of God should cover the whole earth (Is. 55:1, 5; 62:1, 2).

Extra-biblical Judaism

In Old Testament times the Jews were surrounded by potent cultural forces. On all sides there were peoples with religions and ways of life all their own. Some see parallels between the religious concepts of the Jews and their neighbors, but it has been pointed out that similarities in concepts and practices are only superficial, since at crucial points there are vast and significant differences.[19]

The Old Testament exhibits a struggle to maintain its distinctive faith and life, for to many Jews the ways of the nations were attractive. (See Ex. 32:4; I Kings 18:21; 19:8, Jer. 2:17-19, 23-28; 17:1-3.)

When the Old Testament was completed, about the middle of the 5th Century B.C. (Ezra 7:6,11,14; Neh. 8:1-5), there emerged a body of writings which have taken a prominent place in the development of Judaism. These writings embody traditions which are purported to be very ancient and in the course of time assumed a place of importance in the religious life of the Jews. As early as 200 B.C. these traditions existed, for a sect known as the Pharisees grew up at about that time, and they, while professing adherence to the Law and the Prophets, rigidly followed the tradition of the fathers (Antiq. 13:10,6), which were codified regulations for all aspects of life. Conformity to these laws took a prominent place, so that in time for many these became the essence of their religion. Conflicts arose between these laws or traditions and the Scriptures.

About A.D. 200 these traditions were gathered and committed to writing by Judah Harcase (the prince). This important work for Judaism is known since Bible times as the *Mishnah* which signifies the second exposition of the Law. The *Mishnah* is divided into five parts, and contains the purported oral law of Moses received by him both on Mt. Sinai and elsewhere, as well as deductions from the written law. Also embodied in this work are the decrees of the learned rulers, known as the Sanhedrin, as well as the customs for which divine sanction is claimed.

The text of the *Mishnah* was amplified by many comments and additions. These took literary form in the *Talmud* which means teaching or learning. The *Talmud* (both Palestinian and Babylonian, about A.D. 500) marks the culmination of Jewish tradition. It has maintained itself as embodying the traditions of the earliest post-biblical period, and is regarded as necessary because it is claimed by the Talmud itself that it supplements the Bible. For many modern Jews it has come to have the place of supreme authority in religion. The religion and worship of Judaism under Talmudic influence consists in learning and practicing the 613 commandments of the Talmud. In these the commonest functions of life are regulated and they give direction for the observance of the Sabbath, the festival seasons, and ceremonies in the synagogue and home. The Talmud has assumed a position of importance, despite reactions from time to time, the most notable being that of the Karaites in the 8th to 11th centuries, a body of Eastern Jews who rejected the Talmud and adhered to Scripture alone. (There are still Karaite communities in Eastern Europe and some adherents among the Jews throughout the world.)

A description of Judaism would be incomplete if there were left out of account the part that the expectation of a Messiah has had in it. The *Targums,* which are ancient paraphrases and interpretations of the biblical text, interpret Messianically such passages as Gen. 3:15; 35:21; 49:1,10; Num. 24:17; Deut. 18:15-19; Is. 2:2-4; Ps. 45; Is. 4:2; 9:6; 43:1; Jer. 23:5; Hos. 3:5; Mic. 5:2; Zech. 3:8.

Jewish believers in Jesus Christ as the Messiah of the Jews appealed to the Jewish Scriptures to justify their belief. In this faith they looked upon themselves as continuing in the Old Testament Judaism. (See in New Testament, Matt. 1:22,23; John 1:41; Acts 2:25-36; 26:6; I Cor. 15:4; Heb. 1:5-13.) And they regarded the New Testament itself as a fulfillment of the Jewish Scriptures (Mt. 5:18, 24:34; Lk. 21:32; Mt. 2:17; 21:4; 25:56; Jo. 13:18; 17:12; Acts 1:16; Lk. 4:21).

The great body of Jewish people have rejected the Messiahship of Jesus of Nazareth. They have found it difficult to reconcile Christ as a man and sufferer with the Old Testament predictions of a Messiah possessing the attributes of deity. However, those Jews who did reconcile these seemingly contradictory views of the Messiah pointed to the prediction of these two elements within the Old Testament itself. (Compare Gen. 3:15; 22:18; Ps. 22:6; Is. 9:16; 7:14; 53:9; Dan. 9:9; Zech. 9:9; 13:7 with Ps. 2:6-8; 45:6,7; Jer. 23:6; Dan. 7:13,14.)

In the modern world there are essentially two types of Judaism—Orthodox and Reformed. Orthodox Judaism is the same as it has been for about two millenniums. The Old Testament Scriptures are held to be divine revelation, but tradition as embodied in the *Mishnah* and *Talmud* also possesses divine authority for faith and practice. Salvation is attained by repentance and by observance of the laws both biblical and talmudical. Much importance is attached to diet and dress, the festive seasons, and the tokens of the covenant, which are circumcision, the Sabbath, and the Passover.

Reform Juadism marks a departure from the old pattern. The *Torah* or the Bible is tested by human judgment. The enlightened modern mind determines what is factual and what is meaningful. Miracles are excluded and are to be interpreted allegorically or teleologically. There is some claim that the Jewish Scriptures are inspired but only to the extent that they present truth and goodness. And in the doing of good, man works out his own salvation. Reformed Judaism still clings to ancestral pieties, sentiments, and group loyalties. Tradition is respected because it contains the findings of men in quest for the true and good. Nationalism and idealism are the unifying principles.

What is known as Conservative Judaism is not so well defined. It seeks to maintain a mediating position between the Orthodox and the Reformed.

3. *Christianity*

Christianity is the religion of the New Testament. There is contained its origin, its tenets and its history. The New Testament is the primary written source material available for an understanding of Christianity. The language of the New Testament is plain and perspicuous. Both learned and unlearned have understood it since its appearance over 1900 years ago. Any religion which may properly be called Christianity can be tested and should be tested by the New Testament.

Does the New Testament propound a different set of religious ideas from that of biblical Judaism?

The authors of the New Testament were all Jews, with the possible exception of Luke, the author of the Gospel which bears his name and of the Book of Acts. The New Testament writers considered themselves as holding the faith of their believing ancestors and countrymen. Never at any time is there any indication that they diverged from the religion of the Old Testament. The Scriptures they possessed were the books of the Old Testament, and to these the early Christian believers appealed for their faith (Acts 1:16; 2:16; 3:18; 18:24; 28:23; Pet. 1:21). Christ himself certified his person and his work by appeals to the Old

Testament Scriptures. He said, "Think not that I am come to destroy the law, or the prophets: I am not come to destroy, but to fulfill. For verily I say unto you, till heaven and earth pass, one jot or one tittle shall in no wise pass from the law, till all be fulfilled" (Matt. 5:17, 18). The faith of the New Testament writers was new in so far as it was the fulfillment of the Old Testament (Acts 1:16; Rom. 15:4; I Cor. 15:3, 4). And their life was unique insofar as it was regulated by both Testaments (Acts 20:32; II Tim. 3:15; Jas. 1:21). Since the Old Testament was believed to be the revelation of God, the New Testament, its fulfillment, was placed on the same high plane of authority (I Cor. 15:1, 2; Gal. 1:8). Both the Old and the New Testaments were the authoritative revelation of God.

There is not to be found any divergence in views concerning God, man and salvation in both Testaments. When Jesus Christ said, "Ye have heard that it was said by them of old time, Thou shalt not kill . . . But I say unto you . . . Thou shalt not commit adultery: But I say unto you . . ." (Matt. 5:21, 22, 28, 29) he did not mean to negate the requirements of the Jewish Bible, but rather as the context shows, he sought to clarify the true meaning of the Old Testament as over against distortions. And it must be remembered that as the Messiah and the Son of God, which Jesus claimed to be, he thought of himself as having the right to inaugurate any new legislation or change in emphasis. But even here there is no sharp clash of viewpoint. Jesus' teaching moves in the orbit of Old Testament religion. Jesus lived and taught as a true "son of Abraham" (Matt. 1:1). What is said of the Jewishness of Christ's teaching can be said of all the other writers of the New Testament (Acts 2:14-36; 7:1-53; 22:1-3; 23:1; 25:8; 26:1-7; Heb. 1:1,2; I Pet. 1:10; Jn. 1:41, 49).

The person of Christ and his work is central in the religion of the New Testament. Any quest for a Jesus who is other than the one who moves upon the pages of this document is illusory. The attempt to find another has been made, but the results are confusing and have proven impossible to square with the evidence.

The Jesus of whom we read, in the only source available to us, claimed to be the Messiah of the Jews, and appealed for verification of his claim to the Jewish Scriptures (Matt. 11:1-6; 16:13-20; 17:1-9; 21:1-11; 26:57-68; 22:41-46; Jn. 7:21; 9:3,4; 11:32; 17:4). Jesus claimed to be God in the Old Testament sense. On the lips of a Jew, the name of "God" referred to no demigod, nor to some personalized quality of nature, nor to some abstract notion, but to the personal, almighty creator and upholder of the universe." It is this understanding of God which Jesus claimed for himself, without any hesitation or qualification (Jn. 14:1-11; 5:17, 18, 23; 10:30, 38; 12:45; 16:15). And his followers so understood him (Phil. 2:6-11; I Thess. 3:11; Gal. 1:15,16). For making this claim he was accused of blasphemy and finally put to death (Matt. 9:3; 26:63-65; Lk. 5:21; Jn. 10:33). We shall not ask here whether this was a false claim, as many of his contemporaries thought. However, if it were a false claim, then Jesus' enemies were correct, and Jesus was a blasphemer, a deceiver, and therefore unworthy of emulation and religious trust. Many believed his claim to be God and to have the right to exercise the prerogatives of God. On this basis they could give him honor and devotion (Jn. 20:28). They fully believed him to be God in the way in which their Scriptures spoke of God, as the one, true and living God. The early followers of Jesus were strict monotheists. They saw no contradiction between this faith in Jesus and their belief in the unity of God. They sought to substantiate their understanding of his full deity from the Jewish Scriptures themselves. Never did they think of themselves as departing from the faith of their fathers. They considered themselves to be true Jews and the true Israel, and thought of their countrymen who rejected Christ as having departed from their own heritage of faith (Acts 2:22-36; 24:14).

How could strict monotheists believe the man who was called the Christ, to be the God of Abraham, Isaac and Jacob? We are confronted with the fact that they did so intelligently, soberly and with full conviction. Some did not grasp the full import of his claims immediately but came to their faith in the course of time, as they heard his words, observed his miracles, and according to their witness, saw him alive after he was crucified, dead, and buried (Matt. 16:15,16; I Cor. 15:3-7).

This is not to say that there was no mystery in their belief. But they saw no contradiction in believing in the unity of God and the plurality of persons within the Godhead. Their eyes beheld a supernatural person; therefore they were compelled to see more than one person in the Deity. For their knowledge of what God is in his essential nature, they depended upon the disclosures of God himself. And as we have noted, they found a divine Messiah in their own Scriptures (Jn. 1:45,49).

Properly understood, what is called Christianity, is the Jewish faith come to fulfillment. The New Testament completes the Old. We might again wonder why the Jewish people as a people did not accept Jesus as the Messiah. Why has the Jewish nation not accepted Christ? Many members of the Jewish nation did accept Christ. The early or primitive church consisted of Jews who were the founders of Christianity. The reasons for the rejection of Christ by the majority are found within the New Testament itself. One reason was their lack of humility before their own Scriptures (Lk. 16:31), and another was that Christ failed to meet their expectations of a Messiah. They expected a kingly Messiah who would subdue their enemies and establish them as a powerful kingdom, for was not the Messiah to reign and rule? Even Christ's disciples shared in this belief. They asked the question, "Lord wilt thou at this time restore again the kingdom to Israel?" (Acts 1:6). Jesus did not deny that he was a king and came to rule (Mt. 16:28) but he said, "My kingdom is not of this world" (Jn. 18:36). He came first to give his life a ransom for sinners (Mt. 20:28). First he must redeem his people and then he would rule over them. This representation does justice to the twofold representation of a suffering and reigning Messiah in the Old Testament (Is. 53; Ps. 45:1-7).

What has been said is comprised in what is known as the gospel of Christ. What is declared concerning Jesus is a way of salvation for men. By believing in his death as a sacrifice for the sinner, and by trusting in Christ, as the savior, there is granted to the sinner forgiveness and everlasting life. The sinner does not earn his salvation, as in Islam, but he receives it by God's grace through his faith. And every one who so believes has the assured hope that when he dies he will go to be with Jesus who was raised from the dead and is now in heaven. The hope of the Christian faith is the resurrection of the body and the establishment of the final or eschatological kingdom when Christ returns with authority and power (Jn. 3:15-18; Rom. 4:1-3; 5:1,8; Cor. 15:24,25,51,54; I Thess. 4:16,17).

This is Christianity and the religion of those who are called Christians. In the beginning they were called by various names such as believers, followers, disciples, Christians, saints. When they organized for worship, to carry out the commands of their Master, whom they believed was with them by his Spirit (Matt. 28:20), they were designated the church. The institution of the church is rooted in the organization and practice of the Jewish synagogue. The people elected elders from the congregation to rule over them and chose those who should direct the worship. They were concerned that everything be done "decently and in order" (I Cor. 14:40). Their worship, like that of the synagogue, was quite simple. There was the reading of the Bible, preaching which explained the Bible and applied it to the congregation, and the singing of the Psalms of David. There was no sharp break from the customs of the Synagogue. What was new was the interpretation of the Bible in the light of Christ's Messiahship, and his work as their Savior and Lord. At times they also observed sacraments. One is known as the Lord's Supper or Communion, a commemoration of Christ's death upon the cross. By eating broken bread and drinking wine, they entered into the meaning of his broken body and shed blood, which was shed for their sins, and appropriated to themselves by faith (Lk. 22:17-20; I Cor. 23-27).

The Bible is not a system of theology. The truths which the Christian theologian has to collect, arrange and

147

exhibit in their internal relation to each other are, however, contained in the Bible. What nature is to the natural scientist, the Bible is to the Christian theologian. It is a storehouse of facts. By applying the inductive method to theology, facts are carefully collected with the greatest comprehensiveness possible. The Christian theologian does not wish to impress his theological principles upon the facts, which must be derived from the data of the Scriptures. Biblical theology is, therefore, concerned with nothing other than the facts and the principles of the Bible.

To hold that the task of biblical theology is to exhibit the facts of Scriptures does not necessarily rule out the possibility of natural theology, although what nature teaches concerning God and our duties is revealed more fully and more authoritatively in God's word. The Bible is for all Christians the primary source of knowledge of things divine. The Scriptures of the Old and New Testaments are believed to be the word of God due to the fact that they were given by the supernatural inspiration of the Holy Spirit. The Spirit so exerted an influence upon the minds of certain select men that they became the organs of God; what God said they said. This does not mean that the sacred writers were machines. Their being inspired as the organs of God in no way interfered with the free exercise of the distinctive mental characteristics of the individual writer. The writers of Scripture impressed their peculiarities upon their productions as though they were under no special influence. God spoke in the language of men and he used men as his instruments, each according to his own special gifts according to his own nature. Christians believe that the inspired writer wrote out of the fullness of his own feelings and thought and used the language and expressions which he found most natural and appropriate, and yet, what he wrote was what the Holy Spirit would have him write.

In short, Christian theologians are concerned with the doctrine of God, with our knowledge of his nature and attributes, with the Trinity, the Divinity of Christ, with the nature of the Holy Spirit, the doctrines of Creation and

148

Providence, and with miracles. They are concerned further with anthropology and soteriology, with the origin and nature of man, with the origin of the soul, the unity of the human race, with man's original state, the fall into sin, and with the divine plan of salvation, through the person and work of Christ. The Christian theologian is concerned with regeneration, faith, justification, sanctification, with the moral law, with the means of grace, and finally with eschatology, the last things, the state of the soul after death, the resurrection and the second coming.

The redemption of fallen man can take place solely because God himself has graciously accomplished it through the person and work of Christ Jesus. To the Christian the incarnation of the eternal Son of God was not a necessary event arising out of the nature of God, but an act of voluntary humiliation.

Jesus was truly man, with a real material body, in everything essential like the bodies of ordinary men. He also thought and reasoned like other men. And yet he was truly God, he was perfect man and perfect God and still one person; two natures united in hypostatic union but not mingled or confounded.

To the Christian the name of Christ is the only name by which man can be saved. The design of the incarnation of the Son of God was to reconcile man unto God, and Christ is the only mediator between God and man.

The Christian believes that Christ is truly a priest in that he alone has liberty of access unto God. Sin could not have been taken away by any sacrifice other than his. For it is only through him that God is propitious to sinful men. Christ once offered up himself as a sacrifice to satisfy divine justice, thereby reconciling man to God. Christ suffered vicariously; he suffered in the place of sinners as their substitute. The guilt of the sinner is expiated and the justice of God is propitiated. For Christ's work was of the nature of a satisfaction; it met all the demands of God's law against the sinner, so that the sinner who believes in Christ is no longer condemned by the law and, is delivered from the power of sin and of Satan, and from

149

all evil. The sinner is thus restored to the image and fellowship of God. His guilt is removed and his soul is quickened with a new principle of divine life.

The success of the whole scheme of divine redemption rests upon the fact that Christ rose from the dead with the same, although a changed, body. The ascended body of Christ as it now exists in heaven is glorious, incorruptible, immortal, and spiritual, and yet it retains the essential properties of a body.

Man's salvation is accomplished by the grace of God, which works a subjective change in the soul, thereby causing a spiritual resurrection, a new birth or regeneration. Regeneration is an act of God, an act of his power, in which God is the agent, a quickening of the soul, a communication of a new principle of life. The first conscious exercise of the renewed soul is faith, the persuasion of the truth of the facts and doctrines recorded in the Scriptures on the testimony of the Spirit of God.

Christ is the special object of saving faith, since by receiving the testimony of God concerning him, the salvation of the sinner is secured. For faith is the condition on which God promises to impute unto men the righteousness of Christ, so that when they believe, they are no longer condemned, but are justified by a forensic act, in which God declares that justice has been satisfied so far as the believing sinner is concerned. Most Christians believe that the act of justification is followed by a process of sanctification. A supernatural work of grace, whereby the principles of evil infecting our nature are increasingly removed and the principle of spiritual life grows until our acts, thoughts, and feelings are brought under control, and the soul is brought into conformity with the image of Christ. The soul is thus led to receive Jesus as its saviour, and is delivered from the guilt and power of sin. The soul of the believer is united to Christ; it participates in his merits, and is the abode of the indwelling Holy Spirit, the source of a new spiritual life.

4. *Roman Catholicism and Reformation Protestantism*

A discussion of Christianity would be incomplete without reference to the division within Christianity between Roman Catholicism and Reformation Protestantism. Much present day Neo-Protestantism rejects the authority of the Roman Catholic Church, and the authority of the Bible upon which the Reformation was based.

Both Reformation Protestantism and Roman Catholicism recognize the need of authority in religion. Both regard God as the final authority; they differ as to where and how God's authority is expressed. The appeal to authority is based for both upon rational consideration. For revelation and authority are correlates.[20] The truth about God in Christianity is known because God has revealed himself. To the Christian the Bible is authoritative because it is the Word of God. To the Protestant, the Bible is the only authority in matters of faith and practice. The Reformation regarded ecclesiastical authority as dependent upon the Bible.[21] The Roman Catholic regards ecclesiastical authority as the extension of the mystical body of Christ. Christ is at the head of the church and he rules the church through his visible vicar the Pope.

The Protestant accepts the notion that the church is the mystical body of Christ, but not in the sense of an identity between Christ and the church. The church is not identical with Christ, but it is in *communion* with Christ. Such communion, for the Protestant, is never apart from faith, and it is never apart from the correlation between faith and the Word of God.

Roman Catholics and Protestants agree in rejecting human reason as the sole standard of religious truth. They both admit an objective, supernatural revelation. They differ, however, in that the former contend that the rule of faith consists of tradition as well as Scripture. Roman Catholics believe that the Church is an infallible teacher. Protestants believe that under the guidance of the Holy Spirit, the Scriptures are sufficiently clear for salvation,

151

and can be understood without an infallible interpreter. Protestants generally do not recognize an authoritative oral tradition besides the Scriptures.

> In his treatment of the visible church, John Calvin remarked: . . . . we may learn even from the title mother, how useful and even necessary it is for us to know her; since there is no other way of entrance into life, unless we are conceived by her, born of her, nourished at her breast, and continually preserved under her care and government, till we are divested of this mortal flesh, and become like the angels.[22]
> When by virtue of regeneration God is the Father of the believer, the church may be called his mother.[23]

Not every gathering that called itself a church was to be so regarded.

> . . . the word Church is used in Sacred Scriptures in two senses. Sometimes, when they mention the church, they intend that which is really such in the sight of God, into which none are received but those who by adoption and grace are the children of God, and by the sanctification of the Spirit are the true members of Christ. And then it comprehends not only the saints at any one time resident on earth, but all the elect who have lived from the beginning of the world. But the word Church is frequently used in the Scriptures to designate the whole multitude, dispersed all over the world, who profess to worship one God and Jesus Christ, who are initiated into his faith by baptism, who testify their unity in true doctrine and charity by a participation of the sacred supper, who consent to the word of the Lord, and preserve the ministry which Christ has instituted for the purpose of preaching it. In this Church are many hypocrites, who have nothing of Christ but the name and appearance; many persons ambitious, avaricious, envious, slanderous, and dissolute in their lives, who are tolerated for a time, either because they cannot be convicted by a legitimate process, or because discipline is not always maintained with sufficient vigour. As it is necessary, therefore, to believe that Church, which is invisible to us, and known to God alone, so this Church, which is visible to men, we are commanded to honour, and to maintain communion with it.[24]

The marks of a true church are the pure preaching of the word of God, and the sacraments administered according to the institution of Christ.

A local church may have many faults and even errors, and yet a believer may still belong to it.

> For all the articles of true doctrine are not of the same description. Some are so necessary to be known, that they ought to be universally received as fixed and indubitable principles . . . such as, that there is one God, that Christ is God and the Son of God; that our salvation depends on the mercy of God; and the like. There are others which are controverted among the Churches, yet without destroying the unity of faith.[25]

Subsequent Reformation Protestantism concurred in Calvin's view of the church. The church, as a divine institution, owes its origin to Christ, not to man. It was framed by divine appointment. The church is a spiritual instrument designed for the spiritual good of man.

The one church of Christ exists in two aspects, the one invisible, comprised of all the elect, the other visible, consisting of all who profess the faith of Christ. The invisible church, the whole number of true believers, is to be regarded as catholic, i.e., as not confined to any people or place. The visible church, insofar as it is made up of those who profess the true religion, is also to be regarded as catholic.

The marks of a true church are to be tested by the Protestant principle that the Bible is the sole standard in matters of faith. The church has been established for the publication of the gospel, for the salvation of sinners. A corrupt faith corrupts the church, and if a society apostatizes entirely, it ceases to be a church.[26] Sacraments, ordinances, the ministry and the outward administration of the church are essential to its well-being, but not to its being.

> The only true and infallible note or mark of a Church of Christ is the profession of the faith of Christ. Whatever be the differences in other respects,— whatever be the distinction in outward form or administration, in ordinances, in government, in worship,—

153

these things are subordinate to the one criterion of the profession of the true faith, which marks by its presence a true church, and declares by its absence an apostate one. It is not the succession of outward forms and ordinances, the hereditary derivation from primitive times of a ministry and sacraments, that constitute a Church of Christ, or lay the foundation for its character and privileges . . . .

It is the succession of the truth alone that marks out a Christian Church . . . . the heritage of that faith which apostles first taught and published.[27]

As the Westminster Confession puts it "The visible church consists of all those throughout the world that profess the true religion, together with their children."

For Protestants a person becomes a member of the church by professing the gospel with his lips and with his life and conduct. It is not sufficient simply to submit to the authority of the church visible, and then to expect that "the grace communicated by its outward ordinances, are enough of themselves, independently of a voluntary profession of faith and corresponding conduct, to constitute a man a member of the Christian Society."[28]

The well-being of the church requires the exclusion from membership of those who neither profess the faith, nor live a corresponding life.

It is of interest to raise the question:

What is the situation within "Protestant churches" (especially in the U.S.A.) when the latter are compared to the historic 16th Century Reformation view of the church?

From the standpoint of historic Reformation Protestantism the mere presence of several hundred Protestant denominations, and hundreds of independent congregations (although not ideal) does not in itself violate the unity of faith, the unity of the body of Christ. Wherever the basic doctrines of the Christian faith are preached, the church is visible. What divides "Protestantism" today is not simply the number of denominations, but it is the fact that the most basic doctrines of the Christian faith, as embodied in the Apostles' Creed, are openly denied by officials within denominations often claiming the largest membership.

154

Many members of "Protestant Churches," especially among the clergy, are indifferent to or deny the doctrinal basis of Christianity. Some deny all real knowledge of God, others deny his existence as a Supreme Person, maker and active ruler of the world. Still others regard God as the Father of all, but deny the deity of his Son.

Where the doctrine of God has disappeared, the concept of man as a sinner is also lacking. Man is either regarded as a creature capable of attaining perfection, apart from grace, or, at best, sin is simply the human condition or finitude.

For many the Bible is either rejected as the infallible word of God and is regarded as a source book of religious insights, or it may *become* the word of God for those who experience it as such.[29] It is in any case no longer the only infallible rule of faith and practice.

For many Jesus is either the example of faith, rather than the object of faith, or he is the first existentialist. In any case he is not the Christ of Chalcedon. The miracles recorded in the New Testament, including his virgin birth, and his bodily resurrection, are to be extricated from the text—in short they are myths to be removed from the content of faith.[30] Jesus is no longer regarded as the Son of God who redeems us by virtue of what he did, by bearing the guilt of our sins upon the cross. The vicarious, substitutionary atonement is denied. The cross is an example of self-sacrifice, or existential courage, not a propitiatory death for sin. The need for redemption, the reality of hell as everlasting punishment is denied.

For many religion has become a function of the community, or of the state, a moral agency.[31] "Churches" of today have in effect admitted great companies of non-Christian persons, not only into their membership, but into her teaching agencies, and into their ministry.

We know of no Protestant seminary or divinity school at a major university where the majority of its faculty are committed to the defense of historic Reformation Protestantism.[32]

155

There are a few Protestant denominations that exercise doctrinal discipline. The largest denominations, however, welcome to their memberships practically anyone who is willing to join, except those who would disturb the status quo by insisting that the historic standards of Protestantism be maintained.

Within nearly every large denomination there are many individual congregations whose minister and many of its members adhere to the standard confession of their church, but many congregations no longer exhibit the mark of a church. How long such a situation can continue is a matter of speculation. Many orthodox congregations and denominations regard certain denominations as being in such a state of apostasy or corruption that they will not affiliate with the National and World Council of Churches.

The situation within Protestantism is a source of concern to those Protestants who regard the Church to be marked by the preaching of the word, and a profession of the gospel of Christ. To quote one of their leading spokesman

> . . . . how great is the common heritage which unites the Roman Catholic Church, with its maintenance of the authority of Holy Scripture and with its acceptance of the great creeds, to devout Protestants today! We would not indeed obscure the difference which divides us from Rome. The gulf is indeed profound. But profound as it is, it seems trifling compared to the abyss which stands between us and many ministers of our own Church (Presbyterian). The Church of Rome may represent a perversion of the Christian religion, but naturalistic liberalism is not Christianity at all.[33]

[1] J. N. D. Anderson, *The World's Religions* (London, 1951).

[2] Louis Gardet, *Mohammedanism* (New York: Hawthorne Books, 1961), p. 29.

[3] *Ibid.*, p. 32.

[4] Anderson, *op. cit.*, p. 79.

[5] *Ibid.*, p. 81.

[6] *Koran*, trans. by N. J. Dawood, Penguin Classics, 1956, p. 371.

[7] *Ibid.*, p. 370.

[8] *Ibid.*, p. 82.

[9] See Anderson, *op. cit.*, pp. 83ff.

[10] *Ibid.*, p. 85.

[11] *Koran*, p. 363.

[12] *Ibid.*, p. 344.

[13] *Ibid.*, p. 314.

[14] *Ibid.*, p. 270.

[15] *Ibid.*, p. 103.

[16] Anderson, *op. cit.*, p. 86.

[17] *Ibid.*, p. 88.

[18] For a discussion of the relationship between science and religion, see Chapter 6.

[19] See A. Heidel, *The Gilgamesh Epic and Old Testament Parallels*, 1949, 2nd Edition, Chicago, pp. 137-269.

[20] See Bernard Ramm, *The Pattern of Authority*, Wm. B. Eerdmann's Publishing Co., Grand Rapids, Mich. 1957, and *Revelation and the Bible*, edit. by Carl F. H. Henry, especially R. A. Finlayson *"Contemporary Ideas of Inspiration."*

[21] Our discussion in this section borrows freely from the work of Gerrit C. Berkouwer, *The Conflict with Rome*, The Presbyterian and Reformed Publishing Co., Phila. 1958. See also, Karl Adam, *The Spirit of Catholicism.*

[22] John Calvin, *Institutes of the Christian Religion*, BK. IV, Chapter 1, (Phila.: Presbyterian Board of Christian Education) trans. by John Allen, Vol. II, p. 273.

[23] Herman Bavinck, *Our Reasonable Faith* (Grand Rapids, Mich.: Wm. B. Eerdmanns) 1956, p. 514.

[24] Calvin, *op. cit.*, p. 280.

[25] For what here follows see James Bannerman, *The Church of Christ* (London: The Banner of Truth Trust, 1960) Vol. I, especially part I.

[26] *Ibid.*, p. 59.

[27] *Ibid.*, p. 60.

[28] *Ibid.*, p. 72.

[29] For a detailed analysis of such a position see Gordon Clark *Karl Barth's Theological Method*, (1962), and Polman, *Barth*, Presbyterian and Reformed Publishing Co.

[30] See H. N. Ridderbos, *Bultmann*, Presbyterian and Reformed Pub. Co., 1960.

[31] See R. Rushdoony, *The Messianic Character of American Education*, (Nutley, N. J.: The Craig Press, 1963).

[32] There are, of course, many evangelical (orthodox) and denominational schools. For example, Fuller Seminary in Pasadena, Concordia (Missouri Synod Lutheran) in St. Louis, Westminster Seminary in Philadelphia, Gordon Seminary in Massachusetts.

[33] J. Gresham Machen, *Christianity and Liberalism*, (Grand Rapids, Mich.: Wm. B. Eerdmans Publishing Co., 1946) p. 52. What

Machen said of the Liberalism of his day applies to the extreme from of modern neo-Protestantism as exemplified by J. A. T. Robinson, Bultmann and Tillich. For appraisals of Karl Barth, the reader is referred to the works of G. Berkouwer, Polman, C. Van Til and Gordon Clark.

CHAPTER VI

SCIENCE AND BIBLICAL RELIGION

There is a widespread belief that the objectivist view of religion, at least insofar as it is based upon the acceptance of the Bible as divine revelation, has been rendered obsolete by the results of the sciences. Julian Huxley, for example, states that ". . . Darwin's work necessitated the immediate abandonment of the theory of creation in favor of evolution . . . ."[1] Elsewhere he writes, "God can no longer be considered as the controller of the universe in any but a Pickwickian sense. The God hypothesis is no longer of any pragmatic value for the interpretation or comprehension of nature, and indeed often stands in the way of better and truer interpretation. Operationally, God is beginning to resemble not a ruler, but the last fading smile of a cosmic Cheshire cat."[2] And again "I submit that the discoveries of physiology, general biology and psychology not only make possible but necessitate, a naturalistic hypothesis, in which there is no room for the supernatural. . . ."[3]

1. *The Problem of Conflict*

The objectivist thesis, and in particular the notion of a revealed creator God, would be refuted, if some indubitably true propositions contradict such a proposition as "God created the heavens and the earth." To be more specific, anyone who accepts the Old and New Testaments as the word of God is faced with the challenge that the Bible is in conflict with statements that are known by other means.

Let us call the statements of the Bible "B," and let us call the statements of the various sciences "S." The question is whether B contains any propositions R, and whether S contains any propositions Z, such that if R is true, Z is necessarily false, and if Z is true R is necessarily false. The statements made by Mr. Huxley do contradict the statements of the Bible. Let us call such statements as Mr. Huxley makes, H statements. Our first problem is threefold. First, what is the nature of the statements of the Bible? Second, what is the nature of the statements of science? And third, what is the nature of the statements made by Mr. Huxley?

Our second problem is also threefold. First, does the acceptance of a B statement and/or an H statement strictly entail the rejection of an S statement, and if so, why, and if not, why not? Second, does the acceptance of an S statement strictly entail the rejection of a B statement and/or an H statement, and if so, why, and if not, why not? Third, does the acceptance of an H statement strictly entail the rejection of a B and/or an S statement, and if so, why, and if not, why not?

There is no universal agreement as to how the preceding questions are to be answered. The way in which concrete conflicts are dealt with, however, by both Christians and non-Christians does depend to a large extent on an explicit or implicit answer.

To speak intelligibly about any subject it must be admitted that contradictory statements cannot both be true. To state that God alone created the heavens and the earth is to deny that some of the heavens and the earth were not created by God. The truth of a universal affirmative proposition entails the falsity of a particular, negative proposition. A statement of the form, all S is P, is contradicted by the statement some S is not P, where S stands for the concept intended by the subject of the proposition, and P stands for the concept intended by the predicate of the proposition. Contradictory statements cannot both be true and they cannot both be false. A universal affirmative proposition is contradicted by a particular negative proposition and a universal negative proposition of the form no S is P, is contradicted by a particular affirmative proposition, some S is P. Two propositions can contradict

160

each other if, and only if, the terms of their respective subjects and their respective predicates stand for the same concepts. The proposition, all sheep are woolly, is not contradicted by the proposition, some billy goats do not have horns. The two statements are simply incomparable, at least with respect to whether or not they are contradictory. What is true in general about propositions is of importance to the problem at hand. For unless the statements of the Bible, the statements of the sciences, and the statements of Mr. Huxley employ identical concepts, they too are simply incomparable.

2. *The Nature of a Scientific Statement*

Our first question is: what is the nature of a scientific statement? The answer might be given that a scientific statement is any statement that a scientist makes. Such a definition is certainly too broad. When seated at dinner, scientists have been heard to utter such words as "Please pass the mashed potatoes." Let us try again: "A scientific statement is a statement of science." This is a little better, but it is circular, for to know what a scientific statement is, necessitates a prior awareness of what science is. A statement is not scientific simply because a scientist makes it. A scientific statement is a statement of a science, but what is a science?

Rather than stipulate an *a priori* definition of science, note first of all that there are many things that we know that we do not call science. It may be that science is knowledge, but this does not mean that all knowledge is science. Most people know how to find their way home, but such knowledge is hardly what is meant by the statement that science is knowledge. Someone may know how to do something, how to find something, or how to make something, and still not be a scientist. Science is a form of knowledge, but it is knowledge about or of something, of some aspect of our world, of what we experience. It is more than just this, it is what we know about something as a result of using a particular method.

161

It is customary in English to use the word science in a narrow and a broad sense. When used narrowly it stands for the disciplines that examine what is called the physical world. When used broadly it refers to such areas as the science of history, economics, jurisprudence and sociology.

Our concept of science includes within its extension the sum total of what we call the sciences. What is it, however, that makes something one of the sciences? The different kinds of sciences originate because our world of experience has many aspects. The different aspects of our world constitute an integral whole, an indissoluble unity. Within the concrete world, the world in which we actually live, the world of individual things and concrete structures, the biological properties of a tree, for example, are inseparable from its physical, chemical, and aesthetic properties.

The various sciences are the result of abstraction. The different sciences abstract different aspects from the concreate world of actual experience. Consider, for example, some objects in your immediate surroundings, such as the furniture in a room.

The ordinary way of experiencing furniture is free of abstraction. If we wish to abstract, we can begin to utilize our ability to form concepts, and we can regard the pieces of furniture from their numerical aspect. We can count them; we can speak of their number, of their quantity. The concrete pieces of furniture are not thereby exhaustively described. We can proceed further to abstract their physical and chemical properties and we can speak of them in biological terms, as non-living. Furniture may also be of interest to the social psychologist and to the sociologist, since its arrangement may have social and psychological consequences. It may also be of interest to the historian, since it may have belonged to a famous person, or be representative of a period; it may also be of interest to the jurist, since the question of its legal ownership may be the cause of litigation. The economist may be concerned with its monetary value, the aesthetician with its style, and the Christian theologian may regard it as a part of God's world.

There are many different perspectives that may be abstracted from the concrete world of things and events. The various sciences are the results of different ways of looking at such things and events. Their number depends upon the nature of things. Knowledge is always of something.

The sciences do more than abstract from the totality of things and events. The various concepts which are formed as the result of their abstractions are then formulated in propositions, which are then arranged in an orderly systematic way, from which further inferences are then drawn. Such propositions are either true or false, although the evidence that a particular proposition is true may not always be conclusive, so that a degree of probability may be all that is attainable.

With the possible exception of mathematics and logic, the sciences originate in some form of sensory experience, and a proposition is not a proposition of a science unless it is based upon sense experience. Of course, while such knowledge begins with sense experience, it then proceeds to make inferences which go beyond what is immediately given by the senses.

Each of the sciences presuppose the truth of certain propositions which do not fall within the scope of their own field of abstraction. For example, they assume that there is a world of things and events that is knowable, and that they are in a position to know it.

The question as to the ultimate origin of the world of experience is not a scientific question. The sciences are never in a position to observe the origin of the world. Of course it is possible to infer from what is immediately given to the senses, what may have preceded the present state of affairs, but such inferences necessarily have a speculative character and can never ascertain with certainty the origin of what now is. It is logically possible that the world never had an origin, that the world is all that there is, and that the world always was. Whether or not such is the case is not ascertainable by any series of observations. What is observable is what already is. It is not possible to observe what is not.

The nature of a particular science is determined by the object it investigates and by the method that it employs. It begs the question to assume that because a question is not susceptible to the methods of observation that it is therefore a meaningless question. It is justifiable to conclude, however, that if a question is in principle unanswerable by means of any possible observations, such a question is not a question of the sciences; it is not a scientific question.

There may be other questions: metaphysical and/or religious questions. The question as to what is the ultimate nature of our world is not a scientific question. And while it is possible for any given scientist to examine the aspects of our world without directly asking about its ultimate nature, nevertheless, as a human being, the scientist has in fact made certain choices that are non-scientific. As a man the scientist shares certain religious beliefs concerning the nature of the world. There are religious questions that everyone does in fact answer with various degrees of psychological certainty. As a human being every person has a belief about himself and whatever he considers to be the ultimate origin of his world, including himself.[4] If the natural world is all that there is, the world is God.

It is possible to observe certain aspects of the world; it is not possible to know from such observations that there is nothing that differs from what we do in fact see. A person may *believe* that the world is God. Such a belief may be of ultimate concern; it may direct the whole course of his life, but it is not a "scientific" belief. There are no observations that will tend to confirm or disconfirm it.

What one sees will remain the same if one believes that the world is not ultimate, that it is not God, but that God is above nature.

164

3. *Certain Statements of Julian Huxley*

The statements quoted from Julian Huxley at the beginning of the chapter are statements made by a scientist, but are they statements of a science? Are they scientific statements?

Let us consider them. To state that "Darwin's work necessitated the immediate abandonment of the theory of creation in favor of evolution," is a statement *about* Darwin's theory and what Huxley calls the theory of creation. Such a statement expresses a judgment that Huxley has made that evolution and creation are contradictory. For Huxley to be correct in his judgment, the theory of evolution and the theory of creation would both have to be the same type of theory.

Julian Huxley tells us what he believes: that God can no longer be considered as the controller of the universe, that the God hypothesis is of no pragmatic value for the interpretation of nature. Huxley's statement is simply a statement of his own personal belief. When he says that God can no longer be considered as the controller of the universe, then he obviously does not mean that everyone has abandoned the belief that God is the controller of the universe. He does mean that he himself has abandoned the belief, and he is apparently urging everyone else to follow his example. Perhaps Huxley has discovered that he can be a biologist without believing in God. Most Christians would never doubt that you can name frogs and lizards even if you do not believe that God created them. The point is not whether God is useful to Mr. Huxley; the question is whether Mr. Huxley is useful to God. And this depends upon whether or not God exists. Huxley has lost his "faith"—rather he has found a new faith—and he defines his new faith in nature as science. It is this that leads him to think that "the discoveries of physiology, general biology, and psychology not only make possible but necessitate a naturalistic hypothesis, in which there is no room for the supernatural . . ."[5]

Huxley does not mention a single such discovery that necessitates a naturalistic hypothesis. It is our contention that a genuine scientific discovery can be compatible with either a naturalistic or a supernaturalistic hypothesis. Whether or not what is observed is best explained in terms of a naturalistic metaphysics or in terms of a supernaturalistic metaphysics is precisely the point at issue between the Christian investigator of nature and the non-Christian investigator. What they both see is not what is at issue; it is the interpretation of what they see that is the point of contention.

The answer to the question as to what is the nature of the quoted statements made by Huxley is that they are belief-statements, statements which express Huxley's religious and metaphysical views of himself and his world. They are statements of Huxley's personal faith. And such Huxley statements are in conflict with certain statements of the Bible. For, as we shall see, the Bible also contains statements that may be called belief or religious statements.

The statements of Huxley and the statements of the Bible do not contradict because the former are scientific and the latter are not. They contradict each other to the degree that both express ultimate religious and/or metaphysical beliefs about the nature of "God." Huxley's concept of God is that God is the world of nature; the biblical concept of God is that God is distinct from the world, that he is its creator.

Huxley is a naturalist and he is excited about being a naturalist. Some naturalists are very devout believers, and Julian Huxley frankly acknowledges that he is such a believer, for "complete scepticism does not work."[6] Huxley believes in belief. He has faith in faith. He also believes that it is always undesirable and often harmful to believe without proper evidence.[7] And where do we get the proper evidence? Huxley tells us: "I believe firmly that the scientific method, although slow and never claiming to lead to complete truth, is the only method which in the long run will give satisfactory foundations for beliefs."[8] Huxley tells us further, "I believe that one should be agnostic when

166

belief one way or the other is mere idle speculation, incapable of verification . . ."[9] Yet Huxley is not agnostic when he says, "The entire cosmos, in all its appalling vastness, consists of the same world stuff."[10] And what of his belief that the scientific method is the only method which in the long run will give satisfactory foundations for beliefs. Does Huxley intend to verify his belief in the scientific method by the scientific method?

For the naturalist such as Huxley the scientific method is the only way. This attitude toward the scientific method has been described by O. K. Bouwsma[11] in a different context, and since Bouwsma's criticism is inimitable, and penetrating, it deserves being quoted at length. The sentences that Bouwsma is commenting on are similar to those of Huxley. The first, from Edel, is "Reliance on scientific method together with an appreciation of the primacy of matter, and the pervasiveness of change, I take to be the central points of naturalism as a philosophic outlook."[12] The second from Hook: "What unites them all (naturalists) is the wholehearted acceptance of scientific method as the only reliable way of reaching truth about the world, nature, society, and man. The least common denominator of all historic naturalisms, therefore, is not so much a set of specific doctrines as the method of scientific or rational empiricism."[13] Third, from Dewey, "It suffices here to note that the naturalist is one who has respect for the conclusions of natural science."[14]

In commenting on these sentences Bouwsma notes their agreement:

> in identifying naturalism with a certain attitude toward scientific method, variously described as "reliance upon," "wholehearted acceptance of," and "respect for." Every naturalist is one who maintains an attitude similar to the attitude here described. He is excited about something. The excitement may vary in intensity, but in some degree naturalists all share it. This is not difficult to understand. In many cases, no doubt such excitement is the spontaneous overflow of new curiosities looking forward to tomorrow. There are secrets in 10,000 boxes, and you have opened forty, and know now how to go on opening a box a day for

167

the rest of your life. What a feast for eager eyes. Who has not shaken a box and wondered, keyless, what was inside it and later, furnished with a key, found out? Precious key!. Well, a naturalist is a man with 10,000 unopened boxes, newly furnished with a key. No wonder he dances, key in hand up-raised, among the boxes.

But this is idle curiousity, idle secrets for idle eyes, and is only half the motive of the naturalists' dance. For in those boxes smuggled away out of men's sight is the furniture of the land of heart's desire. Here is a box of the beauty that will not fade in the rain. Here is a heart that will not fail, a pump with scrutable controls. Here are pellets for stretching the hours and wobbling all dimensions. Here are new snuffers for old pains and here are new pleasures for old duffers. Besides there are new and quick get-aways, new smashers, new glue better than love, daisies that will tell even what the old ones wouldn't, rapid transit swifter than *gloria mundi*, lightning to keep your orange juice cold, falling water to dry up your feet, shocks to give you peace, a drop or two to make you jump, babies delivered in cellophane, bloodless wars, holocaust by button . . . a new Joseph for all your dreams . . . and so on from 9,000 and more other boxes. So the naturalist does his dazzle dance. Who then would not accept scientific method, and prefer to go to Babylon by candle light? Scientific method is successful.[15]

When Huxley expresses his belief that the scientific method is the only method that will give satisfactory foundations for belief, he is expressing his personal preference. Huxley has this preference because he has made certain religious decisions about the world in which he lives. Huxley is so firmly convinced of his own position that he can write, "But personally, I believe, and believe strongly, that if the standards of good and evil by which we ought to live this life are different from the standards by which we may hope to achieve satisfaction or blessedness in a life to come, then so much the worse for the universe and its government; but I refuse on that account to modify my standards of conduct in this world, for that appears to me an outrage, and a surrender of the highest part of our nature."[16]

168

Huxley's view of the world is controlled by a belief in his own sovereign personality. The belief in the sovereignty of man is opposed to the biblical belief in the sovereignty of God. We have not yet examined the nature of a biblical statement in detail, but it should be apparent from our discussion of the statements of science and of some of those made by Huxley that the latter are not scientific statements at all. Huxley's statements (what we have called H statements) do not entail the rejection of any genuine scientific statement (S statement); they are compatible with the latter, since they are either statements *about* science and not statements *of* science, or they are statements of Huxley's personal faith, statements that are in no way verified by any experimental procedure or by any observation.

4. *Certain Biblical Statements Considered*

Huxley's statements are in conflict with certain biblical statements, since some of the latter do make assertions about the existence and nature of God. Certain biblical statements are simple descriptions of historical events, e.g., "There went out a decree from Caesar Augustus that all the world should be taxed." Others are commands: "Praise ye the Lord." Some statements are literal and some are figurative. Some are phenomenal, that is, they describe things and events as they appeared to the author, e.g., Joshua's description of the sun's standing still. Others speak of God and his nature in terms that we can understand.

No less a commentator than John Calvin, when speaking of the first chapter of Genesis states "For, to my mind, this is a certain principle, that nothing is here treated of but the visible form of the world. He who would learn astronomy, and other recondite arts, let him go elsewhere . . ."[17] "The history of creation . . . is the book of the unlearned."[18] "Moses does not here subtly descant, as a philosopher, on the secrets of nature. . . ."[19]

Christians do not agree among themselves as to whether a conflict does exist between some statements of the Bible and some statements of science. There are many areas in which possible disputes can arise. At present the "conflict" centers around the first few chapters of Genesis and their relation to natural science.

For the first chapters of Genesis to be in conflict with certain scientific theories, they must be interpreted as containing statements that contain the same subject and predicates as the scientific theories in question. There are several possibilities. The statements of Genesis and the statements of science might both be true, they might both be false, or the former might be true, and the latter false, or vice versa.

5. *Different Interpretations of Genesis*

Christians do not agree among themselves as to the degree of literalness that ought to be assigned to the first chapters of Genesis. Those who interpret Genesis as giving detailed information about the same states of affairs as are treated in the sciences are faced with a conflict so that if certain statements of the latter are accepted as true, those of Scripture must be regarded as false.

The alternative, of course, is to regard the statements of Genesis as true and reject the current interpretation of the scientific theories. The latter course has recently been taken by Henry M. Morris and John C. Whitcomb, Jr.[20] Since their position is representative of an important segment of evangelical Christianity, we shall state their argument in some detail.

The main theme of their book concerns the Genesis flood. The conclusions that they reach, however, have many implications for the sciences of anthropology, geology, and for the theory of evolution. The statement of Genesis 7:19-20, "And the waters prevailed exceedingly upon the earth; and all the high mountains that were under the whole heaven were covered. Fifteen cubits upward did the waters prevail, and the mountains were covered," is interpreted by Morris and Whitcomb as being anthropomorphically universal, although they do not necessarily assume

170

that the mountains were as high before the flood as they are now.[21]

The authors oppose the notion that the flood was local on several grounds; e.g. its duration for more than a year, the fact that it produced tremendous geologic upheavals in the oceanic depths, the huge size of the Ark (approximately 14,000 tons), the very need of an ark, the testimony of Peter, and the fact that a local flood could not have destroyed a widely distributed human race.[22]

Morris and Whitcomb are not unaware of the arguments against the universality of the flood. In fairness it is to be remembered that it is not the observed data that is in question but the interpretation of the data. We need to note that their quarrel is not with geology as a whole but solely with historical geology, and that even here they do not quarrel with the observed data but only with the interpretation of such data.

Morris and Whitcomb insist that the paleontological and other geological data can be organized on a different basis by means of the clear and legitimate implications of the Biblical revelation.

> Historical geology is unique among the sciences in that it deals with events that are past, and therefore not reproducible. Since presumably no human observers were present to record and study these events of the past it thus is impossible ever to prove that they were brought about by the same processes of nature that we can measure at present.[23]

Morris and Whitcomb hold that the Genesis record is itself sufficient evidence to deny the uniformitarian view in favor of a catastrophic view. They insist that "Uniformitarianism has simply been assumed, not proved. Catastrophism has simply been denied, not refuted."[24] Moreover, they attempt to show in detail that the principle of uniformity is "inadequate to account for by far the greater part of the geologic phenomena."[25] It is not the facts of geology, but only certain interpretations of those facts, that are at variance with Scripture. These interpretations involve the principle of uniformity and evolution as a framework for the historical evaluation of the geologic data. But historical geology is only one of the many branches of geologic science . . . .[26]

The authors recognize that to interpret the past in the light of the present is a reasonable assumption, unless there is valid evidence to the contrary. They insist, however, that it is an assumption that must always remain an unproven assumption.

> It should be obvious that this principle can never actually be proved to be valid. To be sure, it seems eminently reasonable, because the same principle is basic in other sciences. The uniform and dependable operation of natural processes is the foundation of modern experimental science, without which, indeed, modern science as we know it would be quite impossible.[27]

By accepting the biblical narrative as literally implying a universal flood, they are compelled to reject the assumption that the actual geologic processes that now occur are the same as those that acted in the past, and that no other factors could have been at work. The authors are convinced that it is impossible to harmonize the biblical doctrine of the flood with uniformitarian theories of geology.

> The decision then must be faced: either the Biblical record of the flood is false and must be rejected or else the system of historical geology which has seemed to discredit it is wrong and must be changed. The latter alternative would seem to be the only one which a Biblically and scientifically instructed Christian could honestly take, regardless of the "deluge" of scholarly wrath and ridicule that taking such a position brings upon him. But this position need not mean at all that since historical geology, unlike other sciences, cannot deal with currently observable and reproducible events, it is manifestly impossible ever really to prove, by the scientific method, any hypothesis relating to pre-human history.[28]

They do not attempt to make the Bible accounts fit into the data and theories of science but rather try to understand the geological data in the light of the Bible.

The days of Genesis are understood to be six "real days." And although the biblical account is admittedly not complete in its detail, what was created "had an appearance of age."[29]

To the objection that it would be dishonest of God to create things with an appearance of age, Morris and Whitcomb reply that:

> There could be no genuine creation of any kind without an initial appearance of age.

> If God could create atomic stuff with an appearance of age—in other words, if God exists!—then there is no reason why He could not, in full conformity with His character of Truth, create a whole universe full grown.[30]

Whitcomb and Morris "accept in faith the account of Creation as simple, literal truth."[31] And they believe that they are thereby provided with "a most powerful tool for understanding all the facts of geology in proper perspective. . . ." The recognition of creation and the fall "ultimately lead to a far more satisfactory and scientific explanation of the observed geological field relationships than any evolutionary synthesis can ever do."[32]

Whether such is indeed the case is a problem that need not concern us. It is a problem for the specialist. We need only note that when confronted with interpretations of observed data that conflict with their understanding of Genesis, Morris and Whitcomb accept what is strictly observed, but offer an interpretation other than the assumption of uniformitarianism.

From a logical point of view there is no reason why God could not have created a full grown universe. The observed data would remain the same. And yet many Christians are not convinced that the world was created full grown in six twenty-four-hour days.

Some Christians hold that the days of Genesis are real days but that they may have been of indefinite periods of time. The fact that it is not until the fourth day that God said, "Let there be light in the firmament of the heaven to divide the day from the night; and let them be for signs

173

and for seasons, and for days and years" indicates for some that at least the first three days were of unspecified duration. Still others consider the possibility of long periods of time between the days of creation.

Within Protestant circles, N. H. Ridderbos attempts to defend the notion that the use of seven days is a literary form,[33] a view that is also popular in Roman Catholic circles. Creation in six days is regarded as a mode of presentation.

> The author did not, of course, carelessly scatter God's work over six days but arranged them with a given purpose in mind. In this arrangement the division into two parallel series of three days are certainly not the only principle. It is plain that a progression from the lower to the higher also influences the mode of narration.[34]

It is not his intent, however, to present an exact report of what happened at creation. This eightfold work he places in a framework; he distributes it over six days, to which he adds a seventh day as the day of rest.[35]

If the framework exegesis of Genesis is adopted, the explanations of the natural sciences can be accepted without contradiction, as long as the natural sciences do not confuse scientific description with metaphysical explanation. For even if the framework exegesis of Genesis I is accepted, the latter is still of significance for natural science, in that it "reveals that God is Creator of all things; it calls upon us to reject all materialism, pantheism, etc.; and this is of great significance for natural science. . . ."[36]

A similar conclusion has been reached by Jan Lever, a biologist at the Free University of Amsterdam.[37] Lever rejects the notion that Genesis gives concrete data to which the biologist is bound in his biological research. The truth of scientific data is not measured by statements of Scripture interpreted literally. Genesis is not written in technical scientific language. The "days" of Genesis do not refer to a physical measure of time. . . . Genesis tells first of all that God created everything. Their meaning does not lie in the area of exact science but in the sphere of a decidedly religious faith.[38] Moreover,

Such words as "day," "kind," and "earth" may not be equated with similar concepts defined by natural science. The obvious mistake of fundamentalism is that it takes the account of origins as related in Genesis and reads it as if it were written in the terminology of natural science, and then it turns around and considers the distorted texts as normative for science. When we are once convinced that the concepts of natural science depend on concurrence among men then we see at once clearly that by the method of the fundamentalists we read Scripture wrongly and also that we fetter science unjustly.[39]

Lever would strictly adhere to the Bible as the Word of God and he does not wish to imply that Scripture should have no influence on natural science. He does not hold to two realities, one of faith, and the other of experience.

Genesis has significance for sciences, it gives data that no science can *discover:*

> . . . Scripture is a miracle . . . the Bible gives us data about reality which no science can discover; for example, that there exists a personal God who called all things into being. Scripture is thus in a certain sense a lamp . . . which places reality in the proper light. . . . But the Bible is not a magic lantern which communicates to us exactly scientific data in the form of tables, graphs and concepts. . . ."[40]

For Lever the Bible is not a theoretical treatise, although it deals with the same reality that is open to scientific investigation. Biblical language is concrete:

> We may not consider the language that is used as scientific concepts, indeed not at all as scientifically qualified language. This signifies that the Bible usually tells us *that* something has happened, but not *how* it happened. The "how" sometimes lies in the terrain of science. The Bible gives us the high points, science *sometimes* can discover the lines between them. We can never derive from Scripture exact physical, astronomical and biological knowledge . . . . The Bible simply is not for that purpose.[41]

Genesis is not normative for observational science, simply because that is not its purpose. This does not mean that Genesis is not true; it is true in the sense that it intends to be true, which is in a religious sense. Genesis reveals that "the wealth of structural form of this world did not originate as a game of chance, but that there exists a personal God. . . ."[42] Genesis reveals that the world exists because of the will of God; the world derives its meaning from God and exists for his glory. Genesis reveals that man is not a passing accident, but rather that the entire creation was directed to man.

Since the Scriptures do not give scientific information, although it curtails such erroneous notions as that man is an accident and the world is eternal, Lever holds that the Christian is free to examine the scientific data with complete freedom. The person who believes that creation took place does not know *"how* creation took place and what *in concreto,* is produced through creation."[43]

In dealing with concrete problems, such as the origin of life, Lever does not seek to acquire scientific information from the biblical text. Living organisms are not the result of purely chance processes, although from the scientific point of view they may be spoken of as such. Living organisms came into being according to the plan and purpose of God, and yet such texts as: Gen. 1:11, 12, "And God said, let the earth put forth grass, herbs yielding seed, and fruit trees bearing fruit after their kind, wherein is the seed thereof, upon the earth; and it was so," and vss. 20 and 21: "And God said, let the waters swarm with living creatures," and vs. 29: "And God said, Let the earth bring forth living creatures," do not imply an original act of creation out of nothing. They provide no scientific data. They do not tell us where, when, or how life first appeared.[44]

What is true of the origin of life, for Lever, is also true of the origin of types of living organisms. New types may have originated "through concrete causes (possibly mutations, selections, early ontogenetic type-origin, reconstruction, etc.), but no absolute chance dominated these processes; to the contrary, they all fit as pieces of a mosaic."[45] At the word of God ("God said") the organisms came into existence, each after its kind.

176

How they originated and *what* their nature is, of course, is not communicated . . . . The main point is—and this is revealed and cannot be ascertained scientifically—that all that man can know about the origin and nature of organisms, he can and must subject to the all-predominating influence of the determinative word of God. . . ."[46]

A similar interpretation of Genesis 1:27 and 2:7 is given by Lever. "And God created man in his own image . . . and God formed man of the dust of the ground, and breathed into his nostrils the breath of life; and man became a living soul."

For Lever this does not have the significance of a technical description of man's origin.

> The essence of this communication is again a religious revelation. Here man is told that as a totality he is not eternal and that he is not of divine origin, but only a revelation that man owes his existence to creation and that in every respect he is linked with that which has been created. The "dust of the earth," therefore, does not have to be at all the dust as we find it along the road, existing of grains of sand, dried particles of plants, the spores of unicellular organisms, but it may just as well be all that which is earthly and temporal. This means, keeping in mind for a moment the fact that we cannot use texts for conclusions of that nature, that the possibility definitely is not eliminated here that use was made of an animal, which, as is related a few verses earlier, also is brought forth out of the earth.[47]

The positions represented by Lever and Ridderbos, on the one hand, and by Morris and Whitcomb, on the other, agree insofar as both accept the biblical record as the authoritative word of God. They differ in that the latter look to the Bible for scientific data, whereas the former do not. If one agrees with Lever and Ridderbos, the acceptance of a biblical statement does not entail the rejection of a statement of science, but it does require the rejection of the naturalist statements of the Huxley variety which often pretend to be genuine scientific statements. On the other hand, if one accepts a position similar to that of Morris and Whitcomb some statements of science must

177

then be rejected together with the statements of a naturalistic metaphysics.[48] The reader ought to remember that it begs the question to assume that scientific theories are necessarily right, while theological theories are necessarily wrong. Morris and Whitcomb do not necessarily question the observed data, they simply question the theoretical explanation of the data.

It is not necessary for us to take sides on this issue. To evaluate the detailed arguments put forth in favor of each position requires specialized knowledge in many scientific fields.

The sole point that we would make is that it is in no way necessary to assume that the natural sciences afford evidence that would necessarily undermine the objectivist thesis. It may be the case that religious statements are simply irrelevant to scientific statements, in which case conflict is excluded in principle, or it may simply be the case that certain theories, not observed states of affairs, are in conflict with certain interpretations of the biblical text. It is in any case clear that a naturalistic view of the nature of what is ultimately real is in conflict with a super-materialistic view. Between two such metaphysical positions there is an irreconcilable conflict and tension.

Some Christians do not feel hindered by their acceptance of Scripture in their acceptance of scientific hypotheses. Some Christians do reject certain scientific theories because of their religious beliefs. What is often overlooked, however, is that whereas some supernaturalists feel free to accept or reject certain theories that are offered in explanation of some observed states of affairs, the naturalist must proclaim certain theories as a dogma. The theory of evolution may become for some a deduction from a naturalistic metaphysics, rather than a generalization from experience.

To explain the origin of living organisms, for example, the supernaturalist may be willing to entertain the notion of instantaneous divine intervention, or a gradual unfolding of certain potentialities created by God at the beginning and sustained by his providence. The naturalist, however, in spite of the admitted difficulties, must find some theoretical justification for spontaneous generation. For if God is ruled out, there may be no other way of accounting for living organisms.

For example: A Christian and a naturalist may both observe a kangeroo's pocket the former may interpret it as the result of design and the latter as the result of chance. What they both see is the pocket. One does not see "chance." The naturalist might well consider the question as to whether his notion of chance is what he knows from looking at the pocket.

Theories of change or evolution need not be in conflict with the biblical texts, either because the notions of the uniformitarians are wrong, or because some theologians are wrong in seeking scientific data in the biblical text.

The choice between these two alternatives must be decided on the basis of many considerations, both scientific and exegetical. The conclusion has been reached by some that wisdom lies in "learned ignorance." It may be that such matters will never be understood with any degree of certainty. The main point at issue, the concern of the philosopher of religion, is to examine the viewpoints of the naturalists and the supernaturalists, of the subjectivists and the objectivists. It is our conclusion that the data of science does not support the subjectivist thesis. Let us suppose for a moment that some form of evolution was not simply a theory but an indisputable statement of fact (something that is often naively assumed and proclaimed by dogmatic naturalists), let us even suppose that we had in our possession a photograph of the entire process of change, from some gaseous mass to the present state of our universe, from fish to farmer. Apart from the difficulties of measuring the time required for the various sequences to unfold, let us suppose we could study the pictures. Would they decide the real issue? Did this strange panorama take place according to the creative act and under the purposive plan of a divine creator, or did it just happen to be there? There is nothing on the

179

film to decide the case of the naturalist and supernaturalist. The photos are not in question. It is the metaphysical and religious interpretations that are at stake.

6. *Science and Scientism*

The description of the history of vertebrates, of reptiles, of mammals, of the primates; the rates of evolution, of the "forces" and "progress" of evolution may in itself, as description, be a matter of indifference. Imagine, again, that we are in possession of a strip of motion picture film on which is recorded the exact description of the entire evolutionary process, authentically dated at every point. Let us suppose that there can be absolutely no question of the genuineness and accuracy of the film. Its record is absolutely certain; it is not in any way an hypothesis, but a record beyond dispute, without any gaps or deficiencies. Every person agrees as to what it shows and understands the chemical, physical, and biological changes depicted. Everyone is in full agreement on what took place from a physical, chemical, and biological point of view.

Now let us suppose that the first part of the film begins by showing the formation of our present earth from a gaseous mass and that we could witness the origin of our earth and solar system as it actually occurred. Suppose we could see the changes that took place on its surface over the course of millions of years. Suppose we could witness the transformation of inorganic material into organic material by "chance" combinations that we could describe in terms of mathematical laws of probability and bio-chemical combinations. And suppose we saw the origin of all the phyla, and could witness every change within the individual phylum, that we saw the gradual appearance in the exact order of marine fauna, shelled animals, land plants, corals, armored fishes, amphibians, land flowers, ancient sharks, insects, primitive reptiles, modern insects, land vertebrates, dinosaurs, birds, flying reptiles, flowering plants, archaic mammals, higher mammals, man-apes, man. On the basis of the regularity portrayed we could

180

describe the various stages in terms of laws, progress, adaptation, opportunism, chance, probability, necessity, etc. We would then have a complete, recorded history of the actual processes of nature. Our scientific knowledge of the past would be complete.

Imagine an imaginary dialogue between a subjectivist and a Christian theologian after seeing the film for the first time.

Non-Christian: "Well! Now don't you see what a fool you have been making of yourself."

Theologian: "Hold on, my friend, I would be careful in calling anyone a fool. Just what do you mean by that remark?"

Non-Christian: "You know very well what I mean. All that nonsense in Genesis about the world being created in six twenty-four-hour days. If you are at all honest, not a hypocrite, or a complete fool, you certainly must restrict your religion to the field of ethics from now on."

Theologian: "Just a minute. I'll admit I used to think in such terms, before I saw this film. But that was partly your fault ... Remember a few hundred years ago you scientists believed that leaving a few old rags in a dark corner would produce mice. Remember until recently neither one of us had any reason to think the earth was so old or to even suspect what we have just seen."

Non-Christian: "You mean you no longer believe in that God of yours."

Theologian: "Not so fast, I believe more in him now than I ever did. His power is overwhelming. I can only say with the psalmist: 'What is man that thou art mindful of him'?"

Non-Christian: "But the film!"

Theologian: "What has the film to do with it?"

181

Non-Christian:	"Everything. It disproves Genesis. Did you see your God in it?"
Theologian:	"Now my friend, let us take one thing at a time. Of course, I 'saw' *God* in the film. But not in your scientific sense of 'seeing.' God is not an object to be photographed. He is the power, the director of the whole performance we have just witnessed. Not only did he create the stage and provide the background, but he is directly responsible for every change in setting, for every character that appeared, and that last fellow, man, was what he had in mind at the very beginning."
Non-Christian:	"You didn't see that on the film!"
Theologian:	"Of course not, if you persist in using the term 'see' in a scientific sense. But God is not known by perception. God's existence is known to me because in faith I accept his revelation in the Bible."
Non-Christian:	"That collection of fairy tales, again. I thought we had discarded Genesis, at least!"
Theologian:	"Oh, no, we haven't! Genesis does not give a scientific account, like we have just seen, but it gives a religious interpretation of the film far more important and significant than any strips of film. It tells me that God is not found within the process we have witnessed. It tells me that the 'chance' and 'necessity' of the film is not blind and that I have been made to love and serve God; that he is not hostile or indifferent and I have been created for a purpose."
Non-Christian:	"Well, I don't believe that; it's not scientific."
Theologian:	"Of course it is not. It's a religious answer to a religious question. The film answered our scientific questions.

Only faith can answer our religious questions."

Non-Christian: "I have no faith."

Theologian: "You have a faith. It's not the same as mine, but it's a faith. There is nothing in the film to indicate that the process we have witnessed is ultimate, final. The film itself doesn't tell us there is nothing beyond nature. It takes faith to believe that 'nature' is 'God'. What separates us is not the strip of film, but our different faiths. You believe in 'nature'. I believe that beyond 'nature' there is a God who has created it."

Such a strip of film is non-existent, and it may be legitimate for science to seek to reconstruct the entire film from the broken strips we now possess. The identification of the reconstructed film with "God," however, is not a scientific description, as our imaginary dialogue indicates; it is an act of faith, a commitment, an answer to the religious question: What is the origin of all existence? What is "God"? To identify God and nature is to deify nature; it requires the exercise of faith, and if the identification is made uncritically and dogmatically proclaimed as the only interpretation of the evolutionary process, it is the scientist that fails to be scientific, not the Christian, in his refusal to accept religion under the guise of science. The admission that all scientific knowledge is the result of what is known by scientific method does not warrant the conclusion that what is not capable of being known via scientific method is not knowledge. All of reality does not coincide necessarily with what we are able to know scientifically. God is admittedly "known" indirectly by revelation, not by scientific observation. From the process of evolution we can learn that life is a unity. But the deepest meaning of nature, the origin of its laws, and the religious meaning of man cannot be learned from a description of the process. That man is related to every other organism and to nature does not in itself disclose the meaning of man and nature.

Man may be classified within the animal kingdom, within the vertebrate sub-phylum, as a member of the mammalian class, but such classification does not answer the religious question of man in his relationship to God.

There is nothing in the evolutionary process itself to warrant the conclusion: "Man is the result of a purposeless and materialistic process that did not have him in mind. He was not planned. He is a state of matter, a form of life, a sort of animal, and a species of the order primates, akin nearly or remotely to all of life and indeed to all material."[49]

Even if one admits that man is a state of matter, a form of life, akin to all other forms of life, it does not logically follow that the nature of reality excludes the hypothesis that the evolutionary process is the very plan described in religious terms in Genesis, the very method by which God accomplished his purpose.

The question is not what are the laws and forces at work in nature. The question is whether these laws are self-sufficient and autonomous, ultimate and without any conscious purpose, or whether in the beginning God created nature with its laws and "chance operations."

To assume that the operations of natural processes are capable of operating independently of any other controlling factor is the expression of a basic conviction, a world view, a religious faith. It is a metaphysical commitment about the nature of things, and is not subject to verification. It is an assumption of "evolutionism," of scientism. Even if one were able to describe the past history of the world of nature, it would not follow that all plan, purpose, and ethical norms are merely human. The historian of culture and civilization may be able to describe the past of civilization with a great degree of accuracy. His description of events has no bearing, however, on the question as to whether there is a God who is concerned with human history. The descriptions of natural science are equally irrelevant to the religious question.

It is a fundamental confusion to assume that purely scientific description and method can solve religious ques-

tions. Darwin's *Origin of Species* may be significant to
the extent that it prepared the way for an understanding
of organic evolution but in failing to restrict itself to an
examination of the organic structure of living organisms,
it opened the way to *evolutionism*, the extension of biological explanation to all of experience, including religious experience.[50]

Every Christian rejects *evolutionism*, a pseudo-religi-
ous form of scientism, which seeks to find a metaphysical,
interpretation of the cosmos and man within the evolutionary process. The Christian is committed at least to the
doctrine that initially, at the act of creation, described in
Genesis 1, God placed within his initial creation the potentiality of all further development, which then subsequently
occurred according to his plan and purpose. Any process
of development is, therefore, an unfolding process, the con-
tinuity of which is directed and sustained at every point
by God's providence.

A Christian might agree that as a process, evolution,
in the strict biological sense, is an indisputable event of
nature, in which living organisms undergo changes, from
lower to higher structural forms. Or a Christian might
reject the evolutionary process. But in any case, the Christian is unable to accept a naturalistic view of reality which
seeks to explain evolutionary development solely in terms
of an absolutization of the material aspect of nature and
in terms of the principle of natural causality.

Evolutionism is a faith in matter: In the beginning
was matter and matter was God. All things evolved because of matter, and without matter was not anything
evolved that was evolved. In matter was life and life
developed into man.

Some Christians agree that the reality of organic
"evolution is an indisputable fact." What is frequently forgotten in text books on evolution, when it is stated that
"evolution is an indisputable fact," is that a naturalistic
materialistic interpretation of the evolutionary process,
cannot be an indisputable "fact." It is not a "fact" at
all, but an interpretation, ultimately dependent upon meta-

physical commitments. The evolutionary process is not the unique discovery and property of evolutionism. A materialistic interpretation is not the only legitimate interpretation of the evolutionary process.[51] All Christians are not opposed to "evolution," but all Christians are opposed to the materialistic interpretation of evolutionism.

No one living in the 20th century can escape the impact of modern science. Its practical achievements in the field of technology, medicine, atomic research, and automation, and its theoretical advance on the frontier of human knowledge makes a tremendous impression. The proper attitude of the Christian, when confronted with the achievements of science in the theoretical and practical area, is that of joyous thanksgiving.

Science is a human activity which investigates the structure of the world in which man lives. It investigates the world of nature and civilization. It includes the natural sciences, physics, chemistry, biology, and psychology, and the realm of history, economy, language, jurisprudence, art, ethics, and theology. It develops the symbols of mathematics and logic as instruments to conduct its investigation, and in all its activity, it reveals to the Christian the nature of God's world.

The modern scientific attitude and method are a recent achievement. The Bible is written in a language which is often poetic, as in the Psalms; it is often commanding, as in calls to repentance. Its language is much closer to life than that of science. It appeals to man as a person and offers answers to questions which science and philosophy may not ask or answer. It deals with ultimate questions of faith, of life, and death. It purports to be a religious book, a divine book, reporting God's redemptive dealings with mankind.

The statements that it makes are final and authoritative. They offer a universal norm of faith. But the knowledge of faith is not the knowledge of science. The knowledge of faith is final, it satisfies man's desire for salvation. It provides a resting point for the human heart, and answers to questions of the utmost significance to man. Its central questions and answers are religious in the deepest sense.

Science accepts the world as it appears to the senses. It does not go beyond what is sensory and what is in principle reducible to sense experience. The Bible provides a religious answer to questions which science is unable to ask. Science deals with the world as it appears. The Bible asks the question: What is the origin of the world? This is not a scientific question in the strict sense, since no observations can be made of the origin of the world.

The Bible reveals that the world is not "God," but that God is the creator of the world. Science can describe the world as it appears. The Bible gives a religious answer to the question: Why does the world exist? Science can describe the human situation. The Bible asks: What is man? Science can describe how man acts. The Bible gives a religious answer to the question: How ought man to act? Science can describe man's birth and death. The Bible gives a religious answer to the question: Why was man born, and what is his final destiny?

Conflicts arise when the scientist asks questions that he cannot answer as a scientist. Conflicts arise when a scientist unscientifically misrepresents religious questions and answers as scientific questions and answers.

The desire for knowledge is a fundamental constituent of human nature. It is human to desire to know. There is something inhuman in a person who lacks the curiosity to seek to learn new things.

The thought processes of the scientist and of the average person do not differ in principle. The scientist is a man like everyone else. Whenever we generalize on the basis of a few repeated experiences we have in fact performed the operation of induction. If from past experience we have repeatedly observed that certain cloud formations generally result in rain, we may further deduce the general principle that dark skies probably mean it is going to rain. Scientific reasoning is like our everyday reasoning except that its observations are more general and its conclusions are of greater consequences.

Observation and experiment are the key words in modern rational scientific method. The scientist looks, and looks carefully. Scientific observation is more exact than everyday observation. The scientist seeks to correct his errors by repeated experiments. The scientist selects facts which recur and he notes their recurrence with precision, and assumes that the future will be like the past, so that he can under given conditions predict the future.

Science is not a mystical activity but a necessary integral aspect of modern civilization. The scientist is aware of the possible relations between propositions. He knows the necessary conditions of valid inference. Logic is, however, not the whole of science. Logic is a formal discipline. Reasoning about a subject matter cannot establish *a priori* truth with regard to it. There are no factual *a priori* statements that can be made in the field of scientific endeavor. The material of a science depends upon experience, apart from which its propositions are empty. Logic enables the scientist to conclude that a proposition is true, if other propositions are true, but it does not establish the truth of his premises.

Cohen and Nagel in their *Introduction to Logic and Scientific Method* rightly restrict the term "science" to such knowledge which is general and systematic, to such knowledge that deduces specific propositions from a few general principles.

The scientific method is a means by which the search for truth is carried on. Science asks what conditions must hold to establish the truth claim of a set of propositions. It is a method by which our impressions and opinions are tested in terms of supporting evidence. Essentially scientific method is the quest for truth.

Habit, inertia, appeal to authority, and intuition are not sufficient ground to establish our beliefs and to settle our doubts. Scientific investigation seeks clarity, order, and accuracy. It requires a method independent of our subjective desires and volition. It restricts itself to what can be tested by everyone. Science is progressive; it is

188

never certain of its results. It chooses the most probable hypothesis to interpret facts of observation.

Scientific investigation examines problems capable of solution. On the basis of previous knowledge it seeks to select what is of significance. It formulates explanations; it makes hypotheses which direct its search for order and which may be a probable solution to the problem.

A good hypothesis permits deductions to be made and a decision to be reached as to whether it explains the facts. When it enables predictions to be made it is verified, but it is never proven beyond a shadow of a doubt. Nevertheless, a scientific hypothesis must be verifiable and falsifiable in principle, at least. Its consequences are open to observation. Mere observation is not sufficient. Our observations constitute the basis of generalizations so that each observed fact enables the scientist to predict others. Generalizations are hypotheses. Such ought not to be multiplied more than is necessary.

The explanatory principles of science can be tested. They are not mere expressions of emotion, but are relative to confirming evidence and must always be revised in the light of new evidence.

The scientist is able to give an accurate description of individual facts or events as immediately observed. By formulating empirical laws he is able to ascertain functional relations between what is observed and by constructing theories he can interpret the facts as formulated in empirical laws.[52]

Hypotheses give an explanation when a problem demands a solution. A guess and an elaborate theory are examples of hypotheses. A scientific hypothesis must be logically possible, and if concerned with the world, it must be physically possible, and must entail consequences capable of being tested. When such consequences are in harmony with the facts of observation, the hypothesis is confirmed or verified with a certain degree of probability.

Within the natural sciences verification requires experiment or sense observation. Knowledge is therefore not a mere collection of facts. The term "fact" is ambiguous.

It may refer to elements of sense experience, to interpretations of sense experience, to things and relations between things experienced.[53]

Scientific method seeks to discover what facts are and is itself guided by the facts discovered. It is used when a problem is encountered that requires its use, if a solution is to be obtained. The scientist formulates hypotheses suggested by his subject matter and required at every stage of his investigation. Hypotheses suggest possible connections between facts and may occur without limit. The task confronting the scientific investigator is to determine which hypothesis is in best agreement with the facts. No hypothesis is absolutely true. The scientist is content with the most probable hypothesis but he continues to search for factual evidence that will increase or decrease the probability of his hypothesis.

A radical doubt of all things is impossible because doubt itself presupposes a standard or criterion in terms of which particular things or experiences are doubted. Scientific method is not sceptical in any final sense but it questions what lacks evidence. It is ready to abandon any theory at any time, and no single proposition is beyond doubt. Only approximate verification is attainable in scientific inquiry.

But simply because science abandons one theory and posits another in no way implies the weakness of science. Its open character is its very strength and essential feature. Because of its openness it is self-corrective. It does not pretend to assert everything about its subject; it selects and abstracts.

Science is analogous to a game. Its canons and method are the rules. They are respected or disregarded. Its rules are rules of evidence: observational, experimental, inductive, deductive, circumstantial, and testimonial.[54] No one needs to play the game, but if a person chooses to do so he must either obey the rules or be guilty of cheating.

The methods of natural science are adequate to the natural sciences. But when they are extended to all areas of human experience so that the explanations of history, ethics, and religion, for example, are given in terms modeled after the natural sciences, the nature of the historical, ethical, and religious disciplines are distorted.

When natural scientific methodology is applied to history it is forgotten that science itself has a history and is in need of historical explanation. When applied to ethics, it is forgotten that it is dogmatic to assume that ethical theory can only describe, and that what actions ought to be can only be deduced from desired goals set up by man, individually or within society. And when natural scientific methodology is made the norm of religion, it is forgotten that the religious question is a different question than what can be asked or answered by any form of scientific inquiry. For religion is an area in which the question is asked concerning what it is, if anything, which makes experience possible. Religion asks and answers the question of salvation. To seek salvation within the area of science, which properly satisfies the desire for knowledge of the world, is to answer a religious question in an area where such answers cannot be given.

Not every person is a scientist, but every person is religious. One is not able to choose whether or not he wishes to be religious. Everyone chooses between religious hypotheses which are meaningful for him and which are forced upon him. The decision he makes is momentous in that to some degree his further thinking is necessarily affected by the choice made, whether consciously or unconsciously. When Bertrand Russell, in the *Scientific Outlook*, ridicules the religious belief in creation, he does not act in the capacity of a great mathematician and philosopher of science, but he speaks as a lay theologian and expresses his religious convictions.

Russell admits that science does not provide a correct conception of the ends of life and does not guarantee progress, although it is an essential ingredient of the latter. And he correctly points out that statements made by scientists in support of religious beliefs are not made in their capacity as scientists; but in confessing his own faith in rationalism and optimism, Russell seems to forget that his own attacks on the Christian faith are not scientific arguments. The question as to whether there is a creator God is a religious question. Its affirmation and denial is a religious act.

It is interesting to note that Russell can derive no comfort from the hypothesis that the world was made by a creator. Russell's personal testimony to his personal convictions are irrelevant to the religious question.

Russell's hatred toward the Christian God, who if existent would be an "Almighty Tyrant," is as childish, as the supposedly childish comforts of a less adult age sought after by Christians. But Russell's feelings have no more value to the religious question of man's existence than the feelings of an idiot or a pig. They are totally irrelevant and of biographical interest only.

Russell has answered the religious question in terms of human experience. The universe is ultimate for him. No questions can be asked or answered which go beyond what he considers "natural." Man as a part of nature is in the last analysis the final judge of his own experience and action. Such is the religious credo pre-supposed in Russell's non-scientific, religious faith in man.

We have stressed the fact that scientific method within the field of sciences can be accepted by the objectivist. The conflict between subjectivists and objectivists in religion is not a struggle between science and religion but a struggle between one form of religion and scientism, a pseudo-religion. The latter transgresses the boundaries of science and expands the scientific method of thinking to cover the entire universe. It equates all of reality with what it can discover. To the objectivist it is perhaps the most dangerous pseudo-religion and pseudo-theology ever formulated.

When science is adored to the degree that its results are looked upon as miraculous, and when it plays the role of the universal savior of mankind, it fulfils a religious longing, and becomes the expression of a religious faith.[55]

Scientism has given the masses of mankind the impression that what science has discovered about the nature of man and of the world makes Christianity superfluous. God has not been discovered in science's search of the heavens and the earth. Nature is ruled by mathematical laws and blind forces unaware of man. Organic life and man obey natural laws. Man is simply an animal whose values and moral standards change with the chance situation in which he finds himself. Even his conscious life is governed by the unconscious instincts of the unconscious. Man and civilization are the result of natural forces. Happiness, that is salvation, is to be found in this world, not in a future existence. Trust is to be placed within one's self. Man is the captain of his own fate. Religion threatens human accomplishment. Man can understand everything in terms of his own thinking and actions.[56]

Scientism is, however, not the same as science. "Science" as an activity, may be neutral, but it is an activity performed by men, and as a human being each man makes religious decisions. When a scientist seeks to explain himself and the world in terms of the world, he goes beyond pure science and answers a religious question. For he assumes that there is nothing beyond the world and that the latter contains its own explanatory principle. Scientific observation can disclose the way in which the world appears to man. It can never disclose that the world is ultimate, that it is itself "God." To assume the ultimacy of the world is not a religiously neutral act but a non-scientific commitment.

The attack on the objectivist's position is not only made in the name of the natural sciences. Frequently, such sciences as psychology and sociology are thought to provide evidence for the subjectivist's point of view. It is hardly worthwhile answering such a charge. The reader need only note that even if the psychologist could show that the idea of God originates in a certain psychological way, it commits the genetic fallacy to assume that because you discover the origin of an idea you can therefore dismiss it.

The issue between the subjectivist and the objectivist is a metaphysical one and the ultimate nature of reality does not depend upon human psychology. Let us suppose that a certain individual, Mr. Z., believes in God to satisfy his need for a father image. Mr. Z is insecure, he has anxieties, he is afraid, and neurotic. A psychiatrist finds this out. Can he argue that God does not exist because Mr. Z. is neurotic? Let us imagine another person, Mr. Y. Mr. Y. never had a father. He was the first man who ever lived. (Someone had to be first.) Mr. Y. lived long before there were any psychiatrists or psychologists to examine him. Mr. Y. was afraid. Some psychiatrists may *now* say that Mr. Y. invented God, even though they never talked to Mr. Y. How could a psychologist know that Mr. Y. invented God? He does not know it from talking to the first man that ever lived. Does he find out from one of his patients? The study of human feelings can reach conclusions about human feelings. It cannot reach conclusions about the existence or non-existence of God. Man's beliefs are accompanied by feelings of certainty or uncertainty, doubt or despair; certain experiences may have produced certain beliefs, but the truth or falsity of such beliefs does not depend upon the emotional states of the believer. The question is not how someone came to believe such and such to be true; the issue is whether what is believed to be true is true. A person may come to believe in God in many ways. He may also stop believing in God for many different reasons, some of which may be psychological as well as social. The psychological or social conditions under which a person believes or disbelieves in the existence of God is of interest to anyone interested in the study of human behavior. It is simply irrelevant to the objectivist or subjectivist thesis.

What is true of psychology is also true of sociology and anthropology. The sociologist may study the religious beliefs and practices of a single society or of many societies. He may find points of difference as well as similarities. What he discovers may be interesting and of some importance to anyone interested in what certain groups of

194

individuals believe. Whether what people believe is true is true, is not a sociological question. It is not a question that can be answered by observing the structure of a society. It is again a metaphysical question, a question about the ontological status of certain religious beliefs.

It is our conclusion that the sole science that is necessarily relevant to the objectivist thesis is the science of history. And this is only relevant to such religions that make historical as well as religious statements.

---

[1] Julian Huxley, *Religion without Revelation*, (New York: Menton Books) 1958, p. 52.

[2] *Ibid.*, p. 59.

[3] *Ibid.*, p. 187.

[4] Cf., what is said of "faith" in Chapter 4.

[5] *Ibid.*

[6] *Ibid.*

[7] *Ibid.*

[8] *Ibid.*, p. 15.

[9] *Ibid.*, p. 17.

[10] *Ibid.*, p. 190.

[11] "The Present Status of Naturalism" in *The Journal of Philosophy*, Vol. XLV., No. 1. Jan. M48.

[12] *Ibid.*

[13] *Ibid.*

[14] *Ibid.*

[15] *Ibid.*

[16] Julian Huxley, *op cit*, p. 19.

[17] *Calvin's Commentaries*, Vol. I. Genesis (Grand Rapids, Mich: Wm. B. Eerdmans, 1948, p. 79.

[18] *Ibid.* p.80.

[19] *Ibid.* p. 86.

[20] *The Genesis Flood* (Phila.: The Presbyterian and Reformed Publishing Co.) 1960.

[21] *Ibid.*, p. 2.

[22] *Ibid.*, p. 34.

[23] *Ibid.*, p. 131.

[24] *Ibid.*, p. 37.

[25] *Ibid.*, p. 200.

[26] *Ibid.*, p. 118.

[27] *Ibid.*

[28] *Ibid.*, p. 214.

[29] *Ibid.*, p. 233.

[30] *Ibid.*, p. 238.

[31] *Ibid.*, p. 239.

[32] *Ibid.*

[33] *Is there a Conflict between Genesis I and Natural Science?* (Grand Rapids, Mich: Wm. B. Eerdmans) 1957.

[34] *Ibid.*, p. 33.

[35] *Ibid.* p. 45.

[36] *Ibid.* p. 69.

[37] *Creation and Evolution,* (Grand Rapids: International Publications) 1958.

[38] *Ibid.*, p. 16.

[39] *Ibid.*, p. 18.

[40] *Ibid.*, p. 20.

[41] *Ibid.*, p. 21.

[42] *Ibid.*, p. 22.

[43] *Ibid.*, p. 23.

[44] *Ibid.*, p. 57.

[45] *Ibid.*, p. 96.

[46] *Ibid.*, p. 139

[47] *Ibid.*, p. 197.

[48] For a detailed criticism of the literary framework hypothesis, see Edward J. Young, "The Days of Genesis" in *The Westminster Theological Journal*, Vol. XXV, Nos. 1 and 2. Young insists that the six days are to be understood in a chronological sense. He admits that the length of the days is not stated, and that the first three days are not solar days.

"The purpose of the six days is to show how God, step by step, changed the uninhabitable and unformed earth of verse two into the well ordered world of verse thirty-one."

"Genesis one is not poetry or saga or myth, but straightforward history, and, inasmuch as it is divine revelation, accurately records those matters of which it speaks," (p. 171).

[49] Simpson, *op. cit.*, p. 344.

[50] Cf. J. J. Duyvene De Wit, *De Mens in zijn Verhouding Tot Het Dierenrijk En Als Beelddragen Gods.* Unpublished manuscript).

[51] Cf. De Wit, *op. cit.*, p. 144ff.

[52] Cf. Herbert Feigl, "Some Remarks on the Meaning of Scientific Explanation," *The Psychological Review*, 52, 1948.

[53] Cf. Cohen and Nagel, *An Introduction to Logic and Scientific Method.* (N. Y.: Harcourt, Brace and Co.), p. 217ff.

[54] See C. J. Ducasse, "Are Religious Dogmas Meaningful?" in *Academic Freedom, Logic, and Religion*, Univ. of Pa. Press, 1953.

[55] Cf. Richard Kroner, *Culture and Faith*, University of Chicago Press, 1951, pp. 111ff.

[56] Cf. Erich Frank, *Philosophical Understanding and Religious Truth*, Oxford University Press, N.Y., 1945, pp. 3ff.

CHAPTER VII

FURTHER OBJECTIONS TO REVEALED RELIGION

1. *The Deism of Matthew Tindall and Thomas Paine*

There are objectivists in religion who believe in God, the creator, but who do not believe in revelation. Such people are usually called deists.

The deists espoused a religion which any man at any time is capable of discovering by reason.[1] God, according to deism, has provided mankind with the means of knowing what he requires of them. Natural religion, the religion man can discover, differs from revealed religion only in the manner of its being communicated. Because God is unchangeable, infinitely wise and infinitely good, natural and revealed religion can differ in nothing as far as their content is concerned.

God has initially given mankind a rule or law for their conduct, the observance of which renders them acceptable to himself. And what originates with a perfect, all-wise God, must itself be perfect, so that an absolutely perfect religion cannot be altered. The original religion of man is as immutable as God its author. Revelation can add nothing to a perfect religion.

Man is capable of knowing what God's infinite goodness would have him know. God was always willing that every man should come to the knowledge of true religion. The name "Christianity" is of recent origin, but the true "Christian" religion has existed from the beginning; it is as old and extensive as human nature; it is in fact the law of creation, implanted in us by God himself. According to Tindall, God, at the beginning and ever since, has given all men sufficient means to know, believe, profess, and

197

practice Christianity. Every man has the means to know what is sufficient for the circumstances he is in.

God judges mankind to the degree they are rational; his judgment is exactly proportional to the use men make of their reason. The use of reason is the means by which God would have us know what to profess and to practice, for God has made us rational creatures. Our reason tells us that it is the will of God that we act up to the dignity of our natures, and it is reason that tells us when we do so. What God requires us to believe must be reasonable, and whether what is offered to us as such is really reasonable, must itself be judged by reason. Reason is the judge of what is reasonable. Nothing should be admitted into religion except what our reason tells us is worthy of having God for its author.

Nothing is required of men by God but what is founded on the nature of things and the immutable relations they sustain to each other. When men sincerely try to discover the will of God, they become aware of a law which is common or natural to all rational creatures. This law is absolutely perfect, eternal, and unchangeable. The gospel did not intend to add or to detract from it. The gospel aimed to free men from their own superstition, so that true Christianity is not a religion of yesterday; it is rather what God dictated at the beginning and still continues to dictate to all men.

Jesus has set us a noble example by living what he taught, and as he was highly exalted for so doing, we too may expect a suitable reward, if we do our best to follow the divine moral precepts which are the same whether revealed in the gospel or discovered by reason.

God has given to men the light of understanding by which they can discover what makes for the good of their souls. Man is capable of perceiving eternal truths and of knowing what will contribute to his temporal and eternal happiness.

The true gospel is not a new religion but a republication of the religion of nature. Natural religion is able to demonstrate the existence of an absolutely perfect being, the source of all other beings and of their perfections. That such a being exists is as certain as our own existence. It is, moreover, equally demonstrable that no creature can add or detract from the happiness of a being who is infinitely happy in himself.

Tindall holds that God requires nothing of us, unless it contributes to our happiness, and God forbids only that which leads to our hurt. His laws can lead only to our good, and his infinite power can bring to pass what he designs for our good. To sin against such a being is to act against ourselves and against our reasonable natures.

Reason can demonstrate the existence of God, the nature of the divine perfections, and the nature of the duties God requires of us, in relation to himself, to ourselves, and to one another.

Revelation is superfluous, for by recognizing that God has endowed us with such a nature that we desire our own good, and by realizing that God could not require anything that would do us harm, we know that we should act in relation to ourselves in such a way that our natural appetites are so regulated as to be conducive to the exercise of reason, the health of the body, and the pleasure of the senses.

Our duty to our fellow man is readily ascertainable, if it be remembered that God is the common parent of all mankind, and that the whole human species is under the divine protection, so that God will punish anyone who injures anyone else. A person's duty is to deal with others as he would have them deal with him in like circumstances. Men are so constituted by God that they are able to assist each other in the concerns of life, and by nature men are framed to be useful to each other. The seeds of pity are sown in the human heart by God, who has implanted in man, his image bearer, a love for his species and a desire to perform acts of benevolence.

The deists held that our duty to God and man is unalterable. It is always plain and clear; it is never changed in whole, or part, so that no person, if he comes from God, can teach any other religion, or give us any precepts other than those of natural religion. True religion is thus a constant disposition of the mind to do all the good we can; and by so doing, to render ourselves acceptable to God in answering the end of his creation.

The religion of nature is absolutely perfect; revelation can neither add nor subtract to its perfection. In fact the truth of all revelation is to be judged by the latter's agreement with natural religion. All particular precepts that fail to contribute to the honor of God or to the good of man fail to carry any obligation.

By failing to make reason the judge concerning the nature of God and the duties he requires of us, man has invented all sorts of superstitions, bigotry, and intolerance. God has been debased by clothing him in our own infirmities, and man's individual conscience has been placed in the hands of corrupt men, in the hands of priests and clerics. True religion is the imitation of the perfections of God. To insist upon rules or practices other than those discovered by reason is to suppose that some men who obey the law of nature may yet suffer eternal punishment for not obeying additional laws. God never requires what the law of nature does not. It is superstition to represent God as damning men to eternity for mistaken opinions about such things as have no foundation in reason.

To magnify revelation is to weaken the force of reason and nature; it is to strike at all order for there cannot be two conflicting standards of divine government. Fortunately, the deists believe the bulk of mankind is able to distinguish by reason between religion and superstition and can extricate themselves from the superstition in which they have been indoctrinated.

The work of Tindal which we have summarized briefly marks the high point of deism. Unlike such later authors as Thomas Paine, Tindall did not explicitly reject the biblical records. Miracles were simply unnecessary for the man guided only by reason. They were superfluous to a religion that consisted essentially in the practice of duties.

The thesis of Tindal, and other deists, is that a man can at any time discover his duties by exercising reason. The deists held that there is a natural religion as old as creation. This thesis was to collapse subsequently under Hume's assertion in his *Natural History of Religion* that the religion of primitive man consists of a medley of crude superstitions.

The optimism of deism, with respect to evil tendencies in human nature, has to a large extent been rendered obsolete by two world wars, Hitler's concentration camps, and fear of atomic holocaust; nevertheless, the subjection of revelation to the tests of reason exerted and, as we have seen, continues to exert its influence upon liberal Protestantism. Its optimism has been carried over to many forms of secular liberalism. There is, moreover, a cultural lag between the most advanced stage of historical development and opinions that are popularly held. During the period in which deism was developed, the man on the street still believed in revelation; today when naturalistic atheism is fashionable among many intellectuals, the man in the street is often a deist.

Mention must be made of *The Age of Reason* by Thomas Paine, since it helped to popularize deism. Like other deists, Paine believed that the existence of God could be proved from the bible of nature. The Scriptures of the Old and New Testaments allegedly carry no evidence in themselves that God is the author of any of them; in nature God is to be found.[2]

Paine hoped for life after death, and believed he was in the hands of his creator, and would be disposed of in a manner consistent with his justice and goodness.[3] In all such judgments Paine recognized no authority higher than what he calls "the reason that God has given me," and he modestly adds, "and I gratefully know that He has given me a large share of that divine gift."[4]

Reason is a gift and God has given it to Paine. How does Paine use the word "reason"? He regards it as some kind of a weapon against error, as the means by which false theology can be distinguished from true theology. Paine confesses,

201

I believe in One God, and no more; and I hope for happiness beyond this life. I believe in the equality of man; and I believe that religious duties consist in doing justice, loving mercy, and endeavoring to make our fellow-creatures happy.[5]

Paine's reason did not prevent him from having a creed; he did not believe in the creed professed by any church. Apparently Paine's reason did not keep him from such puzzling utterances as "My own mind is my own church."[6] Of course, it is possible to give such an expression a meaning, but it is rather odd. Going to church in your own mind is almost like not going to church at all; it's like taking a walk while sitting in one's own chair, which is like not walking at all.

By reason, Paine seems to mean that he is sometimes in possession of some magical power which enables him to have opinions before examining the "facts." Of course, if he only means that he understands the basic principles of logic, and that contradictions are absurd, and if he only means that beliefs supported by evidence are more reasonable than beliefs without evidence, then we could readily understand him and would in fact be in agreement. There is a sense in which anyone is free to hold any opinion that he wishes. No one wishes to put a student in jail because he adds two plus two and gets five, but he might flunk the course.

When Paine says "All national institutions of churches, whether Jewish, Christian, or Turkish, appear to me no other than human inventions, set up to terrify and enslave mankind and monopolize power and profit,"[7] this is a very interesting statement by Paine, but it tells us nothing about the origin of *all* churches. I presume Paine did not examine every church, nor could he know every motive that went into their establishment. Whether every church is a human invention ought to be an open question, at least to someone who confesses he believes in a Creator God. Such opinions however, are apparently beliefs which Paine has. Other people "have the same right to their belief as I have to mine."[8] Apparently, Paine does not know that all churches are simply human inventions. He thinks so, and he is against hypocrites, who believe one thing and say something else.[9] Who isn't?

The claim to revelation by Judaism, Christianity, and Islam is simply a pretense. "Revelation," as conceived of by Paine, when applied to religion, means something *immediately* communicated to man from God.

It is admittedly within God's power to reveal himself to a certain person, but after the initial event, revelation becomes hearsay; it is revelation only to the first person; to everyone else it is second hand information.[10]

The belief that Moses received the moral law from God or that Jesus was born of a virgin depends upon the acceptance of testimony. The notion that Jesus is the Son of God fits in with pagan mythology and was rejected by the Jews. "The Christian theory is little else than the idolatry of the ancient mythologists."[11] Jesus was a virtuous man, though similar systems of morality had been preached by others. The account of his resurrection and ascension and other Christian doctrines are frauds and fables, erected by Christian mythologists, fables which are derogatory to the almighty, inconsistent with his wisdom and contradictory to his power.

The writings of the Old and New Testament were collected by the mythologists of the Church. The Old Testament is, for the most part, a history of the grossest vices, a collection of paltry tales, more like the word of a demon, than of God; the books of the New Testament are no more trustworthy; they contain disagreements, and are anecdotal.

The true word of God is the creation we behold. The universe is governed by fixed and unalterable laws, which are discovered by man in the sciences.[12] "The Almighty Lecturer, by displaying the principles of science in the structure of the universe, has invited man to study and to imitate."

The nature that Paine saw was not that of tooth and claw, of the survival of the fittest; it was one from which man could learn of God's munificence to all "to be kind to each other."[13]

It is not necessary to repeat every detailed answer that has been given.[14] Paine's argument stands or falls with deism in general. The allegations against the trustworthiness of the biblical text will be considered, however, in this chapter.

The discussion of Chapter Eight on miracles also constitutes in part a Christian answer to Paine's assertions; he has no arguments, the latter require evidence. It is here sufficient to note that in the eighteenth century the existence of an intelligent author of nature, and a natural governor of the world was not at issue. There was then, as there is now, an ever increasing conviction that Christianity was a fit subject for ridicule.

2. *The Analogy of Religion of Joseph Butler*

Joseph Butler in his *Analogy of Religion* sought to prove there is strong evidence for the truth of Christianity, and that it is at least impossible to prove that Christianity is false. His *Analogy* seeks to answer the deists by applying analogical reasoning to religion. It of course assumes premises which deists were willing to admit.

Butler held that degrees of likeness between things or events yield probable evidence which in distinction to demonstrative evidence admits of degrees and produces a presumption, an opinion, or a full conviction. To an infinite intelligence, no possible object of knowledge is merely probable, but for finite creatures "probability is the very guide of life."

For anyone who presupposes the existence of an author of nature, the analogy between the system of revelation and the known course of nature makes it probable that they have the same author, and to the extent that the teachings of religion are shown to be like the course of nature, such analogies will either amount to a practical proof of their truth or will serve to answer objections against them.

Butler answers the objection to the doctrine that mankind has been appointed to live in a future state by showing that there is no reason to hold that death destroys living agents, or even suspends their powers of reflection. It is rather likely that we shall live on in a future state where everyone shall be rewarded and punished. We are now governed in our present life in such a manner that one course of action is followed by the reward of pleasure, and another by punishment of pain. It is not incredible to suppose that the future will be like the past, and that an infinite being is a righteous governor, who will continue to punish and reward men in exact proportion to their virtues or vices, to their personal merits or demerits.

The principles of a moral government are discernible in nature, so that the final judgment of man, in terms of distributive justice, differs only in degree from what we now experience. There is a strong presumption that our present life is a probation for a future state, and that we are now under God's moral government, and must later give an account of our actions, both in our natural and our moral capacity.

The light of nature accepted by deists in nowise minimizes the importance of Christianity and the necessity of revelation. That revelation is not useless is shown by the condition of men in the heathen world, by man's skepticism in matters of importance, and by the general ignorance and inattention of men. Even if it were possible for man to reason out the whole system of natural religion, there is no probability that he would, and he would still need to be reminded of it. The very best of men are in need of supernatural instruction.

In answer to the deists, Butler argues that to minimize the importance of the Christian revelation is to forget that it has been given by God, and that in addition to restating the truths of natural religion with increased light attested to by the authority of miracles and prophecy, it also contains a record of what is not discoverable by reason, namely, a disclosure of the particular dispensation of God's providence in the salvation of a fallen humanity, enacted by the Son and the Holy Spirit.

The disclosure of God's special dealings with men places man under the moral obligation to render worship to our Sanctifier, our Mediator and the Holy Spirit. Such duties cannot be neglected with impunity.

Butler argued that Christianity is credible to reason. For there is no presumption against revelation in general, on the ground that it is not discovered by reason or experience, since many things in the natural and moral system of the world are beyond our natural faculties. There is also no reason to hold that everything that is unknown must be like what is known. Nor is there a presumption against the miraculous character of revelation. The power exercised to make a world at the beginning, before there was a course of nature, could be further extended to make a revelation. And even after nature received its appointed course, there is no presumption against the occasional occurrence of miraculous interpositions.

Butler maintained that there are, as a matter of fact, no valid objections against the Christian revelation. Objections against Christianity are based upon the supposition that we possess *a priori* knowledge as to what God's revealed dispensation ought to be, a knowledge that we do not even possess with respect to the natural governance of the world.

Butler contends that the situation with regard to revelation is analogous to that of natural information. We have no *a priori* knowledge of what God will permit us to know, of the means to be used, or of the degree of evidence it will have.

The real issue, as Butler saw it, is not whether the Christian revelation is what we might have expected God to reveal, but whether or not it is real revelation. The authority of Scripture can be overturned if, and only if, it can be shown that there is absolutely no proof of the miracles originally wrought to attest its authority, that there is nothing miraculous in its success, and that it contains no prophecy of events that human wisdom could not forsee.

Butler held that serious objections to Christianity are not forthcoming. If objections are to be made they must be made against the evidence for Christianity. For the analogy of nature makes it highly credible that if a revelation is to be made, it must contain many things different from what might be expected. Christianity is a scheme that is beyond our comprehension; it is not to be judged by reason. We do not have sufficient knowledge to protest against its wisdom, goodness or justice.

The presence of a divine mediator between God and man is, moreover, in accordance with the analogy of nature. Our life and its blessings are due to others. Prior to revelation, however, we have no means of knowing whether a mediator was necessary, or how the work of redemption was to be accomplished.

Even doubt puts man on trial, for it presupposes some evidence. Many of our difficulties are our own fault, due to inattention to the evidence, and an overconcern with objections. The man of ordinary ability is capable of being convinced of the truth of both natural and revealed religion.

Christianity is, however, not established solely by meeting objections against it. There is positive evidence for it. The two most direct and fundamental proofs of Christianity are the miracles and the prophecies recorded in the Scriptures.

The accounts of miracles are recorded in books which, until proved to the contrary, are to be regarded as genuine history. From its inception Christianity was accepted upon the basis of miracles, and thus differs from all other religions. We shall see that its success constitutes evidence of the actuality of the miracles recorded, for unless they were fully convinced of the truth of miracles, the Apostles and their contemporaries would not have undergone the sufferings and death incurred by their belief in miracles.

One form of evidence is human testimony, and even when marked by enthusiasm, testimony is not overthrown, unless there is incredibility in the things attested or contrary testimony. The evidence of testimony can be destroyed either by a proof or a probability that the witnesses are incompetent to judge the facts to which they bear witness, or that they are under some indirect pressure in giving evidence. Neither case is likely in Christianity. Because of its importance, people would not want to be deceived themselves and the obligations to truthfulness would prevent them from wishing to deceive others.

Collateral evidence may also be adduced from the character of the Christian revelation, from its content, and from facts relating to it. Butler admits, however, that it is easier to attack Christianity than to defend it, for it is easier to assult a single point than to accumulate the whole mass of evidence in its defense. However, when the positive evidence for Christianity is considered in mass, and the objections against it are carefully considered, as well as the practical consequences of its denial, then if complete satisfaction as to its truth is not given, the most extreme scepticism cannot reach further than a middle position between complete satisfaction of the truth of Christianity and complete satisfaction of its falsity. Whenever the proper evidence for Christianity is presented and considered, the sceptic can not avoid the serious apprehension that Christianity might be true, although he may still doubt whether it be so. As Butler states: "If this be a just account of things, and yet men go on to vilify or disregard Christianity, which is to talk and act as if they had a demonstration of its falsehood; there is no reason to think they would alter their behavior to any purpose, though there were a demonstration of its truth."[15]

Butler's *Analogy* is significant as an attempt to stem the tide of deism and scepticism with respect to the reasonableness of the Christian faith. Its argument exerted considerable influence upon orthodox Christians and commanded and continues to command the respect and attention of its serious opponents.[16]

Its force depends in part upon the acceptance of the premise of the deists that God is the author of nature. Before considering further the Christian claim that his faith is supported by evidence, we shall examine several more recent attempts to render faith in revelation incredible. The question may still arise as to whether everything possible has in fact been said against revealed religion. The question remains as to whether we have treated the deist fairly. Admittedly no treatment of religion can ever be complete and exhaustive, but the objection might be raised that we have thus far failed to do justice to the arguments against biblical religion that purport to show that the Bible is an untrustworthy document, filled with errors and contradictions.

3. *The Trustworthiness of the Biblical Documents*

What is frequently overlooked in all such discussion is that the investigator is never neutral in his approach to the biblical text. For he is already either a complete *subjectivist* or an *objectivist* prior to his investigation of the Scriptures. Anyone who does not believe in an omnipotent God can never believe in a special act of God, that is, in a miracle. If the miracle of divine revelation is ruled out as impossible by the subjectivist, then it is a foregone conclusion that predictive prophecy and supernatural acts will also be rejected. The complete or radical subjectivist approaches the biblical text as he does any other book because he believes that it is like any other book. This is of course precisely the point at issue. It is circular to approach the biblical text with the presupposition of subjectivism and then to pretend that the results of the investigation objectively prove subjectivism, for such conclusions are at least partially the result of an *a priori* rejection of the supernatural.

It is hardly neutral to approach the Old Testament as Robert H. Pfeiffer does in the following opening passage of his book *Introduction to the Old Testament.*[17]

> The Old Testament owes its origin primarily to the religious aspirations of the Jews. . . .Developing from a purely national worship of a tribal god into a monotheistic religion with universal appeal, Judaism never lost its nationalistic character and canonized writings whose appeal was primarily patriotic or literary, besides genuinely devotional literature.

209

It is, therefore, not surprising that in connection with the book of Daniel, Pfeiffer later writes:

This traditional theory, by accepting the book at its face value, necessarily presupposes the reality of the supernatural and the divine origin of the revelations it contains. Such miracles as the revelation to Daniel of the details of Nebuchadnezzar's dream and their meaning (2:19, 30, 31 ff.), the divine deliverance of the three confessors from the fiery furnace (3:24-28) and of Daniel from the lions (6:22-24) and a hand without a body writing a message on a wall (5:5) lie outside the realm of historical facts. Similarly the correct prediction in the sixth century of the course of history down to the second century (2:31-43) belongs to the realm of the supernatural. Historical research can deal only with authenticated facts which are within the sphere of natural possibilities and must refrain from vouching for the truth of supernatural events. In a historical study of the Bible, convictions based on faith must be deemed irrelevant, as belonging to subjective rather than objective knowledge.[18]

Such an approach underlies much of the present day so-called neutral and scientific approach to the entire Bible. A method is adopted which rules out the authenticity of any record of what is miraculous, and then, lo and behold, the modern investigation of the Bible discovers there are difficulties in "understanding" the Bible.[19]

The subjectivist has no other alternative than to reject biblical accounts of miracles. If he is critical and honest, however, he ought to relinquish his claim to neutrality.

Pfeiffer simply assumes the subjectivist thesis about the religion of the Old Testament. Of course, if the miracle-events depicted as occurring did not happen, the historian ought not to be concerned with them. But how does anyone know that such events could never happen? If the biblical God exists, then they could have occurred and they could then be accepted by the historian.

Higher criticism of the Bible need not be destructive. For it can corroborate and illuminate what is found in the biblical texts. However, the critic such as Bultmann who assumes that the supernatural elements of the Bible are to be *demythologized* ought first to prove that the Bible contains myths. Of course if there is no God, then God could not have acted in the course of historical events, and all such claims to the contrary are false. But whether man created God in man's image is, as we have seen, the central problem of the philosophy of religion. Whether the Old Testament owes its origin to God, as Christians and Orthodox Jews believe, or whether it owes its origin "primarily to the religious aspirations of the Jews" is precisely the point in question.

Pfeiffer has told us that "historical research can deal only with the authenticated facts which are within the sphere of natural possibilities and must refrain from vouching for the truth of supernatural events." The issues that are raised by such a statement are simply not dealt with in most biblical criticism. What does it mean to state that historical research can only deal with natural possibilities? Are there no other possibilities? If there are no other possibilities, does one know this? Where is the evidence? Perhaps Pfeiffer's statement is not a proposition that is meant to be true. It may simply be a proposal disguised as a proposition. Maybe he simply means to say "Let us call what deals with 'natural possibilities' historical research." Such a proposal could then simply be followed or rejected. Or again perhaps the statement is simply a conceptual definition in which Pfeiffer tells us what he means by "historical research." Someone else might mean something different.

If there are no possibilities other than natural ones, then Pfeiffer's restriction makes sense, but if there are "supernatural events" then it is possible to examine the record of those who were witnesses to such events. It makes little difference what such "research" is called, the point is that such investigation can yield objective knowledge that is neither "irrelevant" nor "subjective."

There have been many changes in Old Testament criticism in recent decades. It is impossible to discuss this field without oversimplifying. On detailed questions there is no longer a consensus of opinion. The reconstruction of the history of Israel's religion in terms of Hegelian philosophy and the documentary hypothesis[20] as expressed by Wellhausanism is scarcely found in its classical form.[21] The documentary hypothesis itself is frequently modified or abandoned and where it is held it is not used to support a neat pattern of the evolution of Israel's religion.[22]

This does not mean, however, that biblical critics have become more critical of their own philosophical presuppositions. There is in some circles a greater recognition of the necessity of permitting the ancient sources to speak for themselves.[23] But the text is frequently marred by the reading into it of such current movements as existentialist philosophy.[24] It is seldom realized that the Scriptures are, as far as anyone *knows,* just what the authors claimed them to be. Anyone who follows the laws of evidence used in our courts of law can intelligently presume with Robert Dick Wilson:

> That the prima facie evidence of the documents of the Old Testament is to be received as true until it shall have been proved false. I hold, further, that the evidence of manuscripts and versions of the Egyptian, Babylonian, and other documents outside the Bible confirms the prima facie evidence of the Biblical documents in general both as to text and meaning; and that this text and meaning cannot be corrected or changed simply in order to be brought in harmony with the opinions of men of our generation. To demand that we should verify every statement of any ancient document (or modern for that matter) before we can reasonably believe it, is demanding the impossible.[25]

Pfeiffer is correct that to accept the book of Daniel "at its face value, necessarily presupposes the reality of the supernatural and the divine origin of the revelations it contains." It is, of course, the reality of the supernatural that Jews and Christians presuppose and which subjectivists in religion do not.

Anyone who does not accept the supernatural cannot consider himself a Christian or a Jew in any historical sense of the term. For to deny the supernatural is to deny

212

the very essence of the Judaism and Christianity that is found in the Old and New Testaments.

Biblical criticism does not necessarily afford any evidence in support of the subjectivist thesis. Lower criticism or textual criticism simply investigates the text of a document in order to determine its truth and original form. Higher criticism begins where lower criticism ends. Upon the assumption that the correct text has been determined, "the higher critic seeks to ascertain whether the claims which are made regarding it, by the document itself or by other evidence which bears upon it, are well grounded in fact, whether its alleged authorship and date are correct, whether its statements are trustworthy and credible."[26] The higher critic who simply eliminates the supernatural is uncritical as long as he pretends to be neutral with respect to philosophical and religious assumptions. We are not suggesting that the subjectivist in religion can approach the Bible with the presuppositions of the objectivist, but whether one is a subjectivist or an objectivist is no neutral matter.

Biblical higher criticism "is not in itself destructive; it can confirm and illuminate the biblical text just as well as it can cast doubt upon it or devaluate it. Insofar as historical and literary evidence can be used to find out exactly what the Bible means and to remove difficulties in understanding it, the study is beneficial. If it has been harmful, the fault is that of the critic rather than the method." . . .[27]

The scholar is at liberty to search for evidence, to classify, and to interpret it. In investigating the historicity and trustworthiness of the Scriptures, the purpose for which they were written must always be considered. "The writers of the Bible did not include more than their purpose of writing demanded, nor did they explain contemporary phenomena for the benefit of scholars in the twentieth century. . . ."[28]

Because the Bible does not accord with every bit of historical or scientific information that we possess does not necessitate the conclusion that the Bible is incorrect. All the necessary evidence may simply not be available.

> The narratives of the Bible do not pretend to give a complete account of all the events that took place, nor even to deal exhaustively with the phenomena that concern them most.... Many statements of the Scriptures cannot be corroborated because they have hitherto remained the sole witness to the sole facts of which they speak, but they need not consequently be regarded with suspicion. As new discoveries enlarge the knowledge of the ancient world, they tend to confirm rather than contradict the Bible.[29]

In the middle of the last century, the Tübingen school of New Testament criticism, headed by F. C. Baur, utilized philosophical presuppositions to reach the conclusion that the Gospels and the book of Acts did not exist before the thirties of the second century A.D.[30]

The evidence for the historical authenticity of the New Testament documents is, however, greater than that of any other ancient document. The New Testament was complete or substantially complete by about A.D. 100, the majority of its writings being finished twenty to forty years earlier. There are about 4,000 Greek manuscripts of the New Testament in whole or in part, the best of which go back to about A.D. 350.[31] We have only nine or ten good manuscripts of Caesar's *Gallic War*, the oldest of which is 900 years later than Caesar's day; of the 142 books of Livy's *Roman History*, only 35 survive in about twenty MSS, only one of which contains fragments as old as the fourth century; of Tacitus' (A.D. 100) fourteen books of histories, four and a half survive; of his *Annals*, ten in full, and a part of two others survive, the text of which depends on two manuscripts, one of the 9th century, the other of the 11th. Thucydides' history (460-400 B.C.) and that of Herodotus also survive in a few manuscripts belonging to around A.D. 900. "Yet no classical scholar would listen to an argument that the authenticity of Herodotus or Thucydides is in doubt because the earliest MSS of their works which are of any use to us are over 1300 years later than the originals."[32]

In addition to the two excellent 4th century MSS of the New Testament, the earliest of some thousands, we have considerable fragments 100 to 200 years earlier. The Chester Beatty biblical papyri consists of eleven codices, three of which contain most of the New Testament writings. Two of these belong to the first half of the third century, and the third to the second half of the third century. Other papyrus fragments are dated not later than A.D. 150. The earliest fragment of John is dated in the reign of Hadrian (A.D. 117-138), so that the latest Gospel which was written, according to tradition between A.D. 80 and 100. at Ephesus, circulated in Egypt within forty years after.

In addition to the early manuscripts and fragments, the historical authenticity of the New Testament documents is evident from the early church fathers whose works afford evidence that they were acquainted with most of the books of the New Testament.[33]

The great number of manuscripts enables the textual critic to correct the errors made by copyists, so that no material question of historical fact or doctrine is affected by various readings. In the words of Sir Frederick Kenyon:

> The interval then between the dates of original composition and the earliest extant evidence becomes so small as to be in fact negligible, and the last foundation for any doubt that the Scriptures have come down to us substantially as they were written has now been removed. Both the authenticity and the general integrity of the books of the New Testament may be regarded as finally established.[34]

The books of the New Testament did not become authoritative because they were included in a list of canonical books by the Church, but they later were included in a list because they had always been regarded by Christians as revelation. When disputes arose, and one or two books were questioned, it then became necessary for Christians to state which books had apostolic authority.[35]

It is not necessary for our purposes to enter into the question as to the sources of the Gospels.

> The evidence indicates that the written sources of our Synoptic Gospels are not later than c. A.D. 60;

some of them may even be traced back to notes taken of our Lord's teaching while His words were actually being uttered. The oral sources go back to the very beginning of Christian history. We are, in fact, practically all the way through in touch with the evidence of eyewitnesses . . . .[36]

There has been much controversy concerning the fourth Gospel. The traditional view, held with few exceptions until the 18th century, conforms to the second century testimony of Justin Martyr, Tatian, and Irenaeus. It assumes that the Gospel was written by John, the apostle, in his extreme old age at Ephesus. Some scholars of the nineteenth century thought they discovered that the Gospel of John was written by an unknown Greek who lived in Egypt in the middle of the second century. The fourth Gospel was not regarded as authoritative or historical in content, but rather as a fusion of Greek philosophical speculation and Jewish Messianism.

Today both external and internal evidence point to the traditional view; there is less objection to ascribing the fourth Gospel to the disciple of Jesus.[37] The internal evidence reveals an author who was an eyewitness, with an accurate knowledge of Palestine, a thorough acquaintance with Jewish customs and law, and with an understanding of the events he records. The external evidence attests to its early date; Ignatius who was martyred around 115, alludes to it; Justin Martyr (c.A.D. 130) quote it, Tatian (c.A.D. 170) includes it in his *Diatessaron*.

Several second-century writers, Irenaeus, Clement of Alexandria, Theophilus of Antioch, Tertullian, and Herocleon, attest to the general ascription of the gospel to John the apostle.[38]

A more serious charge is often made that the Christian religion is the result of the genius of the Apostle Paul. The Christian explanation of the relationship between Paul and Jesus accepts what Paul presupposes about Jesus, namely, that he was a heavenly being who entered human history to suffer and die for the sins of mankind, so that Paul merely recognized as divine one who really was divine.

216

Jesus of Nazareth, according to the liberal view, was the greatest of the children of men. His greatness centered in his consciousness of standing toward God in the relation of son to Father. . . .He urged men, not to take him as the object of their faith, but only to take him as an example for their faith; not to have faith in him, but to have faith in God like his faith.[39]

Under the influence of such men as Wrede and Gunkel, Gospel criticism underwent a transformation, and the unity between Paul and Jesus was broken, and Paul becomes an innovator of a religion of redemption, and the attempt was made to find the origin of Paul's transcendent Christology in specific segments of Judaism current in Paul's day.

Wilhelm Bousset and Richard Reitzenstein suggested that the key to understanding Paul was to be found within the Hellenistic mystery religions.

After a period of time, however, the so-called parallels were unable to make very much impression. Especially in connection with Christology, the redemptive facts proclaimed by Paul and the Hellenistic mystical cults were so formally and materially different that one can hardly speak of parallels, let alone speak of genetic connections. To mention only a few points: whereas Paul speaks of the death and resurrection of Christ and places it in the middle of history, as an event which took place before many witnesses, in the recent past, the myths of the cults in contrast, cannot be dated; they appear in all sorts of variations, and do not give any clear conceptions. In short they display the timeless vagueness characteristic of real myths. Thus the myths of the cults, even though they speak of the death and resurrection of the deity, for the majority at least, are nothing but depictions of annual events of nature in which nothing is to be found of the moral, voluntary, redemptive substitutionary meaning, which for Paul is the content of Christ's death and resurrection was proclaimed by Paul as a forensic and ethical emancipation. The entire meaning of the mystery religions is expressed in the *athanasia*, the conquering of natural death, the escaping of the power of fate, and the return of the divine-in-man to its origin and end. Whereas, in the view of Paul, faith and repentance occupies an indispensable place, within the mystery religions, it is

217

entirely superfluous, or insofar as it can be spoken of, it bears an entirely different character: The magical rules everything. Paul speaks of walking in love, humility, mercy, and good works, whereas a physical, dualistic world view is at the foundation of the mystery religions, and salvation is accomplished by the transfer of a divine vital force, expressed sometimes in asceticism and at other times in the most unrestrained libertinism. And we still have said nothing of the cleft between the material employed in the myths of the cults, in order to portray the re-living of the deity, and the preaching of the passion, the death, and resurrection of Christ. When still in 1933 Lietzmann appeals to the Isis mysteries to prove that the conception of dying with Christ and rising again with him (Rom. 6, vs. 3, 4) could not have developed out of the Jewish purification ceremonies, but must be viewed as an "Hellenistic material," one must then remember that at the foundation of the Isis mysteries, the myth of the cult speaks first of the murder of Osiris, by his brother Seth, after which his dead body is cut and hacked into pieces. And finally, when the scattered limbs of Osiris are again brought together, from all directions, the re-living of Osiris takes place, and his identification with Isis follows. It is no wonder that the apologist Theophilus of Antioch already made fun of a comparison of the resurrection of Christ with the reliving of Osiris, a conception apparently already introduced in his own time.[40]

A more recent attempt to explain the religion of Paul has been followed by Rudolph Bultmann. In agreement with Albert Schweitzer, Bultmann assumes that the preaching of Paul and Jesus has a common basis in an eschatological view. Jesus looked forward to the kingdom of God and the Messianic office; Paul viewed Jesus' death as the arrival of the new era. The entire New Testament theology is thus to be explained in terms of the entrance into the eschatological situation. Paul now appears as a gnostic existentialist. The gospel according to Bultmann is concerned with the decision before which mankind is placed by Jesus. It is supposed to be stripped of all supernatural elements; these are simply discarded as mythology, the very issue in question. The faith of the church simply expressed in mythological concepts the choice that man has between clinging to the visible things of the world, and existential freedom.[41] Jesus provides an escape from the pessimistic anthropology of existentialist philosophy; he is the example, the preacher. Ridderbos correctly points out that Bultmann's view is simply a speculative rejection of Christianity; it need not concern us further here.

The writings of Paul are not an alien or speculative addition to the original gospels but are simply an explication and consequence of it. Whether they are accepted or rejected depends in the final analysis upon whether one finds Christianity credible and worthy of acceptance, a subject to which we shall return in the final chapter, but first we shall consider two further objections to revealed religion, the alleged problem of evil, and some recent developments in philosophical theology.

4. *The Problem of Evil*

Subjectivists often take the presence of "evil" as evidence for their position.[42] The objectivist is frequently challenged by statements and questions such as:

> The presence of evil in the universe is incompatible with the existence of God.
>
> The existence of a wise, omnipotent, loving heavenly power is incompatible with the evil condition of the world.
>
> How can a good God permit the anguished cry of a single innocent child?
>
> How can there be evil men like Eichmann, Hitler and Khrushchev, if God is in the heavens?

Such sentences, however, either make no sense or they presuppose the points at issue in such a manner that they in no wise constitute evidence against biblical religion.

There are, of course, those who would deny that there is an objective basis for religion and also deny that there is evil in the world. There can be no problem of reconciling God and evil if the reality of both are denied. There can also be no problem of reconciliation if evil is thought to be real and the reality of God is denied, nor if the reality of evil is denied and God alone is thought to be real. The problem of theodicy, of reconciling the reality of God and the reality of evil occurs if, and only if, there is a dualism between two ultimate metaphysical principles, namely, God and evil.

Consider the first of the preceding statements: "The presence of evil in the universe is incompatible with the existence of God." What is here meant by the term "evil"? Does the reader understand this sentence?

To understand what the term "evil" means, we first need to discover how people do in fact use it. It is easy to assume that the above statement is readily understood and that everyone understands the same thing by it. The term "evil" is frequently used to refer to what is detrimental to or destructive of living organisms. Evil may be identified with whatever causes or contributes to suffering or it may simply be equated with physical suffering and/or death.

The term "evil" is used in a second sense when it is said that a particular person is evil or that a certain act is evil. Here the term is used in a *moral sense* to describe an act which *ought* not to have been performed or to describe what is judged to be an undesirable character.

Now in addition to the physical and moral senses in which the word evil is used, the term is thought to have a "metaphysical" sense. The question is asked, What is evil? And then when such answers are given that cancer is evil because it destroys human life, that Hitler was evil because he murdered innocent people, the questioner snaps back, "But that is not what I want to know. I want to know what *evil* is." And both the questioner and the answerer do not know what to say. They are both puzzled, profoundly puzzled. "Maybe evil is a privation," says the one. No says the other, "It's equally ultimate with the good." "Ah," says the third, looking very wise, "How is the presence of evil compatible with an all powerful God?" And so on and on it goes. We chase the word "evil," looking for a thing behind a word, a game of hide-and-seek-a-thing-behind-a-word, a metaphysical scrabble, a cosmic grab bag. Step up and pull out a substance in return for a substantive! Hurry, it may be your last chance.

Consider a parallel situation in which the question is asked, What is strength? The answer is given that John has strength, because he can lift more horseshoes than any other blacksmith. Other similar answers are given in which even greater feats are mentioned. The questioner understands every answer. He, too, knows how to use the word "strength," but he still wants to know what is strength? What does he want to know that he doesn't already know? Why is he puzzled? Would he know the answer if someone could tell him? Why does he keep asking, What is strength? Perhaps he's curious. It's very odd to be curious unless you are curious *about* something.

What is one curious about when he asks, What is evil? The question makes no sense, unless the questioner is satisfied with such answers as: Death is evil, pain is evil, Hitler is evil. Of course, the word evil may be given new usages, but evil is not a thing or event over and above the things and events that we experience. The word may be given a meaning when it is used to refer to certain acts, events, and people, but it has no meaning when the word "evil" is used to refer to *evil*. For evil is not a thing distinct from certain concrete states of affairs.

Upon closer examination the sentence, "The presence of evil in the universe is incompatible with the existence of God," makes no sense if "evil" is used in its so-called metaphysical sense. For the term "evil" here simply fails to designate. It is as if one were to say: "The presence of boojums is incompatible with the existence of God," without first explaining what is meant by boojum.

If the word "evil" is used in its physical or moral sense, the sentences under consideration are at least intelligible. It then remains to be seen whether physical suffering, death, and men like Hitler are incompatible with the God of biblical revelation. Do pain and evil men constitute evidence against the God of the Bible?

221

In what sense is physical and moral evil incompatible with the God of biblical religion? Is there anything about physical and moral evil that necessitates the non-existence of the biblical God? If so, what is it? Or, what is there about the nature of the biblical God which would necessitate a universe without physical and moral evil?

It is to be noted first of all that unless the biblical God is accepted, moral evil is reducible to likes and dislikes. For unless God is the author of moral norms, what is meant by saying that "Hitler is evil"?

There are three possible sources of moral standards: God, man, and physical nature. If God is eliminated man and nature alone remain. Moral standards or norms can then be derived either from man or nature. It is difficult to see how nature can help. Neither rocks, rivers, rattlesnakes, planets, plants, nor even little fish can tell man what he ought to do. What is "nature"? The word is sometimes hypostatized and used as though it referred to something other than sticks and stones, "Mother Nature!" We have already seen that persons alone are capable of free conscious, purposive behavior. To formulate a norm as to what ought to be done requires nothing less than a person.

Unless nature is personified, when God is rejected, man alone is the standard of what is right and wrong. Since men differ in what they want, there are then as many possible standards as there are human differences. The terms "right" and "wrong" may then be used to refer to the feelings that a particular person has with respect to a particular action, what pleases the individual or groups of individuals. "If there is no God, then in a moral sense, all things are possible." Of course, the values that are then adopted may be the same values that were in vogue when men thought God existed. In business, honesty may still be the best policy; stealing, lying, murder, rape, and pillage do not help everyone, and without God one can still live as though God had said, "Thou shalt not." When a particular individual or group of individuals persists in acting contrary to the norms accepted by the majority, or by those in power, sanctions may be imposed against the non-

222

conformists. To say that Eichmann or Hitler were wrong means that according to the usually accepted standards of Western society, Eichmann and Hitler were wrong. They violated the commonly held moral norms. In other words, "We don't like Hitler and Eichmann." "Why?" "Because they killed people without any reason, and we don't like killing because after people are killed, they are dead." "But what is wrong with dead people?" "We like them alive better." The problem, of course, was that Eichmann didn't, a slight difference of opinion between Eichmann and six million Jews.

The point is that unless moral standards have the approval and sanction of God, unless God is the moral lawgiver, there are no unchanging moral standards. Moral evil is simply what certain people do not like. Most people do not like suffering and death, so in most cases, moral evil will be identified with physical evil.

If moral evil is reducible to what Adam and his brothers don't like, it is difficult to see how "the presence of evil in the universe is incompatible with the existence of God." For if "evil" is used in its moral sense, it then means that what Adam and his brothers don't like is incompatible with the existence of God. The likes and dislikes of Adam and his kinfolk do not necessitate the existence or non-existence of anything.

If God is denied, what remains is personal likes and dislikes and physical evil, that is suffering and death. What does it mean, however, to call suffering and death evil? Here, too, if God is denied, evil is what most men other than sadists do not like. What else can "evil" here mean other than what people do not like? And what is there about human likes and dislikes that is incompatible with the biblical God?

Perhaps what is really meant in saying that the evil condition of the world is incompatible with an omniscient, omnipotent God is simply the "modest" admission that "if I were God I would do things differently." The world is a place in which physical death and suffering occur. It is not a place where there are anguished innocent cries, not if biblical revelation is true.

The Bible does have an answer for the presence of physical suffering and death. Death and pain are abnormal. They are God's punishment for man's disobedience. The subjectivist may neither like nor believe the biblical answer. But then what answer does he have? To die is as normal as to live. The very presence of living organisms is simply an accident. The death of physical organisms has no meaning. Man does not like to die; he does not like pain either. The universe could not care less.

The Bible does have an explanation of "evil." It denies metaphysical evil; it regards physical pain and death as the after effects of man's own act of disobedience. But, as we have seen in Chapter 5, biblical religion is concerned with sin and redemption, not simply with the effects of sin.

Men like Hitler and death and pain do not constitute evidence against the God of biblical revelation; the latter provides rather a basis for the condemnation of Hitler, and it offers an escape from the consequences of sin, namely, eternal life.[43]

5. Some Recent Developments[44]

Our consideration of objections to revealed religion would certainly be inadequate if no mention were made of recent discussions of our problem. Some older forms of logical positivism simply ruled out the possibility of "religious knowledge" together with metaphysics.[45] It was thought to be absurd to state that "God exists" and equally absurd to state that "God does not exist," and until recently very little room was allowed for discussion. At present, however, there is throughout the English-speaking world, considerable discussion of religious questions. The background of this discussion is provided by Alfred Jules Ayer's now famous book *Language, Truth and Logic*. We shall begin, therefore, by stating Ayer's argument of 1936. We shall then briefly set forth certain more recent developments that have to a large extent been provoked by Ayer's original position.[46]

Ayer's original accusation that religious utterances are nonsensical stemmed from his general attitude toward metaphysics. The latter was to be disposed of, not by a criticism of the way in which it comes in being, but by a criticism of the nature of its statements.[47]

The metaphysician and, for Ayer, the theologian utter sentences which do not measure up to the standards which alone constitute a sentence as "literally significant." The condition that every sentence must meet, if it is to be regarded as a significant proposition, is the criterion of verifiability in principle. A sentence is factually significant, if and only if, there are specifiable observations which warrant its acceptance as true and its rejection as false. Unless a sentence is a tautology, it is devoid of sense, if there is no observation relevant to the determination of its truth and falsity. Thus for any proposition to be factual it must be an empirical hypothesis, i.e., it must be relevant to a future experience. Meaningful sentences either express tautologies or empirical hypotheses, but metaphysical sentences are neither tautologous, nor expressive of an empirical hypothesis; therefore, they are nonsensical.[48]

Any knowledge of God is precluded for Ayer by his objections to metaphysical sentences in general. To those who would prove demonstratively that God exists, the question can be asked, what are the premises for such a demonstration? If the conclusion that God exists is to be certain, the premises must also be certain, but if they are certain, then they are *a priori,* and if they are *a priori,* they are tautologies, and from a tautology, only a tautology can be deduced. It is not possible to deduce a statement about the existence of anything from *a priori* statement. And an empirical proposition can never be more than probable. Ayer is, however, not willing to admit that it is possible to prove that God probably exists. If it were probable that God existed, the statement would be an empirical hypothesis, from which certain experimental propositions could be deduced. And since there are no such experimental propositions, it follows that God cannot be said to exist even probably.[49]

For Ayer it is not meaningful to talk about God as a transcendent being who although knowable through certain empirical manifestations is, however, not to be defined solely in terms of such manifestations. Such talk is metaphysical talk, in which the term "God" is a metaphysical term, and statements about metaphysical terms are not genuine propositions. They cannot be true or false, they simply make no sense at all, i.e., they are nonsense.

Ayer believes his position to be incompatible with the atheist's and the agnostic's position, as well as with that of the believer. For it is as nonsensical to assert that God does not exist as it is to assert that he does. A statement that lacks significance cannot be significantly contradicted.

Even the agnostic makes the mistake of regarding the question as to whether or not God exists as a meaningful question, although he is not sure of the answer.

Some religious people may believe they can answer Ayer by agreeing with him that God's existence is not a matter of scientific proof. It might be argued that religion is a matter of faith in a being whose nature is mysterious, since God transcends our human understanding. But Ayer is not so easily put off, for he holds that to admit that something transcends the human understanding is to admit that it is unintelligible, and if it is unintelligible then it cannot be described significantly. And truth about any matter of fact must lead to verifiable propositions, capable of being incorporated into a system of such propositions. But for Ayer there are no religious sentences which meet his criterion of what is meaningful.

We shall return to Ayer's position in the final section of this chapter, but first it is necessary to set forth certain additional objections that have been made against the possibility of *meaningful religious discourse.*

To most Christians, it is reasonable to request that they be able to state what they mean and what they do not mean when they confess their faith.[50] Traditionally, when a Christian stated that he believed in God, he understood by

226

"God" a being who is necessary, in contrast to all other beings, which are contingent. God is traditionally thought of as his own being, and his own goodness. However, against those who hold that it is meaningful to state "God is his own goodness," the objection is raised that such a statement is simply bad grammar, a meaningless combination of words, because meaningful statements can be made, if and only if, the same word is not used as both an abstract and a common noun. It is quite legitimate to say either that "The people were very happy," or "The people's happiness was great," since both statements have the same meaning. But to say "God is his own goodness" is like saying "people are happiness." The term "God" in the expression "God is his own goodness" appears to refer to a person or thing of which qualities can be predicated, that is to say, the word "God" appears to be a proper noun. But to say that God is identical with that which is predicated of him is to use the same term as a proper noun and as an abstraction.

We can say nothing about God because we are unable to make sense when we talk about him. We are unable to attribute any quality to God *because of the limitations of our language.* It is not even possible to say that God exists, since existence is not a predicate that can be applied to things. To say something exists is not like saying that so-and-so has a property. For example, it is possible to say, "some cows moo," and to ascribe mooing to cows is to say something about them, but to say "some cows exist" is not to say something about cows; it is simply to say "there are cows." To say "some cows do not moo," is clear, but to say, "some cows do not exist" supposedly lacks any clear meaning.

The reasons for stating there is a God allegedly presuppose that the term "God" refers to a necessary being, whereas we can in fact speak solely of contingent beings. Existential statements are possible only with respect to what can be and not be. The notion of necessity can not be ascribed to anything which is. Propositions alone are necessary; things can never be necessary, any more than a square can be round.

It should at this point be clear that Ayer rejected religious statements as nonsensical primarily because they were metaphysical, while in recent discussion certain writers have stressed the alleged impossibility of religious utterances due to the limitations of our language. This does not mean, however, that everyone has now abandoned Ayer's demand that a sentence is factually significant if, and only if, certain observations would warrant its acceptance as true and its rejection as false. For it is possible to detect Ayer's influence at work in a recent discussion of the problem of *Theology and Falsification*, a discussion that occurred at Oxford in 1950 and 1951, and which is reprinted in *New Essays in Philosophical Theology*.

The discussion got under way by John Wisdom's article "Gods," in which a parable appears. The parable has been summarized by Anthony Flew as follows:[51]

> Once upon a time two explorers came upon a clearing in the jungle. In the clearing were growing many flowers and many weeds. One explorer says, "Some gardener must tend this plot." The other disagrees, "There is no gardener." So they pitch their tents and set a watch. No gardener is ever seen. "But perhaps he is an invisible gardener." So they set up a barbed-wire fence. They electrify it. They patrol with bloodhounds. (For they remember how H. G. Wells' *The Invisible Man* could be both smelt and touched though he could not be seen.) But no shrieks ever suggest that some intruder has received a shock. No, movements of the wire ever betray an invisible climber. The bloodhounds never give cry. Yet still the believer is not convinced. "But there is a gardener, invisible, intangible, insensible to electric shocks, a gardener who has no scent and makes no sound, a gardener who comes secretly to look after the garden which he loves." At last the sceptic despairs, "But what remains of your original assertion? Just how does what you call an invisible, intangible, eternally elusive gardener differ from an imaginary gardener or even from no gardener at all?"

The parable as interpreted by Flew illustrates that what starts out as an assertion is finally qualified to such an extent that its qualifications reduce it to a "picture preference."

Such utterances as "God has a plan," "God created the world," "God loves us as a father loves his children," appear at first to be cosmological assertions. But to assert any proposition, p, is equivalent to a denial of its negation, not p. Whenever there is any suspicion that an utterance is not really an assertion, one way of putting it to a test is to ask what could count against the truth of the utterance in question. For an utterance is not really an assertion unless it denies something. An utterance which does not deny anything does not assert anything either.

For Flew, Wisdom's parable illustrates that the believer's original utterance was so qualified that it did not assert anything. Nothing could count against it. The believer who would assert, for example, that "God loves us" ought to be able to state what would have to occur to disprove that "God loves us." Flew would thus have the believer state what would be evidence against an assertion as well as what would be evidence for it. The believer is not simply asked to give reasons for his faith, but he is also asked to specify what would be evidence against his faith. Flew's question is "What would have to occur or to have occurred to constitute for you a disproof of the love of God, or of the existence of God?"[52] The objection to religious utterance is that they are alleged to be compatible with every possible state of affairs. It is held that for an assertion to be an assertion it must make the claim that things stand in one way and not in another. And likewise any explanation must explain why one particular thing occurs and not something else.

Thus, whereas such older logical positivists as Ayer immediately ruled out theological statements as pseudo-statements, as nonsense, it is now fashionable first to ask how theological statements are verified? What would confirm them and what would refute them. The Christian may now be accused of holding two contradictory beliefs and of holding to both of them simultaneously, for he confesses his faith in a loving God while living in a heartless world.

The Christian's utterances are held to be incapable of falsification, since all contrary evidence of the love of God is simply qualified to the degree that nothing is allowed to count against God's love. The Christian refuses to recognize that every moral defect in the universe and every evil human act is the responsibility of God, since his omnipotence does not allow the Christian to say God would like to help but cannot, and his omniscience does not allow the Christian to say that God would help, if he only knew. "Indeed an omnipotent, omniscient God must be accessory before (and during) the fact of every human misdeed. . . .[53]

Yet for the Christian the statement that "God is love" is compatible with any state of affairs. No argument is allowed to count against it. As a result religious statements are held not to be fully meaningful. For while they appear to assert that such and such is in fact the case, they are permitted to be compatible with any and every possible condition. But utterances which do not "mark out" some one state of affairs are not really statements. In short to know what something means implies that we know what it does not mean. Thus to summarize what has been said, whereas Ayer rejected religious utterances because they were metaphysical, the present trend is to reject religious utterances either on the ground that the limitations of language do not permit us to assert them, or on the ground that they are incapable of falsification. It now remains for us to subject the position surveyed to criticism.

The older attack on religious statements, represented by Ayer, rejects such statements as "God exists" because they are metaphysical. The assumption is that any metaphysical statement is devoid of meaning because it is not verifiable.

It has been pointed out that Ayer's original position would lead to the rejection of certain generalizations made in science, and that it has, therefore, been made the subject of criticism and has undergone modifications, so that it is now regarded by many as a proposal or definition. Ayer, himself, in the introduction to the second edition of *Language, Truth, and Logic,* admits that the verification principle is not an empirical hypothesis, but a definition, which is, however, not entirely arbitrary.

Ayer is willing to distinguish between a "strong" and "weak" sense of verifiable: "a proposition is said to be verifiable in the strong sense of the term, if and only if its truth could be conclusively established in experience, but it is verifiable, in the weak sense, if it is possible for experience to render it probable."[54] Ayer now reformulates the principles of verification to be that any non-analytic statement that is literally meaningful must be directly or indirectly verifiable. It is directly verifiable "if it is either an observation statement, or is such that in conjunction with one or more observation statements it entails at least one observation statement which is not deducible from these other premises alone . . . ."[55] It is indirectly verifiable if, in "conjunction with certain other premises it entails one or more directly verifiable statements which are not deducible from these other premises alone; and secondly, that these other premises do not include any statement that is not either analytic, or directly verifiable, or capable of being independently established as indirectly verifiable".[56]

By permitting the "other premises" to include analytic statements, in the case of indirect verification Ayer would make room for scientific theories that do not designate anything observable.

"For while the statements that contain these terms may not appear to describe anything that anyone could ever observe, a dictionary may be provided by means of which they can be transformed into statements that are verifiable; and the statements that constitute the dictionary can be regarded as analytic."[57]

Metaphysical statements are still excluded by Ayer because they "do not describe anything that is capable, even in principle, of being observed, but also that no dictionary is provided by means of which they can be transformed into statements that are directly or indirectly verifiable."[58]

Thus Ayer's position in the second edition to his *Language, Truth, and Logic* is as hostile to what he calls metaphysics and theology as was the first edition. However, his hostility is now more readily seen to be a fact about Ayer's preferences rather than a fact about metaphysical statements. For Ayer admits the necessity of detailed analyses of particular metaphysical arguments if metaphysics is to be effectively eliminated, and he admits that his defense of the criterion of verifiability is the defense of a methodological principle; but if such be the case, why must anyone else adopt Ayer's methodogical principle? Mascall has correctly pointed out that Ayer's admission that particular metaphysical arguments need the support of detailed analysis before they can effectively be eliminated, reduces the verification principle to a generalization from experience, and as long as some metaphysical propositions remain unexamined, it is possible that one of them may turn out to be valid. Ayer now regards his principle of verification as a definition, and yet it is not arbitrary, or it is not supposed to be entirely arbitrary. But why is Ayer's criterion not arbitrary? Mascall remarks, "For the assertion that the principle is a definition makes it impossible to question its truth, while the assertion that it is not entirely arbitrary suggests that some ground for its assertion is to be found in experience."[59] "Ayer rapidly oscillates between a number of positions, treating the verification principles at one moment as a definition, at another as a truth of logic and at another as an empirically verified generalization . . . ."[60] Mascall concludes that to be convicted of this, is to make Ayer guilty of what he condemns in others. For Ayer's basic doctrine rests upon "the absolute distinction between truths of logic and statements of empirical fact."[61]

The verification principle is a deduction from Ayer's basic assumption that what is meaningful is, in the last analysis, to be defined solely in terms of some form of human experience. By secularizing the Christian doctrine of creation, man alone is thought to be the creative source of meaning. Man is freed from any obligation to recognize

232

his creaturehood, and what is not the creation of his own theoretical activity is at most regarded as probable.

Ayer absolutizes two special forms of scientific thought, the logical and the psychological. It is for this reason that he brands as meaningless any statement that is not a tautology or which is not directly or indirectly related to an observation report. This restriction of experience to what is directly or indirectly observable makes man's observations the origin of what is meaningful. It is itself the absolutization of an aspect of the fullness of our experience. The world exists whether it is experienced or not. It is not our observation of the world that makes it what it is, but it is what the world is that makes it possible for us to know it.

A truly "empirical" approach to any object employs a method that is suitable to the nature of that object. To assume that the only method that will yield knowledge is the method of observation, assumes that to be knowable is to be directly or indirectly observable. Such an assumption rules out the possibility of our knowing anything about what is not so observable. It fails to take into account the nature of theological statements. For the latter, in the case of Christian theology, are statements that occur within the aspect of faith. Their norm is not to be found in their verifiability in Ayer's sense, but in their conformity to the revealed word of God. Admittedly their truth is not demonstrable by an appeal to any present observable event. They are rather that by which the religious significance of all observable events are interpreted. To say that the statement "God exists" is meaningless because we cannot point to "God" simply begs the question. It assumes that what we can point to, the world, is ultimate, and that our experience legislates for what is, or at least what is knowable.

Ayer's own position, while pretending to be anti-metaphysical, is itself metaphysical. It presupposes that there is nothing, at least nothing knowable, that is not identical with some aspect of the natural world. Ayer rules out theological statements, because he has ruled out

233

a God that ultimately justifies them. Statements about
God are meaningless for Ayer because Ayer believes that
what is meaningful must ultimately derive its meaning
from man.

Ayer's position rests upon an *a priori* of faith; an *a
priori* which in apostasy from the God of revelation places
its trust in Man's own sovereign personality.

We have not tried to show that the content of Ayer's
faith is false. It is sufficient here simply to show that
Ayer's principle of verification is not a "neutral," "philosophical" or "scientific" assumption; it is rather a "dogma"
that Ayer happens to share with many others, a dogma
which fortifies Ayer's religious conviction that "thou shalt
have no other gods higher than Ayer," thou shalt not bow
down to them, nor serve them, for the dogma of human
autonomy is a jealous "God."

Much that has been said about Ayer is also true of the
more recent alleged impossibility of religious statements
due to the limitations of our language. A theory of
language does not occur in a vacuum, and the theory of
language that refuses to admit the possibility of statements about God presupposes a particular view about the
origin, nature, and the purpose of language, which in turn
rests upon a view of man, the world in which he lives, and
the origin of the world.

Either man is a creature of God or he is not. If he is
not, then it makes no sense for man to utter statements
about a non-existing creator. But if man is a creature of
God, then he was created by God with the power of speech
that is adequate for man to express his faith.

Gordon Clark deals with this problem by stating:
"If God created man in his own rational image and endowed him with the power of speech, then a purpose of
language, in fact, the chief purpose of language, would
naturally be the revelation of truth to man and the prayers
of man to God. . . . Language was devised by God, that is,
God created man rational for the purpose of theological
expression. Language is, of course, adaptable to sensory
description and the daily routine of life, but it is unneces-

234

sary to invent the problem of how sensory expressions can be transmuted into a proper method of talking about God."[62]

We need not fully agree with Clark that language has a chief purpose, but we can agree that it is unnecessary to invent the problem as to how sensory expressions can be transmuted into a proper method of talking about God. Such a difficulty arises when the linguistic aspect, together with sense perception, is absolutized and made the common denominator of all experience, so that the aspect of faith, in which religious utterances are made, is reduced to a matter of linguistics and sense experience.

It is of course true that when a Christian confesses his faith he does not give an exhaustive, precise, scientific definition of God, a definition in which all mystery is removed. Some Christians, at least, have always held that while there is no mystery in God, our definitions of God do not exhaust his inner nature. The assumption that we can say nothing about God because we cannot say everything begs the question.

If a person confesses his faith, he does not claim that he exhausts God in his definitions. Language is admittedly inadequate to express fully the nature of God. The God of the Bible can never be fully known by philosophical analysis. If we worship the biblical God, what we worship is not fully comprehensible, philosophically. It must be recognized that the very attempt to make God fully comprehensible is itself equivalent to a denial of the biblical God.

In other words, if the biblical God exists, then he is not fully known, which implies that any God that is fully known is not the biblical God. It has correctly been said that no creature can know all that is proper to God and no creature can give an exhaustive statement of all that God is.

Christianity does not necessarily claim to comprehend both the essence and the attributes of God; nor does it claim to know exhaustively all of God's attributes, nor to understand fully the relation in which these attributes stand to God, and the way in which God is related to the world.

The Christian holds that his knowledge of God is imperfect, but yet it is true as far as it goes. God really is what we believe him to be, so far as our idea of him is determined by the revelation which he has made of himself in his works, in the constitution of our nature, in his word, and in the person of his Son.

And yet even when the Christian exercises proper caution, his attempt to speak of God does not go unchallenged. For if he says that "God is a spirit, infinite, eternal, and unchangeable, in his being, wisdom, power, holiness, goodness and truth," he is still told that such a statement is bad grammar, a meaningless combination of words, like round square, cat no six, all mimsy were the slithy toes and the momeuraths outgrabe. We are not simply told that the statements that we make about God are false, we have become accustomed .to this; we are told rather that the attributes that we ascribe to God are pseudo-concepts, and the statements or judgments that we make about God in which such concepts appear are pseudo-judgments.

Let us try to gain some deeper insight into what is here meant. If I say, "This table is green," when in fact it is not green, the term "green" is not a pseudo-concept and the judgment, "This table is green" is not a pseudo-judgment, it is simply false. For while this table is not "green" the notion of "green" is a property which can be ascribed correctly to other states of affairs, such as grass. In fact, if we were to state that "the square root of 6 is very red," even though such a statement is preposterous, it would still not be a pseudo-statement, since some other things are very red.

Thus if the propositions of theology are pseudo-propositions, then theologians must be very confused indeed. For while they think they are making sense, they are in fact simply giving vent to feelings and attitudes, which they express in combination of words that have no meaning.

Such an attack can be countered by the simple answer that questions of existence are prior to questions of the meaning of words. The rules of grammar describe the way in which we speak in a given language, they do not determine *what is*.

There may have been a time when there was no human speech, and yet there were things that could have been described, if man had been present, but man's description does not constitute the nature of things.

A normal infant comes into the world with the potentiality of speech, and it reaches a stage in its development where it is capable of making any sound that a human being can make. From this point it goes on to imitate and learn the meaning of words, but its ability to speak and the limitation of the language it learns has no bearing upon the nature of the world. Likewise, man as such has entered a world that he did not make. And either this world of space and time is all that there is, or it is not. Either this world is "God" or it is not. God is the world or he is not. And the decision that is reached here is prior to any questions concerning our ability to describe God adequately.

When we say that "God is his own goodness," we confess our faith in a being beyond the contingent finite realm. To say that "God is his own goodness" is not to give an exhaustive definition of God. Admittedly our language is inadequate to describe God fully. Negatively, at least, the meaning of the expression is clear: we mean that there is no standard or source of goodness—no Platonic realm— upon which God is dependent, i.e., God is really God. The term "God" refers to that which is beyond our temporal world, to that which is the origin of all that we experience as temporal. The rules of grammar apply to a segment of human experience, they do not legislate for the universe.

Language ought not to be confused with reality. Either God exists or he does not. If God exists then he exists prior to and independently of our ability to signify what he is. The nature of the universe could only depend upon our ability to express it, if man were himself God. For the Christian our words are not the Word. The Word who became flesh is not subject to our words; the reverse is true. Our words and our rules of grammar ultimately depend

237

upon the Word that has dwelt among us, for it is he that hath made us and not we ourselves.

This brings us to our final criticism. It concerns the objection to religious discourse on the ground that religious statements are not capable of falsification, and are not assertions at all. Wisdom's parable is supposed to show that the believer qualifies what he asserts to the point that he does not assert anything.

In our judgment the demand that a religious statement be capable of immediate falsification in terms of immediate experience completely distorts the very nature of a religious statement, such as "God is love."

To meet this objection we must ask when a statement is properly qualified by the adjective "religious." We have seen in Chapter One that statements dealing with the religious experience of a person may presuppose religious statements, but are not themselves religious. A proper religious statement is qualified in the *pistical* aspect of experience, i.e., it depends in the last analysis solely on our faith. For the Christian norm is the revealed word of God, the Holy Scriptures. It has no other source by which it can be verified or falsified.

Religious statements are justified solely in terms of a person's most basic presupposition concerning the origin of everything we experience, i.e., the origin of the world, of ourselves, of what we are, and of what we ought to become.

We have noted previously that a characteristic of a religious proposition is that its truth or falsity is not capable of being decided by a limited appeal to the senses. Statements used to support religious statements may in principle be open to a direct and immediate test, but genuinely religious statements are not.

Since a genuine religious statement is not verifiable by any direct test, the person who equates the meaning of a proposition with the method by which it is put to an empirical test, will dismiss religious statements as lying outside the domain of what can be true or false. They will deny that they are assertions. Such a denial is a deduction

238

from a naturalistic assumption, and in the last analysis is the result of a humanistic *a priori* of faith.

---

[1] See Matthew Tindall, *Christianity as Old as Creation*.

[5] Thomas Paine, *Age of Reason*, Wiley Book Co., N.Y., 1942, p. 6. of *Thomas Paine*, edit. by Philip S. Foner. (N.Y.: Citadel Press), Vol. II, pp. 749ff.

[3] "My Private Thoughts on a Future State," *loc. cit.* Vol. 2, p. 892.

[4] *Ibid.*, p. 893.

[5] Thomas Piane, *Age of Realson*, Wiley Book Co., N.Y., 1942, p. 6.

[6] *Ibid.*

[7] *Ibid.*, p. 7.

[8] *Ibid.*

[9] *Ibid.*, p. 8.

[10] *Ibid.*, p. 9.

[11] *Ibid.*, p. 11.

[12] *Ibid.*, p. 47.

[13] *Ibid.*, p. 52.

[14] For example, the reader is referred to R. Watson *An Apology for the Bible*, in a series of letters, addressed to Thomas Paine.

[15] *Op. cit.*, p. 319.

[16] For a criticism of Butler's method, see C. Van Til, *The Defense of the Faith*, Presbyterian and Reformed Publishing Co., Phila., 1962.

[17] Harper & Bros. N.Y. 1948, p. 3.

[18] *Ibid.*, p. 755.

[19] See H. Ridderbos, *Bultmann*, Presbyterian and Reformed Publishing Co., Phila. 1962.

[20] The documentary hypothesis as propounded during the latter half of the 19th century held that the first six books of the Bible were a composite of four documents. The earliest Yahivistic document (J) was dated about the middle of the 9th century, the second, the Elohistic document (E), about the middle of the 8th century, Deuteronomy (D), in the 7th century, and the priestly code (P), dating to the exile and immediately after. (See N.H. Ridderbos, in *Revelation and the Bible*, p. 336)

[21] See John Bright, "Modern Study of Old Testament Literature" in *The Bible and the Ancient Near East*, Essays in honor of William Foxwell Albright, edited by G. Ernest Wright. (N.Y.: Doubleday & Co., 1961), pp. 17ff.

[22] *Ibid.*, p. 21.

[23] See Cyrus H. Gordon, *The World of the Old Testament*, 2nd Edit., (N.Y.: Doubleday and Co., 1958).

[24] For a critique of such distortions in the field of theology see, D. H. Freeman, *Tillich*, in International Library of Philosophy and Theology, Presbyterian and Reformed Publishing Co., Phila., 1962.

For a detailed discussion of Biblical Criticism see: Robert D. Wilson's *A Scientific Investigation of the Old Testament;* Oswald Allis, *The Five Books of Moses;* Herman Ridderbos, *Bultmann,* and *Paul and Jesus;* J. Machen, *The Origin of Paul's Religion, Revelation and the Bible,* edited by Carl Henry.

[25] Robert D. Wilson, *A Scientific Investigation of the Old Testament.* (Phila.: The Sunday School Times Co., 1926), p. 7.

[26] O. T. Allis, *The Five Books of Moses.* (Phila.: Pres. & Reformed Pub. Co., 1949), p.3.

[27] Merrill C. Tenney, "The Limits of Biblical Criticism," *Christianity Today,* Vol. V, Number 4, Nov. 21, 1960, p. 5.

[28] *Ibid.,* p. 8.

[29] *Ibid.,* p. 6.

[30] For our discussion of the reliability of the New Testament documents, see F. F. Bruce, *Are the New Testament Documents Reliable.* Grand Rapids, Eerdman's, 1954.

[31] *Codex Vaticanus, Codex Sinaiticus* are the two most important; also of importance are the *Codex Alexandrinus,* 5th century, and *Codex Bezae,* 5th or 6th century, containing the Gospels and Acts in Latin and Greek.

[32] F. F. Bruce, *op. cit.,* p. 21.

[33] See *The New Testament in the Apostolic Fathers.* (1905), cited by F. F. Bruce, *op. cit.,* p. 23.

[34] *The Bible and Archaeology,* pp. 288 ff. quoted by F. F. Bruce, *op. cit.,* p. 23.

[35] See F. F. Bruce, *op. cit.,* and H. N. Ridderbos, *The Authority of the New Testament Scripture.*

[36] See F. F. Bruce, *op. cit.,* p. 51.

[37] See M. C. Tenney, "Reversals of New Testament Criticism," *Revelation and the Bible,* p. 361.

[38] See F. F. Bruce, *op. cit.,* pp. 55ff.

[39] J. Gresham Machen, *The Origin of Paul's Religion,* (Grand Rapids: Wm. B. Eerdmans, 1947), p. 25.

[40] See Ridderbos, *Paul And Jesus,* pp. 6-20.

[41] *Ibid.* p. 24.

[42] The following remarks on evil appeared previously in: Freeman, *Recent Studies in Philosophy and Theology* (Presbyterian and Reformed Publishing Co., 1962).

[43] For a fuller treatment of revelation and morality see Gordon H. Clark, *Religion, Reason and Revelation.* (Presbyterian and Reformed Publishing Co., 1961), especially pp. 151 to 191.

[44] This section originally appeared in Freeman, *Recent Studies in Philosophy and Theology.*

[45] Alfred J. Ayer, *Language, Truth, and Logic.* N.Y.: Dover Pub., 1946), pp. 114ff.

[46] Cf. E. L. Mascall, *Words and Images.* (N.Y.: The Ronald Press, 1957).

[47] Ayer, *op. cit.*, pp. 34ff.

[48] *Ibid.*, p. 41.

[49] *Ibid.*, pp. 115ff.

[50] Cf.   A. N. Prior "Can Religion be discussed?" in *New Essays in Philosophical Theology*, edited by Anthony Flew and Alasdair Mac Intyre.   (N.Y.:   MacMillan Co., 1955).

[51] "Theology and Falsification" in *New Essays*, p. 96.

[52] *Ibid.*, p. 99.

[53] *Ibid.*, p. 107.

[54] *Op. cit.* p. 16.

[55] *Ibid.*, p. 9.

[56] *Ibid.*, p. 13.

[57] *Ibid.*

[58] *Ibid.*

[59] *Op. cit.*, p. 9.

[60] *Ibid.*, p. 8.

[61] *Ibid.*, p. 9.

[62] "Special Divine Revelation as Rational," *Revelation and the Bible*, edited by Carl Henry (Presbyterian and Reformed Publishing Co., 1958), p. 40.

241

Chapter VIII

THE END AND THE BEGINNING

1. *Difficulties Still Remain*

The goal of a philosophical examination of religion is to determine the truth about religion. The path to the achievement of this end is, as we have seen, beset with the difficulty that there is no agreement as to what religion is. The situation is further complicated by the existence of many conflicting religions. It is, therefore, not surprising if the reader is confused and annoyed because he does not know how to decide the issues that have been raised.

The *subjectivist* regards religion as having no real basis other than some aspect of human experience, whereas the *objectivist* believes that man is related to something outside of himself. We have seen, however, that it is possible to be a *partial subjectivist,* and hold that many religions are in fact without any objective basis, while at the same time believing that at least one religion is objectively true. The reader may share our contention that such speculative religions as Hinduism and Buddhism do not present a serious claim to truth. In any case, it should be evident that Hinduism and Buddhism move in the world of timeless myth, in a world similar to that of the religions of the ancient Near East. Christianity and Judaism are related to history in a way that Hinduism and Buddhism, for example, are not. Buddhism and Hinduism, and to a lesser extent, Islam, do not offer any evidence that can be tested by the science of history. If they have any objective basis, there is no way that the philosopher could know it in any ordinary sense of the word know.

We have seen that Hinduism, in its traditional forms, breaks with the common sense notion that the world is real. The sole reality is an all-pervading world-substance: *Brahman*. This single world substance is the Self of everything and of everyone. The phenomenal world, the world that appears to the senses is an illusion due to our nescience, and an illusion from which we must seek to escape. Hindu sages may take refuge from wild elephants by climbing trees, but unlike ordinary people, they "know" that they themselves, the elephant, and the tree, are not real. The Hindu pantheon may contain innumerable gods, but the gods themselves not only came into being, but they too have no reality other than Brahman. Everything is Brahman and Brahman is everything. Brahman is the ultimate reality, the sole reality. Brahman is an impersonal absolute that becomes personal solely by being the being of everything. Brahman is not a person that is capable of revealing himself to distinct, concrete, individual persons. The latter become aware of Brahman when they recognize that they do not exist as distinct, concrete, individual persons. That a contradiction is involved here does not seem to bother anyone. For superior knowledge is beyond logic; it is not thought in concepts, and formulated in logically consistent judgments; but it is experienced.

Christianity and Judaism do not deny the validity of the laws of logic. In fact they insist upon them. In this sense, at least, they claim to be rational and the doctrines that they teach claim to be compatible with the rest of our knowledge about ourselves and the world in which we live.

Since our primary problem is to discover the truth about religion, it is sufficient to note that if either Judaism or Christianity is true, then any denial of the doctrine of creation is false.

To hold that if a single religion is true, others must be false, is to run the risk of being accused of intolerance. But such an accusation can only be made when tolerance is identified with indifference. If all religions are false, then it may make no difference which error a person may choose. If he is intelligent, he may shun all of them. But why should anyone care about the mode of anyone else's error? Tolerance is necessary when there is a genuine difference. It is only then that there is something to tolerate. The tolerant person agrees with the intolerant person that there is a difference. The tolerant person recognizes the nature of the difference, and if the difference is religious, then unlike the intolerant person he does not impose non-religious sanctions derived from the State, or any other non-religious sphere, in order to coerce religious beliefs.

Our comparison between Christianity and Hinduism and between Christianity and Buddhism disclosed an essential incompatibility. They all may be false, but they cannot all be true. The Christian doctrine of God is that God is an infinite, eternal, and unchangeable spiritual being. His very nature is to be all-knowing, all-powerful, holy, and just. This single God is one substance, consisting of three persons, the Father, the Son, and the Holy Ghost. And it is this triune God that is believed to be the creator of a real world that is in no sense a part of the divine substance, nor is it an illusion. The entire biblical tradition stands or falls with the distinction between the creator and the creature. And it is this very distinction which is explicitly denied by the Hindu notion that the sole reality is a single all-inclusive world substance, and by the Buddhist's notion of *karma*, and dependent origin.

The biblical view of man is that he has been created to enjoy fellowship or communion with God. Man's loss or original righteousness, his fall from paradise, was due to an act of rebellion against God's command. It originated in man's desire to be like God. Reconciliation between God and man is initiated by God himself, by God, the second person of the Trinity becoming man, by his sacrificial death on the cross, and by his resurrection from the dead. The redemption accomplished by Jesus the Messiah is appropriated by faith, manifested in obedience to the will of God. Man is thereby restored to the fellowship with God for which he was created, but man never loses his personal identity. He is forever man; he is never God, nor nirvana. His future state, which is conditional upon his earthly existence, is either to be in the presence of God, heaven, or to be eternally absent from God, hell. Never is man to become identical with God, a part of God's being, nor does man ever cease to be.

The essence of sin within Christianity is for man to try to be like God, whereas within Hinduism, man's "salvation" is to become aware that he is Brahman, to lose himself in a cosmic all; and in Buddhism it is to follow the path to nirvana. Sin is man's ignorance, salvation is the knowledge that man is not a man, the world is not really real. It consists in the extinction of the self, rather than the reconciliation of the self with a conscious, personal, loving God.

Consequently, unless the principle of non-contradiction does not hold in matters of religion, which would reduce religion to the absurd, the non-biblical religions become improbable to the degree that there is any reasonable ground for the acceptance of biblical religion. It is impossible for the philosopher to examine the evidence for Hinduism and Buddhism when no evidence is offered. That there are Hindus and Buddhists is a fact, but upon what facts do Buddhists and Hindus base their beliefs. Until such "facts" are presented, the further examination of such systems of religious speculation belongs to the realm of the comparative religionist, to the psychology of religion, and to the history of religion, but it is not the primary concern of the philosopher of religion.

2. *The Christian Appeal to the Evidence of Testimony*

The Christian exercises "reason" in inquiries concerning religion[1] but not in the same sense as the deist. The word "reason" is sometimes vaguely used to refer to some mysterious force or occult faculty in man or in the universe. Here it simply means that no religion is worthy of belief, apart from evidence. To use "reason" in religion is to examine the evidence; it is to look at arguments, and to form a judgment as to whether a particular proposition is true.

A proposition does not become true (in the sense in which we use the term) because someone believes it; a proposition is true or false independently of what a particular person believes. A Christian does not say: "Jesus rose from the dead" is true for me; it is true because I believe it to be true. The Christian says rather: "Jesus rose from the dead" is a true proposition, and because it is true, I believe it. Whether it is true or false that Jesus rose from the dead does not depend upon what anyone believes happened. It depends upon what *did* happen.

When the Christian says that "Jesus rose from the dead" is a true proposition, he makes a judgment. To exercise "reason" in religion is simply to look critically at the evidence offered in support of such judgments.

A religious proposition cannot be the proper object of faith, unless it is first judged to be true. The judgment P is true, where P is a religious proposition, presupposes that there is more evidence to support the truth of P than there is to support the falsity of P. The basic assumption of the Christian is that the Old and New Testaments are the word of God. The propositions of the Scriptures are believed because they are held to be true. They are held to be true because they are given by God, and what God declares to be true, is true, since he cannot lie.

To exercise "reason" in the case of the Christian religion is to examine the evidence for the truth or falsity of the proposition, "The Old and New Testaments are the word of God." After this proposition is held to be true, it is possible to say, "I believe it." It would make little sense to say "I believe it, although I know it is false."[2]

The Christian frequently uses the word "believe" where many people use the word "know." When he says "I believe," he may mean, "As far as I can honestly tell, the evidence for the truth of my basic proposition is greater than the evidence against it. The evidence has been examined, if not by me personally then by others whose judgment I trust, and a conclusion on the basis of the evidence has been reached so that when I am asked what my basic religious position is, I can now say I know or I believe that

246

the Old and New Testaments are the word of God."   I
usually prefer to use the word "believe," not because there
is any evidence that causes me to doubt the truth of what
I affirm, but because my assent to the truth of religious
propositions is not detached from my entire person.   What
"I know" *here* affects me more than anything else that
"I know"; it affects my will and my feelings.   I am more
certain of its truth than of anything else.   I will die rather
than deny it.   The word "know" does not convey the trust,
the whole-hearted reliance upon and the importance that
I attach to this proposition.   For I believe *in* and trust a
person; I believe what this person has said, more than any
other person, since this person is not just like any other
person; this person is God.

The Christian claims to have a certain kind of knowledge.   He claims to know that the "Old and New Testaments
are the word of God."   Now where such a claim is made
one can ask for evidence.   A person may think whatever he
pleases.   He may engage in fanciful speculations which are
poetic and filled with imagery.   The reader is free to think
that Vishnu assumed the shape of a boar and told the goddess of the earth that "land is cleansed by scouring, by
plastering it with cow-dung" and that "cows alone make
sacrificial oblations possible (by producing sacrificial but-
ter) ; cows take away every sin."[3]   The reader is free to
think that the urine and dung of cows expiate sins.[4]   The
reader is free to think in the next life, "One who has stolen
cattle, becomes a vulture,"[5] but if he says that he "knows"
this to be the case, then either he is using the word "know"
in a rather odd way, or he should be willing to give some
evidence in support of what he "knows."   If he wishes he
can persist in using the word "know" to stand for what he
"thinks," but there are other senses of "know."   The one
that we are here concerned with is the claim to "know" on
the basis of evidence.

The Christian does not simply assert that he believes
the Old and New Testaments to be true, because he does not
know that they are false; he asserts more.   When he asserts that he believes, he means that he has some kind of

knowledge. He has evidence which is adequate to satisfy his mind, as well as his heart, his intellect, as well as his emotions. Intellect, will, and emotions, may be conceptually distinguishable but they are inseparable within the individual person.

Not every Christian uses the words "believe" and "know" as we are using them.[6] For some the heart may have reasons which the mind does not know. Others may tell themselves they believe because what they believe is absurd. Our present concern is not with those who have made a leap in the dark, but with those who have leaped in broad daylight.

The Christians with whom we are here concerned do not simply "will to believe"; they do not simply *feel* that what they believe is true, but they claim to know that what they believe is true. What they know to be true then affects what they will; it issues in action, and it is accompanied by feelings of peace of mind and security. They do not believe because they have certain feelings; they have certain feelings because they believe, and they do not believe because they will to believe; they believe because of evidence.

The Christian's exercise of reason in religion can be understood when it is contrasted with the appeal to reason that is made by the deists. We have seen that the latter make "reason" the judge of what is true in religion and reject revelation.

The Christian does not decide beforehand what the content of revelation ought to be.[7] He does not find it strange that a revelation contains doctrines which he does not fully understand and which are different from his previous conceptions. What relates to an infinite being is bound to be incomprehensible. The Christian finds it reasonable to accept whatever God declares to be true.[8]

The Christian holds that there is nothing improbable or unreasonable in the idea of a revelation from God. Anyone who believes that a holy, wise and good God exists ought not to find the idea of a revelation from such a being strange. It is not absurd to suppose that an omnipotent being could inspire certain persons and direct them to make known certain truths to others.

One could expect, however, that the first establishment of a revelation might be marked by some evidence which is open to the experience of everyone. Such evidence is usually called "miracles." The Christian claims that the account of miracles that the Old and New Testaments contain attest to their authenticity.

Of course, anyone who does not believe that there is a God cannot believe that a miracle is possible. A person who is uncertain as to what he believes might be led to believe in God because of the account of miracles; however, it is obvious that anyone who is firmly persuaded that God does not exist will never believe that God has acted in a special way in the course of human history.

Many Christians hold that miracles are capable of proof from testimony. This contention has been attacked by David Hume in his *Enquiry Concerning Human Understanding*. Experience is for Hume the only guide in reasoning concerning matters of fact. To be wise a person's belief ought to be in proportion to the evidence. In all questions concerning matters of fact, there are different degrees of assurance, ranging from the highest certainty to the lowest. The testimony of men and eyewitness reports are indeed useful and even necessary to human life. Much of our assurance with respect to matters of fact depends solely upon our observation of the veracity of human testimony. In weighing the value of such testimony certain circumstances need to be considered, e.g., the character and number of witnesses, the manner in which they give their testimony, whether it is free from contradictions, and whether the witnesses have a vested interest.

Up until this point, the Christian might agree with Hume. The value of testimony is indeed dependent upon the character and trustworthiness of the witnesses. Hume argues further, however, that no human testimony can ever have such force as to prove a miracle and make it a just foundation of any religious system.

249

For when testimony is given to establish the extraordinary, the evidence resulting from it diminishes in proportion to the unusual character of the fact reported.

> A miracle is a violation of the laws of nature, and as a firm and unalterable experience has established these laws, the proof against a miracle, from the very nature of the fact, is as entire as any argument from experience that can possibly be imagined.[9]
> Hume holds further that, no testimony is sufficient to establish a miracle, unless the testimony be of such a kind, that its falsehood would be more miraculous, than the fact, which it endeavours to establish.[10]

Hume believed that his argument against miracles would "with the wise and learned, be an everlasting check to all kinds of superstitious delusion, and consequently, will be useful as long as the world endures."[11]

Whether his argument is useful or not depends upon what someone wishes to accomplish. A fallacious argument may succeed in persuading people to abandon a sound position. The question is whether Hume's argument is valid. Does Hume have an argument?

Consider Hume's statement: "A miracle is a violation of the laws of nature . . . ." What does the expression "laws of nature" mean? Congress makes laws, legislatures make laws and "nature makes laws." Motorists violate the laws made by the legislature against speeding; when they are caught they are punished. Miracles should be caught, too; they are troublemakers; imagine violating nature's laws in broad daylight! Presumably these "laws" have been established by a firm and unalterable experience. Whose experience? Hume's own private experience, the experience of all Englishmen, or of everyone Hume has talked to personally?

The issue is: what is nature? Is the world an independent, self-sufficient organism, or machine, a giant self-programing computer? In his *Dialogues*, Hume has Philo remark that it is better never to look beyond the material world. "By supposing it to contain the principle of its order within itself, we really assert it to be God; and the sooner we arrive at that divine Being, so much the better."

Hume may be willing to admit that the causes of order in the universe probably bear some remote analogy to human intelligence,[12] but the connection is vague and unimportant to our understanding of the world. God, if he exists, is simply irrelevant; he's no longer interested in the world and in mankind.

The biblical concept of a miracle is not that of a violation of "laws of nature." The world, the universe, or nature, is sustained and controlled by the providential power of God. The doctrine of creation is inseparable from the doctrine of providence.

Hume's very definition of a miracle implies a world in which God is not necessary. To the unsuspecting reader, it gives the unfavorable impression that some injury has been committed, that some obligation has been violated. To the Christian and to the Orthodox Jew, the "laws of nature," which are to be distinguished from the "laws formulated in the sciences,"[13] are simply the usual way in which the world is governed by God. At every point they depend for their existence and continuation upon the divine will.[14] . . . "A miracle is nothing else than the exertion of the same power in a way different from that which is common; or it may be a mere suspension of that which is common; or it may be a mere suspension of that power which is commonly observed to operate in the world."[15] It is noteworthy that the biblical account of miracles is never accompanied by a scientific explanation as to what took place. It may well be that in some instances, at least, ordinary, as yet undiscovered, "natural" means were utilized to accomplish the divine purpose. The description that is given is merely a report of their occurrence. Nothing is ever said about a "law of nature" being violated.

Hume has simply prejudged the case. In effect, he has told us that he does not believe in a God-controlled universe. His mind is made up. Nothing can change it. Would Hume believe in a miracle if he saw one? Could he trust his senses to accept what did not conform to his usual experience? And what about the next day, or a year later? Could he then believe the testimony of his own

251

memory? Would not he find it more probable that he had suffered an hallucination?

A miracle is by definition unusual and unique. If they occurred everyday and could be performed by everyone, we would become accustomed to them and probably would not call them miracles. Hume objects to the possibility of anything unusual. He will not accept the report of anything that does not occur repeatedly, and then he tells us that there can be no evidence in support of miracles. It is difficult to see how any testimony could ever establish the occurrence of any event which had not already been repeatedly experienced by Hume.

Unless someone *knows* that God does not exist, the only objection that an unprejudiced person can have against miracles is that they have not happened in his own experience. Whether they have occurred in the experience of anyone else is precisely the point at issue.[16]

There is an ambiguity in Hume's appeal to experience. Does he mean his own experience? Does he wish to say that no fact is to be taken on testimony unless he, too, has experienced it? Anyone who takes this as his criterion would cut himself off from the greater part of human knowledge. Or does Hume mean the experience of the whole world? If the term "experiences" refers to the experience of mankind, then how does Hume know that a "dead man has never come to life"? The question in debate is whether miracles have ever been experienced. Hume simply begs the question, " . . . by an argument intended to demonstrate that no testimony can establish them, the main principle of which is that all experience is against them. If miracles have ever occurred, they are not contrary to universal experience; for whatever has been witnessed at any time, by any person, makes part of universal experience. What sort of reasoning is it then to form an argument against the truth of miracles, founded on the assumption that they never existed? If it is true, as he says, that it has never been witnessed in any age or country that a dead man should come to life, then indeed it is useless to adduce testimony to prove the dead have on some occasion been brought to life. If he had a right to take this for granted, what was the use of such a parade of reasoning on the subject of testimony? The very conclusion to which he wished to come is here assumed as the main principle in the argument. Nothing is proved by the argument which promised so much, except the skill of the writer in sophistical reasoning."[17]

To argue that conviction in miracles cannot be produced by testimony because it opposes uniform and unalterable experience presupposes that we already know what universal experience is. But apart from our own personal experience, we know what others experience (universal experience) by testimony. To destroy the testimony in favor of miracles, Hume must in fact appeal to testimony. For otherwise he would not know what "universal experience" is.

When Hume is confronted with testimony that a particular "miracle" occurred, he does not produce witnesses that testify that this particular miracle did not occur. If he did then the problem would be to determine which witnesses were the more credible. Instead Hume introduces witnesses from other countries and other ages, and they then testify that they never saw anything like the miracle in question. Hume's argument amounts to "no more than *non-experience*, a mere negative thing which can never have any weight to overthrow the testimony of positive witnesses. In a court of justice, such a method of rebutting testimony would be rejected as totally inadmissable. If we had sufficient evidence of a fact of any kind, that testimony would not be invalidated if it could be proved that no person in the world had ever witnessed the like before. This want of previous experience naturally creates a presumption against the fact, which requires some force of evidence to overcome: but in all cases, a sufficient number of witnesses, of undoubted intelligence and veracity, will be able to remove the presumption and produce conviction."[18]

Hume's position pretends to consider the probability of miracles, but in fact it assumes *a priori* the impossibility of miracles. For if there is any probability of an event then one must allow for the possibility of the event, whereas Hume rules out the very possibility of a miracle being established by testimony and yet talks about their probability. Does the "empiricist" Hume know *a priori* that miracles are impossible? What is the evidence?

If an omnipotent God exists, then all things are possible to him, and if something is possible it may be believed when the testimony is sufficient. Admittedly, the testimony must be strong in proportion to the improbability of the event to be confirmed.[19]

The Christian believes that the miracles recorded in the New Testament are credible. For this reason, together with the fulfillment of the Old Testament prophecies with respect to the Messiah, he holds that any one who accepts the Old Testament ought also to accept the New Testament. The religion of the New Testament is to the Christian not a new religion; it is the fulfillment of the Old. The possible relationship between the Old and the New Testaments is as follows, both the Old and the New Testaments could be the true word of God as the Christian believes. The Old Testament could be true and the New Testament false, as present day Orthodox Judaism believes. Both the Old Testament and the New Testament could be false, as subjectivists believe. It is impossible for the New Testament to be true, however, and the Old Testament to be false. For the New Testament writers repeatedly affirm their belief in the veracity of the Old Testament.[20] If the New Testament is not the word of God, then Christianity is simply a Jewish heresy. If the New Testament is the word of God, then present day Judaism is a departure from the true religion of Israel and has erroneously rejected the Messiah.

If the testimony of the New Testament writers is not credible concerning the miracles they describe, then Christianity has no evidence in its support, and to believe it is irrational. If the Christian religion is not attended with sufficient evidence, it may still satisfy emotional needs, but it then is not worthy of belief and can readily be dismissed.

The evidence of testimony admits of conceivable degrees, from the weakest probability to the fullest assurance. In some cases our assent is weak, in others we are as certain of what we believe on the basis of testimony as of what we experience directly by our senses.[21] Is there anyone who doubts that Lincoln was President of the United States during the American Civil War? Is there anyone who doubts that Adolph Hitler was the dictator of Nazi Germany? Does anyone doubt that Plato and Aristotle lived in Greece? Many such things are believed with unwavering confidence.

Our conviction, our degree of certainty, does not necessarily depend upon the number of witnesses. Several reliable witnesses who agree and are uncontradicted by other evidence are frequently sufficient to produce conviction. Certain circumstances, especially the consequences of facts reported, often re-enforce the conviction produced by testimony.

It is, of course, always possible to raise objections against the evidence of testimony. In fact, if such and such is asserted to be the case, it should be possible to state what it would be like, if such and such were not the case. To deny the truth of a set of propositions submitted as evidence on the basis of testimony, is to affirm the truth of their contradictories. Frequently, it is overlooked that the denial of the truth of one proposition necessarily asserts the truth of its contradictory. To disbelieve in the veracity of certain witnesses is to believe in their untruthfulness. The person who simply objects to the truth of a position and never considers the objections on the other side often appears to have a strong case. The court of law that exempts the prosecution from answering the arguments of the counsel for the defense because they are not worth replying to is hardly being fair and objective. The most firmly established facts of history can be made to appear highly improbable, if objections are introduced without allowing for any consideration of the evidence for the opposite view.

Because sufficient evidence is presented in support of a position is no guarantee that conviction will inevitably be produced. A person can always ask for more evidence. Strong feelings, prejudices, lack of intelligence, and ill-will may cloud the issue. Many people demand evidence without first asking themselves what evidence they would regard as conclusive proof. It is futile to ask questions, unless a person knows what it is that he wishes to know.

In listening to the evidence of testimony, we presume that a person is truthful. It is easier to tell the truth than it is to lie. Of course, if a person is known to have some sinister end in view, if he stands to gain by his testimony and is a known liar, his testimony may be suspect. We do not generally suppose that anyone will go to the trouble of inventing a lie which they know can bring nothing but misery upon themselves. It is difficult for a series of lies to remain undetected when subjected to close scrutiny.[22]

The person who objects to Christianity frequently ignores the difficulties involved in accepting the consequences of his own position. To deny the evidence of Christianity and to deny that miracles ever existed necessitates that the existence of the Christian Church be explained on other principles.[23]

The basis of Christianity is primarily contained in the twenty-seven books of the New Testament. The latter includes four separate narratives of Jesus' life, miracles, death, resurrection and ascension, an account of the activity of the Apostles in the establishment of the church, and a collection of letters addressed to churches and individuals, as well as a book of prophecy.

The books of the New Testament are certainly not of recent origin. They are quoted in very early sources and can be traced back to the time in which the Apostles lived.[24] Pagan sources mention the existence of Christians as early as Nero who was contemporary with the Apostles.

Tacitus, for example, wrote about seventy years after Christ's death of events that took place thirty years after that event. He mentions how Nero tried to escape blame for burning Rome by blaming the Christians. Tacitus' account is given by William Paley as follows:

> . . . The founder of that name (Christians) was Christ, who suffered death in the reign of Tiberius, under his procurator Pontius Pilate. This pernicious superstition, thus checked for awhile, broke out again; and spread not only over Judea, where the evil originated, but through Rome also, whither every bad upon earth finds its way, and is practised. Some who confessed their sect were first seized, and afterwards by their information a vast multitude were apprehended, who were convicted, not so much of the crime of burning Rome, as of hatred to mankind. Their sufferings at their execution were aggravated by insult and mockery; for some were disguised in the skins of wild beasts, and worried to death by dogs—some were crucified—and others wrapped in pitched shirts and set on fire when the day closed, that they might serve as lights to illuminate the night. Nero lent his own gardens for these executions . . .[25]

Thirty years after the death of Christ many Christians are found in Rome who are willing to die for their faith in what the gospels teach. The writings of the Apostles were accepted as authoritative by the early Christians. They contain numerous references to the geography of Judea, to the manners and customs of the Jews, and although their words are Greek, their idiom is Syro-Chaldaic, the vernacular of Judea at the time of Christ and the Apostles.

Not only is it an established fact that the books of the New Testament are the genuine production of the Apostles and contain their testimony to the miracles described, but these books have not undergone any material change since they were written, as is evident from the general agreement of many copies, versions, and quotations from other sources.[26]

The authenticity of the New Testament documents does not in itself establish the credibility of their testimony. Many events described are miraculous, the raising of the dead, the instantaneous healing of the sick, the feeding of thousands with a few loaves and fishes, and the declaration of all the witnesses that Jesus rose from the dead three days after he had been crucified.

The Apostles could not have repeatedly suffered illusions. For the most part the miracles were performed in public, under the observation of learned, intelligent enemies, in a variety of circumstances, and for several successive years. The miracles performed are characterized by dignity, propriety, and kindness; not by ostentation nor for personal gain. There is every indication that the writers claimed to be truthful and honest. What they relate is set forth as the unadulterated truth, nor do they in any way seek to magnify their own persons, nor betray any appearance of ill-design or evil purpose.

The testimony of the New Testament writers is not impaired by discrepancies among the writers. Different points of emphasis are made, different aspects stressed, and the same fact is sometimes related from a different perspective, but the accounts agree on every substantial point.[27]

Alleged discrepancies in the gospel accounts overlook the fact that the gospels were written two thousand years ago, in a remote country with different customs, so that many difficulties arise from our own lack of knowledge. Moreover,

> The gospels do not purport to be regular histories of events, arranged in exact, chronological order, but a selection of important facts out of a much greater number left unnoticed. The time when, or the place where, these facts occurred, is of no consequence to the end contemplated by the evangelists. In their narratives, therefore, they have sometimes pursued the order of time, in other cases, the arrangement has been suggested by the subject previously treated, or by some other circumstance.[28]

Either the accounts given by the writers of the New Testament are true or they are not. If they are not, then there is no alternative other than to hold that they are intentional frauds, the product of premeditated deceit. The question that then needs to be answered is, what motive could the gospel writers have had for their wilful intention to perpetrate a fraud upon the world? What caused these men to embark upon a dangerous enterprise, to provoke the fury of mobs, the wrath of civil and religious authorities. Their leader was executed. Why would they say he was miraculously alive and had performed miracles? Why were they willing to be persecuted for what they knew to be a lie? Did they expect to become famous by proclaiming a lie? If so, why did they not point to themselves? Were they simply enthusiastic fanatics? Do their writings appear to have been written in a frenzy? And suppose they were motivated by some unknown reason to commit a fraud. How could they gain adherents in the very country and city where the miracles were said to be performed, among those who were in a position to know whether what they said was true? Only a few weeks had elapsed after the death of Jesus, before their testimony was received as true and multitudes became disciples.

In questions concerning matters of fact, it is not possible to give a demonstration similar to the demonstration of a theorem in geometry. The conclusion that the Christian reaches by such considerations is that the testimony for the miracles of the New Testament renders them credible, that it is more probable that such a body of testimony is true than that it is false. The only reason to reject it is the *a priori* assumption that miracles are impossible, and the latter assumption is justifiable solely on the ground that an omnipotent God does not exist.

In summary, the Christian holds that

The miracles recorded are real miracles, that they were performed in an open and public manner, that the witnesses could not possibly have deceived themselves; that enemies had every opportunity and motive for disproving the facts, if they had not been true; that there is every evidence of sincerity and honesty in the evangelists; that the epistles of the apostles furnish strong collateral proof of the same facts; that all Christians from the beginning must have believed in these miracles, and they must therefore be considered competent witnesses; that none of the witnesses could have any motive to deceive; that they never could have succeeded in imposing such a fraud on the world, even if they could have attempted it; that it would

259

have been the easiest thing in the world for the Jewish rulers to have silenced such reports if they were false; that the commencement of preaching at Jerusalem, and the success of Christianity there, cannot be accounted for on any other supposition than the truth of the miracles; that the conduct of the apostles in going to the most enlightened countries and cities, and their success in those places, can never be reconciled with the idea that they were ignorant imposters; and finally, that no contrary evidence exists.[29]

The spread of the Christian religion in spite of persecution is a matter of history, confirmed by pagan historians such as Tacitus, Suetonius, and Pliny, as well as by Christian authors.

It is not necessary for us to enter into the fulfillment of biblical prophecies that have taken place, and which Christians also appeal to in support of their acceptance of the Bible as the word of God. Much has been written on this vast subject,[30] but we need not enter into the Scripture's own witness to itself.

3. *Christianity, Judaism, and Islam*

The Christian regards the fulfillment of prophetic utterances and miracles as evidence in support of his religious faith. To adequately treat Christian evidences requires a separate volume. Our purpose has merely been to indicate the line of argument that Christians employ. It is, however, to be noted that any argument that is presented in support of Christianity is at the same time a refutation of modern Judaism and Islam.[31]

Christians believe that present day Judaism has only a part and the beginning of the truth, that the Jews are the offspring of holy men, that they were often visited by the prophets of God, that the Messiah was born of them, and that they were the first teachers of Christianity.

It is the belief of Christians that Jews ought not to look upon them as their enemies; rather they ought to accept the miracles of Christ as sufficiently attested, and upon the same kind of evidence of testimony, which persuades them of the miracles done by Moses and Elisha. The miracles of Christ ought to be accepted by the Jews as divine, because Jesus taught the worship of the true God, reverenced the writings of Moses, fulfilled the law of Moses when on earth.

Christians believe Jesus ought to be accepted by the Jews as their own Messiah because he fulfills the extraordinary promise of the Messiah which is found in the books of the Old Testament itself. That he was to be of the seed of David, that he was to be born of a virgin, was to heal the sick, was to be the instructor of all nations, and was to suffer and die, is foretold by the prophet.

With respect to Islam, Christians hold that a confrontation of Christianity and Islam discloses that the latter is directly opposite to Christianity. Islam was calculated for bloodshed; it delights much in ceremonies, and would be believed without allowing enquiry into it.

To assert that the Koran is uncorrupted and the writings of Moses and of the disciples of Jesus are corrupted overlooks the fact that copies of the gospels in many languages were immediately scattered over all the world and have been preserved by many sects. Mahomet says that Jesus was the promised Messiah, born without a human father, that he was taken up into heaven, that he healed the sick, and restored the dead to life. Mahomet says that he himself was sent with arms, not miracles; the body of Mahomet remains in the grave. Christianity was propagated by miracles and by the blood of the martyrs; the teachers of Islam did not endure any grievous troubles, nor undergo severe death for their profession. Mahometanism spread by the sword; its precepts allow polygamy, divorce is permitted, revenge is enjoined, and needless rituals and prohibitions are reintroduced.[32]

There is no external evidence that the Koran is a true revelation. Nowhere in the Koran does Mahomet perform a miracle that was public and open to inspection. Stories written centuries later ascribe miracles to Mahomet, but they deny the Koran's own statement that Mahomet was a preacher only.[33] Mahomet may have claimed to have

261

made a night journey to Jerusalem, and from there to heaven, under the angel Gabriel's guidance, but no one saw him go. Centuries later his followers may have believed that stones saluted Mahomet, a bean groaned to him, a shoulder of mutton told him it was poisoned, and a camel complained to him, but no one else was there.[34]

The content of the Koran is not above the capacity of an imposter. "It gives encouragement to the strongest and most vicious passions of human nature; promotes ambition, despotism, revenge, and offensive war; opens wide the door of licentiousness; and holds out such rewards and punishments as are adapted to make an impression on the minds of wicked men. It discourages, and indeed forbids all free inquiry, and all discussion of the doctrines which it contains. Whatever is excellent in the Koran, is in imitation of the Bible; but wherever the author follows his own judgment, or indulges his own imagination, we find falsehood, impiety, or ridiculous absurdity."[35]

The sword is the key of heaven and hell; a drop of blood shed in the cause of God, a night spent under arms, is of more avail than two months of fasting and prayer. Whosoever falls in battle, his sins are forgiven.

The highest heaven was reserved for the warrior. Converts had little choice. "Strike off their heads; strike off all the ends of their fingers: kill the idolaters, whereso-ever ye shall find them."[36]

There is nothing unusual about the spread of Islam. The main point against it, however, is not that it spread by force, but it is intrinsically contradictory. For it claims to accept the Old and New Testaments, which were written centuries before, and yet it contradicts the teachings of the Scriptures. Mary the mother of Jesus is, for example, confused with the sister of Moses.

In the Old Testament at I Chronicles 6:3 we read that Amram was the father of Aaron and Moses and Miriam, but the Koran written six hundred years after Christ says that Aaron (Imran) was the Virgin Mary's father. How did he do that?[37]

262

Christians, Jews, and Pagans admit that Jesus was hung on the cross and executed, but the Koran says that the Jews were deceived. Not only did they not kill Jesus, they did not even crucify him. "But they did not kill him, and they did not crucify him, but a similitude was made for them."[38]

An *eidolon*, an unsubstantial image, a phantom hung on the cross.[39]

Jesus whom Mahomet regards as a prophet taught men to love their enemies, to use peaceful means to spread the gospel; Mahomet prescribed that the hands of a thief be cut off as punishment, and that his enemies "shall be slaughtered or crucified, or their hands cut off and their feet on alternate sides or that they shall be banished from the land."[40]

It is not necessary to multiply examples. The reader need only compare the Old and New Testaments with the Koran to see that they move in a different world. Both texts are readily available. In the final analysis, each reader will have to make his own judgment. One thing will become certain upon inspection, while the reader may reject both the Bible and the Koran as being the word of God, he will not be able to accept the Koran and the Bible as Mahomet purports to do, but then the reader may not have the special assistance of the angel Gabriel at his disposal.

5. *Final Remarks*

Our philosophical inquiry is now at the end, and the end is like the beginning. Throughout its pages the reader has been confronted with a choice between opposing definitions of religion. Various religions have been examined; certain difficulties have been dealt with. And yet no exact formula has been given. The reader may still ask the question: What is the ultimate origin of man and the world in which he lives? He may still presuppose that man is the highest known form of consciousness and that the world in which he lives is all that there is. He may also presuppose that man is related to something higher than himself, and view himself as the creature of an omnipotent revealed God. In the last analysis the final decision may be a personal faith and commitment. Faith is not necessarily a blind leap. When a person believes, he believes in something, and his assent and trust is not necessarily apart from considerations of evidence. The Christian, for example, believes in the God of the Scriptures because he believes in the reliability and trustworthiness of the biblical writers. He bases his faith upon what he considers adequate evidence. He finds that in view of the evidence of the Scriptures, it requires less credibility to believe in their truth, than it does to disbelieve. The evidence is deemed so adequate by the Christian that to doubt the Scriptures is unreasonable. As a juror he sits in judgment. The testimony is presented by Moses, by the prophets, and by the apostles. He does not find it wanting. The verdict is called for. He pronounces their message to be true beyond a reasonable doubt. It is in this sense that the Christian believes. Moreover, when he believes the Scriptures, he attributes the certainty that he has to the operation of the grace of God, whose very Spirit convinces him that the Scriptures are of God.

The Christian finds that the arguments advanced against his belief are based upon misunderstanding and ignorance. They stem in fact from another faith. For the radical subjectivist is in fact a *believer*. The subjectivist does not prove that God does not exist. He does not prove that Moses, the prophets, and the apostles were either liars or were deceived. He does not prove that the world is all that there is. He *believes*. His faith is faith without evidence. He has neither conclusive rational arguments, nor the evidence of testimony. He has no Holy Scripture. He believes himself to be alone in the world. His faith may be accompanied by a psychological conviction of certainty, and he may be unwilling to consider any evidence to the contrary. He may even be unwilling to consider the question: What evidence would he require before he would accept a contrary position? The subjectivist's position may simply be a dogmatic *a priori*, a conviction, a commitment, a belief without evidence. God is dead, as far as he is concerned. Nothing could happen that could cause him to change his mind. It is not a question of evidence at all. He simply believes there is no God, or if God exists, he believes that neither he nor anyone else could know it.

The present day radical subjectivist can find many others who share his conviction. Together they may constitute an informal community of believers. They may then seek to change the political and social structure of the world, or they may simply be content to live and die in their *loneliness*.

The dispute about the nature of religion is not decided by words and arguments alone. Christians are partial subjectivists in that they have chosen the side of biblical religion. They regard non-biblical religions as human fantasy. They believe that the Old Testament finds its fulfillment in the New Testament. Christians do not expect that every reader will necessarily accept their position, but they are convinced that the human heart will remain restless until it finds rest in the living God. Those who are wise and happy seek and find God; those who seek and do not find, are wise but unhappy, while those who neither seek or find remain unhappy and foolish.

The question, what is religion? is a religious question, a question that cannot be fully answered by philosophy, a question that can only be fully answered by a religious faith.

---

[1] Cf. Archibald Alexander, *Evidences of the Authenticity, Inspiration, and Canonical Authority of the Holy Scriptures*, Philadelphia, 1836. In what follows we are greatly indebted to Alexander.

[2] There are of course other uses of "I believe." It would make sense to say I believe P, and I do not know that P is false. The use we are here concerned with is: I believe P and I know P is true, that is, I have sufficient evidence that P is true.

[3] *The Institutes of Vishnu*, in, *Sacred Books of the East*, edit. by Max Muller, Vol. VII, p. 105.

[4] *Ibid.*, p. 146.

[5] *Ibid.*

[6] The terms "believe" and "know" are frequently used in such a way that what is known by a logical demonstration cannot be believed.

[7] Our remarks here would apply, [as far as the Old Testament is concerned], to Orthodox Judaism as well as Christianity.

[8] See. Archibald Alexander, *op. cit.*

[9] David Hume, *An Enquiry Concerning Human Understanding.* (The Open Court Publishing Company, 1945), p. 120.

[10] *Ibid.*, p. 121.

[11] *Ibid.*, p. 113.

[12] *Dialogues Concerning Natural Religion*, edit. by Norman K. Smith (New York: Thomas Nelson & Sons, 1947), p. 227.

[13] The laws formulated in the sciences are at best approximations or partial formulations of the "laws of nature." The latter are, to the Christian, the way in which God actually governs the world.

[14] See Archibald Alexander, *op. cit.*, p. 68.

[15] *Ibid.*

[16] *Ibid.*, p. 70.

[17] *Ibid.*, p. 71.

[18] *Ibid.*, p. 72.

[19] *Ibid.*, p. 88.

[20] Cf. Roger Nicole, "New Testament Use of the Old Testament," *Revelation and the Bible*, edit. by Carl Henry, Philadelphia: (Presbyterian and Reformed Publishing Company, 1958).

[21] See *ibid.*, pp. 89ff. for much of what follows.

[22] See A. Alexander, *op. cit.*, 91.

[23] *Ibid.*, p. 92.

[24] See Alexander, *op. cit.*, for what follows. Also cf. F. F. Bruce, *Are the New Testament Documents Reliable?* Grand Rapids: (Wm. B. Eerdmans Publishing Co., 1954).

[25] *A View of the Evidences of Christianity*, James Miller, N.Y. MDCCCLX, p. 52.

[26] See Alexander, *op. cit.*, p. 98.

[27] See H. N. Ridderbos, *The Authority of the New Testament Scriptures* and his *The Coming of the Kingdom* (Presbyterian & Reformed Publishing Co., 1962).

[28] Alexander, *op. cit.*, p. 109; also H. N. Ridderbos, *TheAuthority of the N. T. Scriptures.*

[29] *Ibid.*, p. 117.

[30] See Bernard Ramm, "Evidence of Prophecy and Miracle," in *Revelation and the Bible.* Also see Paley, *op. cit.*

[31] For a detailed study of the conditions that prevailed among the Jews at the time of Christ, see A. Edersheims, *The Life and Times of Jesus the Messiah.*

[32] See Hugo Grotius, *The Truth of the Christian Religion* (Baynes & Son, 1836).

[33] Cf. William Palely, *Evidences.*

[34] See Alexander, *op. cit.*, p. 174.

[35] *Ibid.*, p. 175.
[36] Sale's *Koran*, ch. VIII, p. 140, quoted by Paley, *op. cit.*
[37] The Koran, *Sacred Books of the East*, 111, 30-35, p. 50:51.
[38] *Ibid.*, Iv, p. 93.
[39] *Ibid.*, p. 53, note 3.
[40] *Ibid.*, Ch. 5. 102.

INDEX

A

Abraham, 54, 129
Acquinas, 82ff.
Agnostic, 12
Angel Gabriel, 125
Anselm, 79
Augustine, 99
Avicena, 99
Ayer, A. J., 224ff.

B

Baur, F. C., 214
Bouwsma, O. K., 167
Buddhism, 56ff.
Bultman, R., 210, 218
Butler, J., 204ff.
Boussett, W., 217ff.

C

Calvin, John, 152ff., 169
Chalcedon, 155
Christianity, 16, 120, 143ff.
Clark, G., 235ff.

E

Egyptian religion, 32ff.
Evil, problem of, 220ff.

F

Faith, 116ff.
Feuerbach, L., 21
Flew, A., 228ff.

G

Gautama, 57ff.
Gunkel, 217

H

Heaven, 139
Hinduism, 16, 41ff.
Hitler, 220ff.
Hume, D., 86ff., 250
Huxley, J. 159ff.

I

Islam, 16, 120ff.

J

Judaism, 16, 120, 127ff., 140ff.

K

Kant, I., 86ff., 121ff.
Koran, 261

L

Lever, Jan, 174

M

Maimonides, 99
Martel, Chas., 121
Marxist, 7
Mascall, E. L., 95, 232
Messiah, 133, 137
Michelangelo, 109
Mishnah, 141
Mohammed, 121ff.
Morris, H. M., 170ff.
Moses, 129

N

Naturalism, 20
Nirvana, 63ff.

O

Old Testament Religion, 39ff.
Ontological Argument, 79ff.
Origin of Species, 185

P

Paine, T., 197ff.
Paley, W., 257
Pfeiffer, R. H., 209ff.
Protestantism, 151ff.